CLIFFS

Praxis I

Pre-Professional

Skills Tests

PREPARATION GUIDE

Jerry Bobrow, Ph.D.

CONSULTANTS
Peter Z Orton, M.Ed.
William A. Covino, Ph.D.
Merritt L. Weisinger, J.D.

Cliffs Notes
INCORPORATED
LINCOLN, NEBRASKA 68501

My loving thanks to my wife, Susan, and my children, Jennifer Lynn 18, Adam Michael 15, and Jonathan Matthew 11, for their patience and support. My sincere thanks to Michele Spence of Cliffs Notes for final editing and careful attention to the production process.

JERRY BOBROW

Cover photograph by Annabelle Breakey / Tony Stone Images

ISBN 0-8220-2052-1

SECOND EDITION

Contents

Part III: Mathematics Review

Part IV: Selective Review of Grammar and Usage

Part V: Two Full-Length Practice Tests

Preface

We know that getting a good score on the PPST is important to you! And because the PPST requires you to use some basic skills that you may not have used in many years, thorough preparation is the key to doing your best. This makes your study time more important than ever. Therefore, it must be used most effectively.

With this in mind, *Cliffs PPST Preparation Guide* was carefully researched and developed by leading test preparation experts and instructors. It is thorough, direct, concise, and easy to use. The materials, techniques, and strategies presented here are presently used in test preparation programs in many colleges and universities.

This guide is divided into six parts:

Part I: Introduction—a general description of the exam, recent format, questions commonly asked, and basic overall strategies.

Part II: Analysis of Exam Areas—focuses on ability tested, basic skills necessary, directions, analysis, suggested approaches with samples, and additional tips.

Part III: Mathematics Review—a brief, but intensive, review in the basics of arithmetic, algebra, and intuitive geometry, with diagnostic tests in each area. Important terminology is also included.

Part IV: Selective Review of Grammar and Usage—a concise review focusing on avoiding some of the most common grammar and usage errors.

Part V: Two Full-Length Practice Tests—two complete, full-length practice tests with answers and in-depth explanations. Each practice test is followed by analysis charts to assist you in evaluating your progress.

Part VI: Testing by Computer—a general description of the Computer-Based Academic Skills Assessments (CBT), an Educational Testing Service Praxis I exam very similar to the PPST that is taken on computer.

This guide is not meant to substitute for comprehensive courses, but if you follow the Study Guide Checklist and study regularly, you will get the best PPST preparation possible.

Study Guide Checklist

_____ 1. Read the PPST information materials available at the Testing Office, Counseling Center, or Credentials Office at your undergraduate institution.

_____ 2. Become familiar with the Test Format, page 3.

_____ 3. Read the General Description and Questions Commonly Asked about the PPST, starting on page 3.

_____ 4. Learn the techniques of Two Successful Overall Approaches, page 6.

_____ 5. Carefully read Part II, Analysis of Exam Areas, starting on page 11.

_____ 6. Review Mathematical Terminology, starting on page 79.

_____ 7. Take the Arithmetic Diagnostic Test, starting on page 87, check your answers, and review the appropriate areas in the Arithmetic Review.

_____ 8. Take the Algebra Diagnostic Test, starting on page 107, check your answers, and review the appropriate areas in the Algebra Review.

_____ 9. Take the Geometry Diagnostic Test, starting on page 115, check your answers, and review the appropriate areas in the Geometry Review.

_____ 10. Study Part IV, Selective Review of Grammar and Usage, page 141.

_____ 11. Strictly observing time allotments, take Practice Test 1, starting on page 161.

_____ 12. Check your answers and analyze your Practice Test 1 results, starting on page 202.

_____ 13. Fill out the Tally Sheet for Questions Missed to pinpoint your mistakes, page 203.

_____ 14. Study **all** the Answers and Explanations for Practice Test 1, starting on page 207.

_____ 15. Have a friend or English instructor read and evaluate your essay using the Essay Checklist, page 205.

_____ 16. Review weak areas as necessary.

_____ 17. Strictly observing time allotments, take Practice Test 2, starting on page 225.

_____ 18. Check your answers and analyze your Practice Test 2 results, starting on page 270.

_____ 19. Fill out the Tally Sheet for Questions Missed to pinpoint your mistakes, page 271.

_____ 20. Study **all** the Answers and Explanations for Practice Test 2, starting on page 275.

_____ 21. Have a friend or English instructor read and evaluate your essay using the Essay Checklist, page 273.

_____ 22. Review weak areas as necessary.

_____ 23. Review Analysis of Exam Areas, starting on page 11.

_____ 24. Carefully read Final Preparations: "The Final Touches," page 291.

PART I

Introduction

Introduction to the PPST
Pre-Professional Skills Tests

FORMAT OF THE TESTS

Test	Minutes	Number of Questions
Reading Test	60	40
Mathematics Test	60	40
Writing Test:		
Multiple-Choice Section	30	45
Part A: English Usage	(10*)	(25)
Part B: Sentence Correction	(20*)	(20)
Essay Section	30	1 essay

Approximate total time: 180 minutes (3 hours)
Approximate total questions: 125 plus one (1) essay

*Suggested time.
Note: Format and scoring are subject to change.

GENERAL DESCRIPTION

The PPST is composed of three tests:

The Reading Test. This test contains about 40 questions and requires the ability to read short passages and answer questions based on them.

The Mathematics Test. This test also contains about 40 questions and requires a cumulative knowledge of the basics of math from elementary school to at least one year in high school and possibly one year in college.

The Writing Test. This test is divided into two sections. Section 1, the multiple-choice section, contains two types of questions, English usage (25 questions) and sentence correction (20 questions), and requires the ability to detect and/or correct errors in standard written English. Section 2, the essay section, requires the ability to plan and write a well-organized essay on an assigned topic.

QUESTIONS COMMONLY ASKED ABOUT THE PPST

Q: Who administers the PPST?

A: Educational Testing Service (ETS) prepares and scores the PPST, but unless otherwise specified, institutions and agencies that plan to use the tests arrange for the administrations with ETS.

Q: What is the PPST?

A: The PPST (Pre-Professional Skills Tests) consists of three tests: the Reading Test, the Mathematics Test, and the Writing Test (multiple-choice and essay). The PPST is designed to measure basic proficiency in each of these areas.

Q: Is the PPST part of the Praxis Series?

A: Yes. ETS has grouped a number of its beginning teacher tests under the title "The Praxis Series." Praxis I includes the PPST and the Computer-Based Academic Skills Assessments (CBT), tests of reading, writing, and mathematics skills that all teachers need. Praxis II includes exams on the specific subjects prospective teachers will actually teach. Praxis III includes tests that evaluate classroom teaching performance.

Q: How is the PPST scored?

A: Each of the tests is scored on a scale ranging from 150 to 190. Separate scores are reported for each test. The Reading Test and the Mathematics Test are scored solely on the number of items answered correctly. The Writing Test score is a composite score adjusted to give approximately equal weight to the number right on the multiple-choice section and the essay score.

Q: How is the PPST score used?

A: The PPST may be used for selection, admission, evaluation, and certification in conjunction with other relevant information. Because each institution or agency may set its own minimum standards and requirements, you should contact the appropriate institution, district, department, or agency to find out if you must take the test and to learn the required standards.

Q: When and where is the PPST administered, and how do I register?

A: Since the administrations are arranged through institutions and agencies that use the exam, registration information (time, place, date, and fees) should be obtained directly from the institution or agency administering the tests.

Q: Are there any special arrangements for taking the PPST?

A: There are some special arrangements available for handicapped individuals. Call or write to ETS long before your test date to inquire about special arrangements.

Q: What materials should I bring to the PPST?

A: Bring positive photo-bearing identification, a watch, three or four sharpened Number 2 pencils, and a good eraser. You may *not* bring scratch paper, calculators (including watch calculators), books, compasses, rulers, papers of any kind, or recording or photographic devices.

Q: How should I prepare for the PPST?

A: Understanding and practicing test-taking strategies will help a great deal. Subject matter review in arithmetic, simple algebra, plane geometry, measurement, and English grammar, usage, and punctuation is also very valuable.

Q: Should I guess on the PPST?

A: Yes. Since there is no penalty for wrong answers, guess if you have to. If possible, first try to eliminate some of the choices to increase your chances of guessing the correct answer. But don't leave any questions unanswered.

Q: Where can I get more information?

A: For more information, write to PPST program, Educational Testing Service, CN 6060, Princeton, NJ 08541-6060.

TAKING THE PPST:
TWO SUCCESSFUL OVERALL APPROACHES

I. THE "PLUS-MINUS" SYSTEM

Many who take the PPST don't get their best possible score because they spend too much time on difficult questions, leaving insufficient time to answer the easy questions. Don't let this happen to you. Since every question within each section is worth the same amount, use the following system.

1. Answer easy questions immediately.

2. When you come to a question that seems "impossible" to answer, mark a large minus sign (–) next to it on your test booklet.

3. Then mark a "guess" answer on your answer sheet and move on to the next question.

4. When you come to a question that seems solvable but appears too time consuming, mark a large plus sign (+) next to that question in your test booklet and register a guess answer on your answer sheet. Then move on to the next question.

   Since your time allotment is about a minute per question or less, a "time-consuming" question is a question that you estimate will take you more than several minutes to answer. But don't waste time deciding whether a question is a "+" or a "–." Act quickly, as the intent of this strategy is, in fact, to save you valuable time. After you've worked all the easy questions, your booklet should look something like this:

$$1.$$
$$+\ 2.$$
$$3.$$
$$-\ 4.$$
$$+\ 5.$$
$$\text{etc.}$$

5. After answering all the questions you immediately can in that section (the easy ones), go back and work on your "+" questions. Change your "guess" on your answer sheet, if necessary, for those questions you are now able to answer.

6. If you finish your "+" questions and still have time left, you can

    (a) attempt those "−" questions—the ones that you considered "impossible." Sometimes a question later in that section will "trigger" your memory and you'll be able to go back and answer one of the earlier "impossible" questions.

or

    (b) don't bother with those "impossible" questions. Rather, spend your time reviewing your work to be sure you didn't make any careless mistakes on the questions you thought were easy to answer.

Remember: You don't have to erase the pluses and minuses you made on your *question booklet*. And be sure to fill in all your answer spaces—if necessary, with a guess. As there is no penalty for wrong answers, it makes no sense to leave an answer space blank. And, of course, remember that you may work in only one section of the test at a time.

II: THE ELIMINATION STRATEGY

Take advantage of being allowed to mark in your testing booklet. As you eliminate an answer choice from consideration, make sure to *mark it out in your question booklet* as follows:

(A)
? (B)
(C)
(D)
? (E)

    Notice that some choices are marked with question marks, signifying that they may be possible answers. This technique will help you avoid reconsidering those choices you have already eliminated. It will also help you narrow down your possible answers.

    Again, these marks you make on your testing booklet do not need to be erased.

PART II

Analysis of Exam Areas

This section is designed to introduce you to each area of the PPST by carefully reviewing

1. Ability Tested
2. Basic Skills Necessary
3. Directions
4. Analysis of Directions
5. Suggested Approach with Samples

This section emphasizes important test-taking techniques and strategies and how to apply them to a variety of problem types. Sample essays are also included in this section as a guideline to assist students in evaluating their own essays and to point out some of the common errors in essay writing.

Introduction to the Reading Test

The Reading Test is 60 minutes long and usually contains 40 questions. It consists of passages of approximately 200 words, shorter passages of approximately 100 words, and short statements of one or more sentences. Each passage or statement is followed by questions based on its content.

The test is composed of the following content areas and *approximate* number of questions.

Literal Comprehension
22 questions
These are the straightforward questions used to determine if you comprehend the passage and its direct meaning:

- its main idea or supporting ideas
- the primary purpose or organization of the passage
- the meaning of words used in the passage

Critical and Inferential Comprehension
18 questions
These are questions requiring you to read "beneath the surface" and understand deeper meanings that are directly implied by the passage:

- the argument's strengths or weaknesses, the relevance of its evidence, or whether the ideas presented are fact or opinion
- implications or assumptions of the passage, or the author's underlying attitude
- generalizations or conclusions that can be drawn or related to new situations

---

ABILITY TESTED

This section tests your ability to understand the content of the passages and any of the following: its main idea, supporting ideas, or specific details; the author's purpose, assumptions, or tone; the strengths and weaknesses of the author's argument; inferences drawn from the passage; the relationship of the passage to its intended audience; supporting evidence in the passage; and so forth.

No outside knowledge is necessary; all questions can be answered on the basis of what is stated or implied in the passage.

BASIC SKILLS NECESSARY

Understanding, interpreting, and analyzing passages are the important skills for this section. The technique of *actively* reading and marking a passage is also helpful.

DIRECTIONS

A question or number of questions follow each of the statements or passages in this section. Using only the *stated* or *implied* information given in the statement or passage, answer the question or questions by choosing the *best* answer from among the five choices given.

ANALYSIS OF DIRECTIONS

1. Answer all the questions for one passage before moving on to the next one. If you don't know the answer, take an educated guess or skip it.

2. Use only the information given or implied in a passage. Do not consider outside information, even if it seems more accurate than the given information.

SUGGESTED APPROACH WITH SHORT SAMPLE PASSAGE

Two strategies that will improve your reading comprehension are *prereading the questions* and *marking the passage*. Readers who become comfortable using these strategies tend to score higher on reading tests than readers who do not use these strategies.

Prereading the Questions

Before reading the passage, read the question or questions that follow it. Do *not* read the multiple-choice answers. Underline or circle the operative phrase in each question, that is, what you are being asked to answer. For example:

The author's argument in favor of freedom of speech may be summarized in which of the following ways?

(A) If every speaker is not free, no speaker is.
(B) Speech makes us different from animals.
(C) As we think, so we speak.
(D) The Bill of Rights ensures free speech.
(E) Lunatic speeches are not free speeches.

In this example, the operative phrase is "author's argument . . . may be summarized (how?)." So you might underline the words "author's argument" and "may be summarized." Thus, prereading allows you to focus on and clarify exactly what you're being asked to answer.

Marking the Passage

After prereading the questions, read and mark the passage. Underline or circle those spots that contain information relevant to the questions you've read as well as other important ideas and details. However, don't overmark. A few marked phrases per paragraph help those ideas stand out.

Short Sample Passage

*By the time a child starts school, he has mastered the major part of the rules of his grammar. He has managed to accomplish this remarkable feat in such a short time by experimenting with and generalizing the rules all by himself. Each child, in effect, rediscovers language in the first few years of his life.

*When it comes to vocabulary growth, it is a different story. Unlike grammar, the chief means through which vocabulary is learned is memorization. *And some people have a hard time learning and remembering new words.

LINE
(5)

*Indicates portions of the passage which refer directly to a question you've skimmed. Also marked are main points and key terms.

1. A <u>child</u> has <u>mastered</u> many <u>rules of grammar</u> by about the <u>age</u> of

   (A) 3   (B) 5   (C) 8   (D) 10   (E) 18

The first sentence of the passage contains several words from this question, so it is likely to contain the correct answer. "By the time a child starts school" (line 1) tells us that the answer is 5. Before choosing (B), you should look at all the answers and cross out those which seem incorrect.

2. Although vocabulary growth involves memorization and grammar learning doesn't, we may conclude that <u>both vocabulary and grammar make use of</u>

   (A) memorization   (D) children
   (B) study skills   (E) teachers
   (C) words

The question asks you to simply use your common sense. (A) is incorrect; it contradicts both the passage and the question itself. (D) and (E) make no sense. (B) is a possibility, but (C) is better because grammar learning in young children does not necessarily involve study skills but does necessarily involve words.

3. The <u>last sentence</u> in the passage <u>implies</u> that

   (A) some people have no trouble learning and remembering new words
   (B) some people have a hard time remembering new words
   (C) grammar does not involve remembering words
   (D) old words are not often remembered
   (E) learning and remembering are kinds of growth

Implies tells us that the answer is something suggested but not explicitly stated in the passage. (B) is explicitly stated in the passage, so it may be eliminated. But it implies its opposite: if *some* people have a hard time, then it must be true that *some* people don't. (A) is therefore the correct choice. (C), (D), and (E) are altogether apart from the meaning of the last sentence.

Another Short Sample Passage

St. Augustine was a contemporary of Jerome. After an early life of pleasure, he became interested in a philosophical religion called Manichaeism, a derivative of a Persian religion, in which the forces
LINE   of good constantly struggle with those of evil. Augustine was even-
(5)   tually converted to Christianity by St. Ambrose of Milan. Augustine's *Confessions* was an autobiography that served as an inspiration to countless thousands who believed that virtue would ultimately win.

1. St. Augustine's conversion to Christianity was probably influenced by

    (A) his confessional leanings
    (B) his contemporaries
    (C) the inadequacy of a Persian religion to address Western moral problems
    (D) his earlier interest in the dilemma of retaining virtue
    (E) the ravages of a life of pleasure

Having skimmed this question, you should have marked the portion of the passage which mentions Augustine's conversion and paid attention to the events (influences) leading to it. (A) requires speculating beyond the facts in the paragraph; there is also no evidence in the passage to support (C) or (E). (B) is too vague and general to be the best answer. (D) points toward Augustine's earlier interest in Manichaeism, and the last sentence suggests that Augustine's interest in retaining virtue continued through his Christian doctrine. Well supported as it is, (D) is the best answer.

2. From the information in the passage, we must conclude that Augustine was a

    (A) fair-weather optimist   (D) failed optimist
    (B) cockeyed optimist   (E) glib optimist
    (C) hardworking optimist

Skimming *this* question is not very helpful; it does not point specifically to any information in the passage. Questions of this sort usually assess your overall understanding of the meaning, style, tone, or point of view of the passage. In this case, you should recognize that Augustine is a serious person; therefore, more lighthearted terms like *fairweather* (A), *cockeyed* (B), and *glib* (E) are probably inappropriate. (D) contradicts Augustine's success as an "inspiration to countless thousands." (C) corresponds with his ongoing, hopeful struggle to retain virtue in the world; it is the best answer.

3. Judging from the reaction of thousands to Augustine's *Confessions,* we may conclude that much of his world at that time was in a state of

   (A) opulence   (D) reformation
   (B) misery   (E) sanctification
   (C) heresy

Having skimmed this question, you should have marked the last sentence of the passage as the place to look for the answer. That Augustine's readers were inspired implies that they *required inspiration,* that they were in some sort of uninspiring, or *negative,* situation. (A) and (E) must therefore be eliminated because they are positive terms. (D) is not necessarily a negative term and so is probably not the best answer. (C), although a negative term, does not describe a state of being which thirsts for inspiration. (B) does, and (B) therefore is the best choice.

GENERAL PROCEDURE FOR ANSWERING READING COMPREHENSION QUESTIONS

1. **Skim the questions,** underlining or circling the word or phrase that stands out in each question. *Don't* read the answer choices.

2. **Read and mark the passage,** paying special attention to information relevant to the questions you've skimmed.

3. **Answer the questions.** Base your answers on *only the material given in the passage.* Assume that the information in each passage is accurate. The questions test your understanding of the passage alone; they do *not* test the historical background of the passage, the biography of the author, or previous familiarity with the work from which the passage is taken.

FIVE KEY QUESTIONS FOR UNDERSTANDING AND INTERPRETING WHAT YOU READ

MAIN IDEA

What is the main idea of the passage? After reading any passage, try summarizing it in a brief sentence. To practice this very important skill, read the editorials in your local paper each day and *write* a brief sentence summarizing each one.

DETAILS

What details support the main idea? Usually such details are facts, statistics, experiences, etc., that strengthen your understanding of and agreement with the main idea.

PURPOSE

What is the purpose of the passage? Ask yourself what the author is trying to accomplish. The four general purposes are (1) to narrate (tell a story), (2) to describe, (3) to inform, and (4) to persuade.

STYLE AND TONE

Are the style and tone of the passage objective or subjective? In other words, is the author presenting things *factually* or from a *personal point of view*? If an author is subjective, you might want to pin down the nature of the subjectivity. Ask yourself, is the author optimistic? pessimistic? angry? humorous? serious?

DIFFICULT OR UNUSUAL WORDS

What are the difficult or unusual words in the passage? Readers who do not *mark* works that are difficult or used in an unusual way in a passage often forget that the words occurred at all and have difficulty locating them if this becomes necessary. By calling your attention to difficult or unusual words, you increase your chances of defining them by understanding their meaning in context.

A PATTERNED PLAN OF ATTACK
Reading Comprehension

SKIM the questions first, marking important nouns and verbs.

READ the passage ACTIVELY, marking main points, names, definitions, important conclusions, places, and numbers.

ANSWER the questions, without spending a lot of time on any one question.

Introduction to the Mathematics Test

The Mathematics Test is 60 minutes long and usually contains 40 questions. The questions are selected from different areas of mathematics including arithmetic, elementary algebra, basic geometry, measurement, and graph and chart reading. Complex computation is not required, and most of the terms used are general, commonly encountered mathematical expressions (for instance, area, perimeter, integer, and prime number).

ABILITY TESTED

This part of the exam tests your ability to use your cumulative knowledge of mathematics and your reasoning ability. Computation is minimal; you are not required to have memorized any specific formulas or equations.

The test is composed of the following content areas and *approximate* percentages.

Conceptual Knowledge	6 questions	15%
Procedural Knowledge	12 questions	30%
Representations of Quantitative Information	12 questions	30%
Measurement and Informal Geometry	6 questions	15%
Formal Mathematical Reasoning	4 questions	10%

Conceptual Knowledge: whole numbers, fractions, decimals, place value, ordering of numbers, and properties of numbers and operations.

Procedural Knowledge: ratio, proportion, percent, probability, equations, inequalities, algorithms, solving problems, computing, and estimating.

Representations of Quantitative Information: interpreting bar graphs, line graphs, pie charts, pictographs, tables, diagrams, and flow charts; seeing trends; making inferences; drawing conclusions; identifying patterns; and making connections.

Measurement and Informal Geometry: systems of measurement, appropriate units of measurement, linear/area/volume measurement, geometric properties, reading scales, and solving problems involving geometry.

Formal Mathematical Reasoning: interpreting logical statements, using deductive reasoning, evaluating the validity of a conclusion, and identifying appropriate generalizations.

DIRECTIONS

Each of the questions or incomplete statements below is followed by five suggested answers or completions. Select the best answer or completion of the five choices given and fill in the corresponding lettered space on the answer sheet.

ANALYSIS OF DIRECTIONS

1. You have 60 minutes to do 40 problems, which averages to just over one minute per problem. Keep that in mind as you attack each problem. Even if you know you can work a problem but that it will take you far longer than one minute, you should skip it and return to it later if you have time. Remember, you want to do all the easy, quick problems first before spending valuable time on the others.

2. There is no penalty for guessing, so you should not leave any blanks. If you don't know the answer to a problem but you can size it up to get a general range for your answer, you may be able to eliminate one or more of the answer choices. This procedure will increase your odds of guessing the correct answer. But even if you can't eliminate any of the choices, take a guess because there is no penalty for wrong answers.

3. Above all, be sure that your answers on your answer sheet correspond to the proper numbers on your question sheet. Placing one answer in the incorrect number on the answer sheet could possibly shift *all* your answers to incorrect spots. Be careful to avoid this problem!

SUGGESTED APPROACH WITH SAMPLES

Here are a number of approaches that can be helpful in attacking many types of mathematics problems. Of course, these strategies won't work on *all* the problems, but if you become familiar with them, you'll find they'll be helpful in answering quite a few questions.

Mark Key Words

Circling or underlining key words in each question is an effective test-taking technique. Many times you may be misled because you may overlook a key word in a problem. By circling or underlining these key words, you'll help yourself focus on what you are being asked to find. Remember, you are allowed to mark and write on your testing booklet. Take advantage of this opportunity.

1. In the following number, which digit is in the thousandths place?

6574.12398

(A) 2   (B) 3   (C) 5   (D) 7   (E) 9

The key word here is *thousandths*. By marking it, you will be paying closer attention to it. This is the kind of question which, under time pressure and testing pressure, may often be misread. It may be easily misread as *thousands* place. Your marking the important words can minimize the possibility of misreading. Your completed question might look like this after you mark the important words or terms.

1. In the following number, which <u>digit</u> is in the <u>thousandths</u> place?

$$6574.12\underline{3}98$$

(A) 2   (B) <u>3</u>   (C) 5   (D) 7   (E) 9

Here are a few more examples.

2. If 3 yards of ribbon cost $2.97, what is the price per foot?

(A) $0.33   (B) $0.99   (C) $2.94   (D) $3.00   (E) $8.91

The key word here is *foot*. Dividing $2.97 by 3 will tell you only the price per *yard*. Notice that $0.99 is one of the choices, (B). You must still divide by 3 (since there are 3 feet per yard) to find the cost per foot. $0.99 divided by 3 is $0.33, which is choice (A). Therefore, it would be very helpful to mark the words *price per foot* in the problem.

3. If $3x + 1 = 16$, what is the value of $x - 4$?

(A) 19   (B) 16   (C) 5   (D) 1   (E) −1

The key here is *what is the value of x − 4*. Therefore, circle $x - 4$. Note that solving the original equation will tell only the value of x.

$$3x + 1 = 16$$
$$3x = 15$$
$$x = 5$$

Here again, notice that 5 is one of the choices, (C). But the question asks for the value of $x - 4$, not just x. To continue, replace x with 5 and solve.

$$x - 4 = ?$$
$$5 - 4 = 1$$

The correct answer choice is (D).

4. Together a sweet roll and a cup of coffee cost $1.25. The sweet roll costs $0.25 more than the coffee. What is the cost of the sweet roll?

(A) $0.25   (B) $0.50   (C) $0.75   (D) $1.00   (E) $1.25

The key words here are *cost of the sweet roll,* so mark those words. Solving this algebraically,

x = coffee
$x + 0.25$ = sweet roll (cost $0.25 more than the coffee)
Together they cost $1.25

$$(x + 0.25) + x = 1.25$$
$$2x + 0.25 = 1.25$$
$$2x = 1.00$$
$$x = 0.50$$

But this is the cost of the *coffee.* Notice that $0.50 is one of the choices, (B). Since $x = 0.50$, then $x + 0.25 = 0.75$. Therefore, the sweet roll costs $0.75, which is choice (C). *Always answer the question that is being asked.* Circling or underlining the key word or words will help you do that.

Pull Out Information

Pulling information out of the wording of a word problem can make the problem more workable. Pull out the given facts and identify which of those facts will help you work the problem. Not all facts will always be needed.

1. Bill is 10 years older than his sister. If Bill was 25 years of age in 1993, in what year could he have been born?

(A) 1958   (B) 1963   (C) 1968   (D) 1973   (E) 1978

The key words here are *in what year* and *could he have been born.* Thus, the solution is simple: $1993 - 25 = 1968$, answer (C). Notice that you should pull out the information *25 years of age* and *in 1993.* The fact about Bill's age in comparison to his sister's age is not needed, however, and is not pulled out.

2. John is 18 years old. He works for his father for $\frac{3}{4}$ of the year, and he works for his brother for the rest of the year. What is the ratio of the time John spends working for his brother to the time he spends working for his father per year?

(A) $\frac{1}{4}$ (B) $\frac{1}{3}$ (C) $\frac{3}{4}$ (D) $\frac{4}{3}$ (E) $\frac{4}{1}$

The key word *rest* points to the answer.

$$1 - \frac{3}{4} =$$

$$\frac{4}{4} - \frac{3}{4} = \frac{1}{4} \text{ (the part of the year John works for his brother)}$$

Also, a key idea is the way in which the ratio is to be written. The problem becomes that of finding the ratio of $\frac{1}{4}$ to $\frac{3}{4}$.

$$\frac{\frac{1}{4}}{\frac{3}{4}} = \frac{1}{4} \div \frac{3}{4} = \frac{1}{\overset{}{\underset{1}{4}}} \times \frac{\overset{1}{4}}{3} = \frac{1}{3}$$

Therefore, the answer is choice (B). Note that John's age is not needed to solve the problem.

Sometimes, you may not have sufficient information to solve the problem. For example,

3. A woman purchased several books at $15 each plus one more for $12. What was the average price of each book?

   (A) $12
   (B) $13
   (C) $14
   (D) $15
   (E) There is not enough information to tell.

To calculate an average, you must have the total amount and then divide by the number of items. The difficulty here, however, is that *several books at $15* does not specify exactly *how many* books were purchased at $15 each. Does *several* mean two? Or does it mean three?

Several is not a precise mathematical term. Therefore, there is not enough information to pull out to calculate an average. The answer is (E).

Plug In Numbers

When a problem involving variables (unknowns, or letters) seems difficult and confusing, simply replace those variables with numbers. Usually, problems using numbers are easier to understand. Simple numbers will make the arithmetic easier for you to do. Be sure to make logical substitutions. Use a positive number, a negative number, or zero when applicable to get the full picture.

1. If x is a positive integer in the equation $2x = y$, then y must be

  (A) a positive even integer
  (B) a negative even integer
  (C) zero
  (D) a positive odd integer
  (E) a negative odd integer

At first glance, this problem appears quite complex. But let's plug in some numbers and see what happens. For instance, first plug in 1 (the simplest positive integer) for x.

$$2x = y$$
$$2(1) = y$$
$$2 = y$$

Now try 2.

$$2x = y$$
$$2(2) = y$$
$$4 = y$$

Try it again. No matter what positive integer is plugged in for x, y will always be positive and even. Therefore, the answer is (A).

2. If a, b, and c are all positive whole numbers greater than 1 such that $a < b < c$, which of the following is the largest quantity?

   (A) $a(b + c)$
   (B) $ab + c$
   (C) $ac + b$
   (D) They are all equal.
   (E) The largest quantity cannot be determined.

Substitute 2, 3, and 4 for a, b, and c, respectively.

$a(b+c) =$	$ab+c =$	$ac+b =$
$2(3+4) =$	$2(3)+4 =$	$2(4)+3 =$
$2(7) = 14$	$6+4 = 10$	$8+3 = 11$

Since 2, 3, and 4 meet the conditions stated in the problem and choice (A) produces the largest numerical value, it will consistently be the largest quantity. Therefore, $a(b + c)$ is the correct answer, (A).

Work from the Answers

At times, the solution to a problem will be obvious to you. At other times, it may be helpful to work from the answers. If a direct approach is not obvious, try working from the answers. This technique is even more efficient when some of the answer choices are easily eliminated.

1. Barney can mow the lawn in 5 hours, and Rachel can mow the lawn in 4 hours. How long will it take them to mow the lawn together?

   (A) 8 hours   (D) 4 hours
   (B) 5 hours   (E) $2\frac{2}{9}$ hours
   (C) $4\frac{1}{2}$ hours

You may never have worked a problem like this, or perhaps you have worked one but don't remember the procedure required to find the answer. In that case, try working from the answers. Since Rachel can mow the lawn in 4 hours by herself, it will take less than 4 hours if Barney helps her. Therefore, choices (A), (B), (C), and (D) are not reasonable. Thus, the correct answer—by working from the answers and eliminating the incorrect ones—is (E).

2. Find the counting number that is less than 15 and when divided by 3 has a remainder of 1, but when divided by 4 has a remainder of 2.

(A) 5   (B) 8   (C) 10   (D) 12   (E) 13

By working from the answers, you can eliminate wrong answer choices. For instance, (B) and (D) can be immediately eliminated because they are divisible by 4, leaving no remainder. Choices (A) and (E) can also be eliminated because they leave a remainder of 1 when divided by 4. Therefore, the correct answer is (C): 10 leaves a remainder of 1 when divided by 3 and a remainder of 2 when divided by 4.

Approximate

If a problem involves number calculations that seem tedious and time consuming, round off or approximate the numbers. Replace the given numbers with whole numbers that are easier to work with. Find the answer choice that is closest to your approximated answer.

1. The value for $(0.889 \times 55) / 9.97$ to the nearest tenth is

(A) 49.1   (B) 17.7   (C) 4.9   (D) 4.63   (E) 0.5

Before starting any computations, take a glance at the answers to see how far apart they are. Notice that the only close answers are (C) and (D), but (D) is not a possible choice, since it is to the nearest hundredth, not tenth. Now, make some quick approximations, $0.889 \approx 1$ and $9.97 \approx 10$, leaving the problem in this form.

$$\frac{1 \times 55}{10} = \frac{55}{10} = 5.5$$

The closest answer is (C); therefore, it is the correct answer. Notice that choices (A) and (E) are not reasonable.

2. The value of $\sqrt{7194 / 187}$ is approximately

(A) 6   (B) 9   (C) 18   (D) 35   (E) 72

Round off both numbers to the hundreds place. The problem then becomes

$$\sqrt{\frac{7200}{200}}$$

This is much easier to work. By dividing, the problem now becomes $\sqrt{36}$. The closest answer choice is the exact value of choice (A).

Make Comparisons

At times, questions will require you to compare the sizes of several decimals or of several fractions. If decimals are being compared, make sure that the numbers being compared have the same number of digits. (Remember, zeros to the far right of a decimal point can be inserted or eliminated without changing the value of the number.)

1. Put these in order from smallest to largest: $0.6, 0.16, 0.66\frac{2}{3}, 0.58$

   (A) $0.6, 0.16, 0.66\frac{2}{3}, 0.58$
   (B) $0.58, 0.16, 0.6, 0.66\frac{2}{3}$
   (C) $0.16, 0.58, 0.6, 0.66\frac{2}{3}$
   (D) $0.66\frac{2}{3}, 0.6, 0.58, 0.16$
   (E) $0.58, 0.6, 0.66\frac{2}{3}, 0.16$

   Rewrite 0.6 as 0.60. Therefore, all of the decimals now have the same number of digits: $0.60, 0.16, 0.66\frac{2}{3}, 0.58$. Treating these as though the decimal point were not there (this can be done only when all the numbers have the same number of digits to the right of the decimal), the order is as follows: $0.16, 0.58, 0.60, 0.66\frac{2}{3}$. The correct answer is (C). Remember to mark *smallest to largest* in the question.

2. Put these in order from smallest to largest: $\frac{5}{8}, \frac{3}{4}, \frac{2}{3}$

   (A) $\frac{2}{3}, \frac{3}{4}, \frac{5}{8}$ (D) $\frac{3}{4}, \frac{5}{8}, \frac{2}{3}$
   (B) $\frac{2}{3}, \frac{5}{8}, \frac{3}{4}$ (E) $\frac{3}{4}, \frac{2}{3}, \frac{5}{8}$
   (C) $\frac{5}{8}, \frac{2}{3}, \frac{3}{4}$

Using common denominators, $\frac{5}{8} = \frac{15}{24}$, $\frac{3}{4} = \frac{18}{24}$, and $\frac{2}{3} = \frac{16}{24}$. Therefore, the order becomes $\frac{5}{8}$, $\frac{2}{3}$, $\frac{3}{4}$.

Using decimal equivalents, $\frac{5}{8} = 0.625$, $\frac{3}{4} = 0.75$ or 0.750, and $\frac{2}{3} = 0.66\frac{2}{3}$ or $0.666\frac{2}{3}$. The order again becomes $\frac{5}{8}$, $\frac{2}{3}$, $\frac{3}{4}$. The answer is (C).

3. Which of the following values is least?

   (A) $\frac{3}{8}$ (B) 38   (C) 0.38   (D) $\frac{8}{3}$ (E) 38%

The least value is choice (A). Choices (C) and (E) are equal, and choices (B) and (D) are each more than 1. The fraction $\frac{3}{8}$ can be changed into a decimal by dividing 3 by 8, which gives 0.375, which is just a little less than choices (C) and (E).

4. On a number line, all of the following fractions lie between $\frac{7}{8}$ and $\frac{19}{20}$ EXCEPT

   (A) $\frac{8}{9}$ (B) $\frac{9}{10}$ (C) $\frac{10}{11}$ (D) $\frac{15}{16}$ (E) $\frac{9}{8}$

Before you get bogged down analyzing each of the first few choices, notice that the last choice, (E), has a numerator larger than the denominator. This means that it is greater than 1, which would mean it does not lie between $\frac{7}{8}$ and $\frac{19}{20}$, each of which are less than one.

Mark Diagrams

When a figure is included with the problem, mark the given facts on the diagram. Marking in this way will help you visualize all the facts that have been given.

1. If each square in the figure has a side of length 1, what is the perimeter?

   (A) 8
   (B) 12
   (C) 14
   (D) 16
   (E) 20

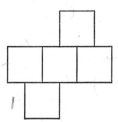

Mark the known facts.

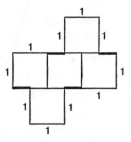

You now have a calculation for the perimeter: 10 *plus* the darkened parts. Now, look carefully at the top two darkened parts. They will add up to 1. (Notice how the top square may slide over to illustrate that fact.)

The same is true for the bottom darkened parts. They will add to 1. Thus, the total perimeter is 10 + 2, or 12, choice (B).

These together total 1

2. The perimeter of the isosceles triangle shown at right is 42". The two equal sides are each three times as long as the third side. What are the lengths of each side?

(A) 21, 21, 21
(B) 6, 6, 18
(C) 18, 21, 3
(D) 18, 18, 6
(E) 4, 19, 19

$\triangle ABC$ is isosceles
$\overline{AB} = \overline{AC}$

Mark the equal sides of the diagram.

$\overline{AB}$ and $\overline{AC}$ are each three times as long as $\overline{BC}$.

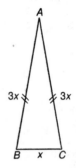

The equation for perimeter is

$$3x + 3x + x = 42$$
$$7x = 42$$
$$x = 6$$

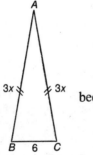   becomes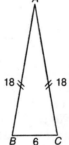

The answer is (D). *Note:* This problem can also be solved by working from the answers given.

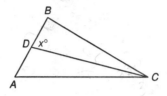

3. In the triangle above, *CD* is an angle bisector, angle *ACD* is 30°, and angle *ABC* is a right angle. What is the measurement of angle *x* in degrees?

(A) 30°   (B) 45°   (C) 60°   (D) 75°   (E) 180°

You should read the problem and mark as follows. In the triangle above, *CD* is an angle bisector (*stop and mark in the drawing*), angle *ACD* is 30° (*stop and mark in the drawing*), and angle *ABC* is a right angle (*stop and mark in the drawing*). What is the measurement of angle *x* in degrees? (*Stop and mark in or circle what you are looking for in the drawing.*)

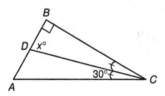

Now, with the drawing marked in, it is evident that, since angle *ACD* is 30°, angle *BCD* is also 30° because they are both formed by an angle bisector (which divides an angle into two equal parts). Since angle *ABC* is 90° (right angle) and *BCD* is 30°, then angle *x* is 60° because there are 180° in a triangle, $180 - (90 + 30) = 60$. The correct answer is (C). **Always mark in diagrams as you read descriptions and information about them. Marking should include what you are looking for.**

Draw Diagrams

Drawing diagrams to meet the conditions set by the word problem can often make the problem easier to work. Being able to "see" the facts is more helpful than just reading the words.

1. If all sides of a square are doubled, the area of that square

    (A) is doubled
    (B) is tripled
    (C) is multiplied by 4
    (D) remains the same
    (E) Not enough information is provided.

One way to solve this problem is to draw a square, double all its sides, and then compare the two areas.

Your first diagram:

Doubling every side,

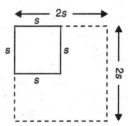

Notice that the total area of the new square will now be four times the original square. The correct answer is (C).

2. A hiking team begins at camp and hikes 5 miles north, then 8 miles west, then 6 miles south, then 9 miles east. In what direction must they now travel in order to return to camp?

    (A) North
    (B) Northeast
    (C) Northwest
    (D) West
    (E) They already are at camp.

For this question, your diagram would look something like this.

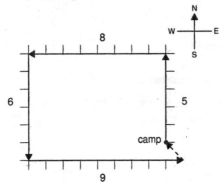

Thus, they must travel northwest (C) to return to camp. Note that in this case it is important to draw your diagram very accurately.

3. If point $P(1, 1)$ and $Q(1, 0)$ lie on the same coordinate graph, which must be true?

   I. P and Q are equidistant from the origin.
  II. P is farther from the origin than P is from Q.
 III. Q is farther from the origin than Q is from P.

(A) I only   (D) I and II only
(B) II only   (E) I and III only
(C) III only

First draw the coordinate graph and then plot the points as follows:

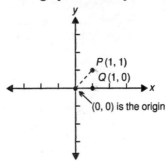

The correct answer is (B). Only II is true. P is farther from the origin than P is from Q.

Try Possibilities in Probability Problems

Some questions will involve probability and possible combinations. If you don't know a formal method, try some possibilities. Set up what could happen. But set up only as much as you need to.

1. What is the probability of throwing two dice in one toss so that they total 11?

   (A) $\frac{1}{6}$ (B) $\frac{1}{11}$ (C) $\frac{1}{18}$ (D) $\frac{1}{20}$ (E) $\frac{1}{36}$

   You should simply list all the possible combinations resulting in 11 (5 + 6 and 6 + 5) and realize that the total possibilities are 36 (6 × 6). Thus the probability equals

$$\frac{\text{possibilities totaling 11}}{\text{total possibilities}} = \frac{2}{36} = \frac{1}{18}$$

Answer (C) is correct.

2. What is the probability of tossing a penny twice so that both times it lands heads up?

   (A) $\frac{1}{8}$ (B) $\frac{1}{4}$ (C) $\frac{1}{3}$ (D) $\frac{1}{2}$ (E) $\frac{2}{3}$

   The correct answer is (B). The probability of throwing a head in one throw is

$$\frac{\text{chances of a head}}{\text{total chances (1 head + 1 tail)}} = \frac{1}{2}$$

Since you're trying to throw a head *twice*, multiply the probability for the first toss ($\frac{1}{2}$) times the probability for the second toss (again $\frac{1}{2}$). Thus, $\frac{1}{2} \times \frac{1}{2} = \frac{1}{4}$, and $\frac{1}{4}$ is the probability of throwing heads twice in two tosses.

Another way of approaching this problem is to look at the total number of possible outcomes:

	First Toss	Second Toss
1.	H	H
2.	H	T
3.	T	H
4.	T	T

Thus, there are four different possible outcomes. There is only one way to throw two heads in two tosses. Thus, the probability of tossing two heads in two tosses is 1 out of 4 total outcomes, or $\frac{1}{4}$.

3. How many combinations are possible if a person has 4 sports jackets, 5 shirts, and 3 pairs of slacks?

(A) 4   (B) 5   (C) 12   (D) 60   (E) 120

The correct answer is (D). Since each of the 4 sports jackets may be worn with 5 different shirts, there are 20 possible combinations. These may be worn with each of the 3 pairs of slacks for a total of 60 possible combinations. Stated simply, $5 \cdot 4 \cdot 3 = 60$ possible combinations.

Interpret Special Symbols

In some problems, you may be given special symbols that you are unfamiliar with. Don't let these special symbols alarm you. They typically represent an operation or combination of operations that you are familiar with. Look for the definition of the special symbol or how it is used.

1. If $\odot$ is a binary operation such that $a \odot b$ is defined as $a^2 - b^2 / a^2 + b^2$, then what is the value of $3 \odot 2$?

(A) $-\frac{5}{13}$ (B) $\frac{1}{13}$ (C) $\frac{1}{5}$ (D) $\frac{5}{13}$ (E) 1

The correct answer is (D). The value of $a \odot b =$

$$\frac{a^2 - b^2}{a^2 + b^2}$$

Simply replacing a with 3 and b with 2 gives

$$\frac{3^2 - 2^2}{3^2 + 2^2} = \frac{9-4}{9+4} = \frac{5}{13}$$

Determine the Method in Procedure Problems

Some problems may not ask you to solve and find a correct numerical answer. Rather, you may be asked *how to work* the problem.

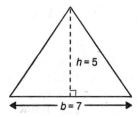

1. To find the area of the figure above, a student could use which formula(s)?

   I. Area = base times height
  II. Area = $\frac{1}{2}$ times base times height
 III. Area = one side squared

(A) I only   (D) I and II only
(B) II only   (E) I and III only
(C) III only

Notice that it is not necessary to use any of the numerical values given in the diagram. You are simply to identify how the problem can be worked. In such cases, don't bother working the problem; it's a waste of time. The correct answer is (B), II only.

2. 51×6 could be quickly mentally calculated by

    (A) $50 \times 6 + 1$
    (B) $51 + 51 + 51 + 51 + 51 + 51$
    (C) $(50 \times 6) + (1 \times 6)$
    (D) $(50 \times 6) + \frac{1}{6}$
    (E) adding fifty-one sixes

Answer (C) is correct. The quickest method of calculating 51×6 is to first multiply 50×6 (resulting in 300), then multiply 1×6 (resulting in 6), and then add the two answers together ($300 + 6 = 306$). Answer choices (B) and (E) will give the correct answer as well (306), but neither is the best way to *quickly* calculate the answer.

Sometimes, however, actually working the problem can be helpful, as in the following problem.

3. The fastest method to solve $\frac{7}{48} \times \frac{6}{7} =$ is to

    (A) invert the second fraction and then multiply
    (B) multiply each column across and then reduce to lowest terms
    (C) find the common denominator and then multiply across
    (D) divide 7 into numerator and denominator, divide 6 into numerator and denominator, and then multiply across
    (E) reduce the first fraction to lowest terms and then multiply across

In this problem, the way to determine the fastest procedure may be to actually work the problem as you would if you were working toward an answer. Then see if that procedure is listed among the choices. You should then compare it to the other methods listed. Is one of the other *correct* methods faster than the one you used? If so, select the fastest.

These types of problems are not constructed to test your knowledge of *obscure* tricks in solving mathematical equations. Rather, they test your knowledge of common procedures used in standard mathematical equations. Thus, the fastest way to solve this problem would be to first divide 7 into the numerator and denominator.

$$\frac{^{1}7}{48} \times \frac{6}{7_{1}}$$

Then, divide 6 into the numerator and denominator.

$$\frac{^1 7}{_8 \cancel{48}} \times \frac{\cancel{6}^1}{7_{\,1}}$$

Then, multiply across.

$$\frac{^1 7}{_8 \cancel{48}} \times \frac{\cancel{6}^1}{7_{\,1}} = \frac{1}{8}$$

The correct answer is (D).

Interpret Data—Graphs, Charts, and Tables

Certain problems will be based on graphs, charts, or tables. You will need to be able to read and interpret the data on each graph, chart, or table as well as do some arithmetic with this data.

Spend a few moments to understand the title of each graph, chart, or table as well as what the numbers are representing. Carefully review the coordinate labels in the graphs and the row and column headings in the charts or tables.

- Identify numbers and facts given on the graph, chart, or table and determine what amount those numbers represent.
- There are three main types of charts and tables. The basic ones focus on information given in rows and columns.
- The amounts in decimal or fractional form on a circle graph always total one whole. The amounts in percentage form on a circle graph always total 100%.
- The amounts written as money or in numerical form on a circle graph always add to to the total amount being referred to.
- Be sure to thoroughly read a paragraph under a graph if there is one and to interpret a legend if one is included.
- On bar or line graphs, it is sometimes helpful to use the edge of your answer sheet as a straightedge so that you can line up points on the graph with their numerical values on the graph scale. Also, look for trends such as increases, decreases, sudden low points, or sudden high points.

Questions 1, 2, and 3 refer to the following circle graph (pie chart).

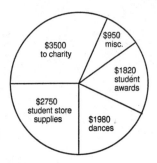

**How the Kettle School Distributed
Its Fundraising Earnings in 1995**

(1995 fundraising earnings totaled $11,000)

1. The amount of money given to charity in 1995 was approximately what percent of the total amount earned?

   (A) 18%   (B) 34%   (C) 45%   (D) 50%   (E) 82%

   The answer is (B). Set up a simple ratio.

   $$\frac{\text{money to charity}}{\text{total}} = \frac{\$3500}{\$11,000} \approx \frac{1}{3} = 33\tfrac{1}{3}\%$$

2. The previous year, 1994, the Kettle School spent 40% of its earnings on student store supplies. This percentage exceeds the 1995 figure by how much?

   (A) 0%   (B) 10%   (C) 15%   (D) 30%   (E) 85%

   The answer is (C).

   $$\frac{\text{student store supplies in 1995}}{\text{total}} = \frac{\$2750}{\$11,000} = 25\%$$

   $$40\% - 25\% = 15\%$$

3. If the Kettle School spends the same percentage on dances every year, how much will they spend in a year in which their earnings are $15,000?

(A) $ 270　　　　　　　　(D) $11,000
(B) $2700　　　　　　　 (E) $15,000
(C) $4000

The answer is (B).

$$\text{In 1995, } \frac{\$1980}{\$11,000} = 18\%$$

So 18% of $15,000 = $2700.

Questions 4, 5, and 6 refer to the following circle graph (pie chart).

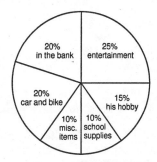

How John Spends His Weekly Paycheck

4. If John receives $100 per paycheck, how much money does he put in the bank?

(A) $2　(B) $20　(C) $35　(D) $80　(E) $100

The answer is (B). 20% of $100 = 0.2(100) = $20.00.

5. John spends more than twice as much on _____ as he does on school supplies.

   (A) car and bike
   (B) his hobby
   (C) entertainment
   (D) miscellaneous items
   (E) It cannot be determined from the information given.

   The answer is (C). School supplies are 10%. The only amount more than twice 10% (or 20%) is 25% (entertainment).

6. The ratio of the amount of money John spends on his hobby to the amount he puts in the bank is

   (A) 1/2   (B) 2/3   (C) 3/4   (D) 5/8   (E) 1/6

   The answer is (C). Set up the ratio.

   $$\frac{\text{amount to hobby}}{\text{amount to bank}} = \frac{15}{20} = \frac{3}{4}$$

Questions 7, 8, and 9 refer to the following bar graph.

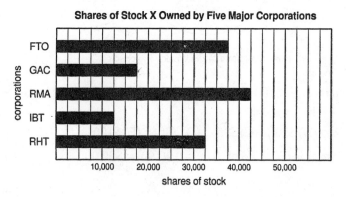

Shares of Stock X Owned by Five Major Corporations

7. The number of shares owned by RHT exceeds the number of shares owned by GAC by

   (A) 10,000   (D) 20,000
   (B) 15,000   (E) 32,500
   (C) 17,500

   The answer is (B).

$$\begin{array}{r} 32{,}500 \text{ RHT} \\ -17{,}500 \text{ GAC} \\ \hline 15{,}000 \end{array}$$

8. The number of shares of stock owned by IBT is approximately what percent of that owned by FTO?

   (A) 18%   (B) 25%   (C) 33%   (D) 42%   (E) 50%

   The answer is (C). 12,500 is what percent of 37,500?

$$\frac{12{,}500}{37{,}500} = \frac{1}{3} \approx 33\%$$

9. The number of shares of stock owned by RMA exceeds which other corporations' by more than 20,000?

   (A) GAC and IBT   (D) IBT and FTO
   (B) FTO and RHT   (E) IBT and RHT
   (C) GAC and FTO

   The answer is (A).

$$\begin{array}{r} 42{,}500 \text{ RMA} \\ -17{,}500 \text{ GAC} \\ \hline 25{,}000 \end{array} \qquad \begin{array}{r} 42{,}500 \text{ RMA} \\ -12{,}500 \text{ IBT} \\ \hline 30{,}000 \end{array}$$

Questions 10, 11, and 12 are based on the following graph.

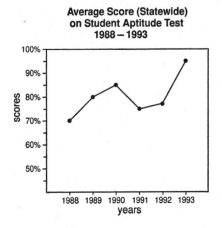

**Average Score (Statewide)
on Student Aptitude Test
1988 – 1993**

10. Between which two years was the greatest rise in average test scores?

(A) 1988 and 1989   (D) 1991 and 1992
(B) 1989 and 1990   (E) 1992 and 1993
(C) 1990 and 1991

The most efficient way to compute greatest rise is to locate the *steepest* upward slope on the chart. Note that the steepest climb is between 1992 and 1993. Therefore, choice (E) indicates the greatest rise in average test scores.

11. In which year was the average score approximately 85%?

(A) 1988   (B) 1989   (C) 1990   (D) 1991   (E) 1992

According to the graph, the average test score was approximately 85% in 1990 (C). In cases such as this, when you must read the graph for a precise measurement, it may be helpful to use your answer sheet as a straightedge to more accurately compare points with the grid marks along the side.

12. Approximately what was the highest score achieved statewide on the test?

(A) 80%
(B) 85%
(C) 90%
(D) 97%
(E) The highest score cannot be determined from the information in the graph.

The first thing you should do when confronted with a graph or chart is read its title to understand what the graph is telling you. In this case, the graph is relating information about *average scores*. It tells you nothing about the *highest* score achieved. Thus, (E) is the correct answer.

Question 13 refers to the following table.

Month	Expenses
January	$121,343
February	101,229
March	380,112
April	91,228
May	499,889
June	9,112

13. A product-development division of a corporation allocated the expenses shown in the above chart for the first half of the fiscal year. Approximately how many thousands of dollars were allocated for expenses in that half year?

(A) 800   (B) 1000   (C) 1200   (D) 1400   (E) 1600

Since the problem asks for an answer in terms of thousands of dollars, drop the last three digits when estimating.

Month	Expenses
January	$121
February	101
March	380
April	91
May	499
June	9

You can now add the numbers exactly or round them off first to make the addition easier.

Month	Expenses
January	$120
February	100
March	380
April	90
May	500
June	9
	$1179

$1179 is closest to 1200, answer choice (C).

Weekly Milk Prices (per quart)

63	65	62	73	68	72	66

14. The range of a set of numbers is the difference between the two most extreme values, and it is found by subtracting the lowest value from the highest value. Listed above are the weekly prices of milk during the course of two months. What is the range of weekly milk prices?

    (A) 3   (B) 9   (C) 10   (D) 11   (E) 12

The highest price in the set is 73. The lowest price is 62. Therefore, the range is $73 - 62 = 11$, or answer choice (D).

Questions 15 and 16 refer to the following table.

**AVERAGE EXPENDITURES
FOR MONTHLY HOUSING EXPENSES**

Metropolitan Area	Mortgage Payment	Property Tax	Hazard Insurance	Utility Cost	Total Monthly Expenses
Large					
Chicago	$291	$ 64	$14	$60	$429
Houston	292	48	26	74	439
Los Angeles	403	99	15	50	567
New York	291	111	25	70	497
San Francisco	445	99	20	50	614
Washington	388	85	14	91	578
All U.S. metropolitan areas with populations of 1.5 million or more	$299	$ 70	$13	$60	$442
All of the United States	$273	$ 54	$13	$60	$400

15. Which city's total monthly expenses were closest to the total monthly expenses for areas with populations of 1.5 million or more?

    (A) Chicago
    (B) Houston
    (C) New York
    (D) Los Angeles
    (E) Washington

First, you must determine the total monthly expenses for all U.S. cities with a population of 1.5 million or more. The last column of the next to the last line shows that the number is $442 per month. The column at the left shows the cities, and the last column shows their total monthly expenses. Second, you must determine which city's total monthly expenses are closest to the $442 monthly figure. The correct answer is Houston (B), which has a total monthly expense of $439.

16. You could conclude which of the following statements from information presented in the table?

(A) Los Angeles residents have larger incomes than residents in New York.

(B) The median mortgage payment in Los Angeles is lower than that in Washington.

(C) Housing dollars would stretch further in smaller cities.

(D) Hazard insurance is higher as the total monthly expenses increase.

(E) It costs more for monthly expenses in Washington, San Francisco, and New York than anywhere else in the country.

To answer this question, you must draw a conclusion from information presented in the table. The information in choice (A) cannot be determined from the data in the table. (Don't choose as an answer information that is not presented in a table, even if the statement might be based on accepted fact.) You can quickly eliminate choice (B) because the mortgage payment table shows that the Los Angeles average is $403, while the Washington average is $388. You can see that choice (D) is false by looking at the Houston hazard insurance ($26), the highest in the chart, and Houston's total monthly expenses ($439), one of the lowest in the chart. Choice (E) is false because Los Angeles has the third highest total monthly expenses ($567).

Notice that the monthly expense column is not in rank order—lowest to highest. The correct answer (C) can be supported by data presented in the table. Notice that all cities with populations of 1.5 million or more have a total monthly expense figure of $442. "All of the United States" (the United States considered as a whole) has a total monthly expense of $400. This means that many small cities reduced the $442 total monthly figure. So you can conclude that housing dollars would stretch further in smaller cities.

Flow Charts

One special type of chart is a flow chart. Following the flow of information is the key to understanding and using this special kind of chart.

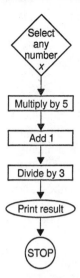

17. If the number chosen, *x,* is equal to 7, what result will be printed in the flow chart above?

(A) 6   (B) 8   (C) 10   (D) 12   (E) 15

If *x* is 7, then the steps in the flow chart are as follows:

7 multiplied by 5 = 35
35 plus 1 = 36
36 divided by 3 = 12

So the printed result is 12, answer choice (D).

Focus on the Words
of Formal Mathematical Reasoning Problems

Some questions will contain formal mathematical reasoning. Be sure to focus on the words used, their meaning, and how they are connected. Don't complicate the problem.

1. In a drawing with five parallelograms, four of the parallelograms are rectangles and one is a rhombus. If the rhombus is not a square, and at least two of the rectangles are squares, which of the following must be true?

   (A) No rhombus is a parallelogram.
   (B) Exactly one rectangle is a rhombus.
   (C) No rectangles are parallelograms.
   (D) Each parallelogram is a rectangle.
   (E) At least three of the parallelograms are rhombi.

Since each square is a rhombus, and at least two of the rectangles are squares, then at least three of the parallelograms are rhombi. Choice (E) is the correct answer.

> Games are played only by children.
> All children have brown eyes.

2. Which of the following conclusions is true if the above statements are true?

   (A) Games are not played by children.
   (B) Children with brown eyes don't play games.
   (C) All brown-eyed people play games.
   (D) Children with brown eyes are the only ones that play games.
   (E) No games are not played by adults.

Since all children have brown eyes, and games are played only by children, then it can be concluded that children with brown eyes are the only ones that play games, choice (D).

> All cats have tails.
> Some cats are furry.
> Chico is a cat.

3. If the statements above are true, which of the following statements is true based on the information given?

   (A) Some furry animals don't have tails.
   (B) Chico has a tail but no fur.
   (C) Cats without tails must be furry.
   (D) Chico has a tail but doesn't have to be furry.
   (E) Chico has fur but doesn't have to have a tail.

Answer (D) is correct. Since all cats have tails, and Chico is a cat, then Chico must have a tail. Since some cats are furry, Chico doesn't have to be furry.

TIPS FOR WORKING MATH PROBLEMS

1. Read the question carefully, circling or underlining what you are looking for.

2. Pull out important information.

3. Draw, sketch, or mark in diagrams.

4. If you know a simple method or formula, work the problem out as simply and quickly as possible.

5. If you don't know a simple method or formula,
   (a) try eliminating some unreasonable choices.
   (b) work from the answers or substitute in numbers if appropriate.
   (c) try approximating to clarify thinking and simplify work.

6. Always make sure that your answer is reasonable.

A PATTERNED PLAN OF ATTACK
Mathematics

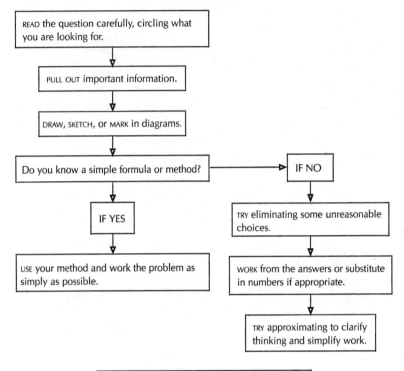

READ the question carefully, circling what you are looking for.

PULL OUT important information.

DRAW, SKETCH, or MARK in diagrams.

Do you know a simple formula or method? ⟶ IF NO

IF YES

USE your method and work the problem as simply as possible.

TRY eliminating some unreasonable choices.

WORK from the answers or substitute in numbers if appropriate.

TRY approximating to clarify thinking and simplify work.

ALWAYS MAKE SURE YOUR ANSWER IS **REASONABLE.**

Introduction to the Writing Test Multiple-Choice Section

The multiple-choice section of the Writing Test is 30 minutes in length and contains 45 questions. It is composed of two parts—Part A, English usage, and Part B, sentence correction.

PART A

Part A, the English usage section, typically contains 25 questions with a suggested completion time of 10 minutes.

The test is composed of the following content areas and *approximate* percentages.

Structure	70%
(noun, pronoun, verb, adjective, adverb problems—15% to 25%)	
(coordination, subordination, structural problems—35% to 45%)	
Diction, Idiom, and Mechanics	30%

ABILITY TESTED

This section tests your ability to recognize errors in standard written English.

BASIC SKILLS NECESSARY

Knowledge of some basic grammar is essential in this section. Review the rules of correctness that have been emphasized in your high school and college English classes.

DIRECTIONS

Some of the following sentences are correct. Others contain problems in grammar, usage, idiom, diction, punctuation, and capitalization.

If there is an error, it will be underlined and lettered. Find the one underlined part that must be changed to make the sentence correct and choose the corresponding letter on your answer sheet. Mark (E) if the sentence contains no error.

ANALYSIS OF DIRECTIONS

1. You are looking for errors in standard written English, the kind of English used in most textbooks. Do not evaluate a sentence in terms of the spoken English we all use.

2. When deciding whether an underlined portion is correct or not, assume that *all other parts of the sentence are correct.*

SUGGESTED APPROACH WITH SAMPLES

Focus on the Verbs

First focus on the verb or verbs.

1. <u>Here</u> on the table <u>is</u> an <u>apple</u> and <u>three pears.</u> <u>No error</u>
     A   B   C   D   E

Focus on the verb (*is*) and ask yourself what the subject is. In this sentence, the subject (*an apple and three pears*) follows the verb. Since the subject is plural, the verb must be plural—*are* instead of *is.*

Check the Verb Tenses

Another sort of verb error occurs when the verb tenses (past, present, future) are inconsistent. If there are two verbs in the sentence, make sure that the verb tense of each is appropriate.

2. He walked <u>for</u> miles <u>and</u> finally <u>sees</u> a <u>sign</u> of civilization.
         A   B   C   D

<u>No error</u>
  E

Walked describes the past; *sees* describes the present. *Sees* must be changed to *saw* so that the whole sentence describes the past. But remember, on this section of the test you don't have to actually make the corrections, and you don't have to know the precise term that describes a given error. You need only recognize the error. Therefore, learning what the errors "look like" is more efficient preparation than memorizing grammatical terminology.

Look for Pronoun Errors

3. We rewarded the workers <u>whom</u>, according <u>to</u> the manager,
                              A   B

  <u>had done</u> the most <u>imaginative</u> job. <u>No error</u>
    C   D   E

To test between *who* and *whom,* try replacing *whom* with either *him* or *them:* "them . . . had done the most imaginative job." To test whether *who* is correct instead, try substituting *he* or *they:* "they . . . had done the most imaginative job." Remember, if *him* or *them* fits when substituted, *whom* is correct. If *he* or *they* fits when substituted, *who* is correct.

Check the Adjectives and Adverbs

4. The mechanic <u>repaired</u> <u>my</u> engine and <u>installed</u> a new clutch
              A   B   C

  <u>very quick</u>. <u>No error</u>
    D   E

Adjectives describe things (nouns and pronouns), and adverbs describe actions (verbs). In this case, actions are being described (*repaired* and *installed* are verbs), so the word that describes those actions should be an adverb, *quickly* instead of *quick*. As you might notice, adverbs often end with *-ly*. The correct use of the adjective *quick* in a sentence occurs in this example: "The quick work of the mechanic pleased me very much." In this case, a thing is being described (*work*), so an adjective is appropriate.

Notice Parallelism

The following sentence contains faulty parallelism.

5. He <u>liked</u> <u>swimming</u>, <u>weight lifting</u>, and <u>to run</u>. <u>No error</u>
   A   B   C   D   E

To run is incorrect. It should be an *-ing* word like the other items.

Consider Idioms

The following sentence contains an error in idiom.

6. The young man <u>had been</u> <u>addicted of</u> drugs <u>ever since</u> his
                  A   B   C
<u>thirteenth</u> birthday. <u>No error</u>
  D   E

The correct idiom is *addicted to,* not *addicted of.*

Watch for Dangling Elements

A dangling element error affects a whole phrase.

7. <u>Stumbling around</u>, the light switch <u>was</u> <u>nowhere</u> <u>to be</u> found.
     A   B   C   D
<u>No error</u>
 E

The sentence seems to say that the light switch is *stumbling around.* In order to change this absurd and humorous meaning, you would need to insert *I realized that* or similar wording so the sentence now reads, "Stumbling around, I realized that . . ." Otherwise, *stumbling around* dangles, not referring clearly to any other element in the sentence.

Pay Attention to Comparisons

A sentence may contain a comparison error.

8. After <u>deliberating</u> <u>for</u> hours, the judges could not decide <u>who</u> was
          A   B   C
   the <u>greatest</u> of the two boxers. <u>No error</u>
       D   E

When only two things are being compared, in this case two boxers, *-er* words (*greater, taller, more beautiful*) should be used; *-est* words like *greatest* are used only when more than two things are being compared. "He was the greatest contender in the history of boxing."

Notice Capitalization and Punctuation

A sentence may contain an error of capitalization or punctuation.

9. We have invested over ten thousand dollars in <u>C</u>anadian postage
                                             A
   stamps <u>,</u> English china <u>;</u> and <u>F</u>rench wines. <u>No error</u>
      B   C   D   E

The capital letters here are correct, but the semicolon (C) should be a comma in a series.

A PATTERNED PLAN OF ATTACK
English Usage

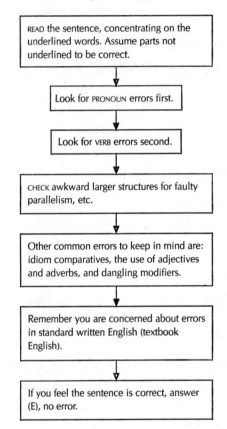

READ the sentence, concentrating on the underlined words. Assume parts not underlined to be correct.

Look for PRONOUN errors first.

Look for VERB errors second.

CHECK awkward larger structures for faulty parallelism, etc.

Other common errors to keep in mind are: idiom comparatives, the use of adjectives and adverbs, and dangling modifiers.

Remember you are concerned about errors in standard written English (textbook English).

If you feel the sentence is correct, answer (E), no error.

PART B

Part B, the sentence correction section, typically contains 20 questions with a suggested completion time of 20 minutes.

ABILITY TESTED

This section tests your knowledge of correct and effective English expression.

BASIC SKILLS NECESSARY

Knowledge of basic rules of grammar and usage is essential in this section.

DIRECTIONS

Some part of each sentence below is underlined; sometimes the whole sentence is underlined. Five choices for rephrasing the underlined part follow each sentence. The first choice (A) repeats the original, and the other four are different. If choice (A) seems better than the alternatives, choose answer (A); if not, choose one of the others.

For each sentence, consider the requirements of standard written English. Your choice should be a correct, concise, and effective expression, not awkward or ambiguous. Focus on grammar, word choice, sentence construction, and punctuation. If a choice changes the meaning or the original sentence, do not select it.

ANALYSIS OF DIRECTIONS

1. Several alternatives to an underlined portion may be correct. You are to pick the best (most clear and exact) one.

2. Remember that in sentence correction questions, there may be *more* than one kind of error in the sentence.

3. Any alternative which changes the meaning of the sentence should not be chosen, no matter how clear or correct it is.

SUGGESTED APPROACH WITH SAMPLES

Focus on the Verbs

As with the usage questions, begin with a careful study of the verb or verbs.

1. The trunk containing <u>costumes, makeup, and props were left</u> at the stage entrance of the theater.

   (A) costumes, makeup, and props were left
   (B) costumes, makeup, and props were all left
   (C) costumes, makeup, and props was left
   (D) costumes, makeup, and props to be left
   (E) costumes, makeup, and props left

   The verb is *were left.* Since the subject is singular (*trunk*), the verb must be singular—*was* instead of *were.* Don't assume that the subject immediately precedes the verb. In this case, the subject and verb are some distance apart.

Check the Verb Tenses

Look carefully at the verb tenses (past, present, future). If there are two or more verbs in the sentence, make sure the verb tense of each is appropriate.

2. He <u>read the recipe carefully, follows</u> directions, and used expensive ingredients, but the cake was inedible.

   (A) read the recipe carefully, follows
   (B) had read the recipe carefully, follows
   (C) reads the recipe carefully, followed
   (D) reads the recipe carefully, follows
   (E) read the recipe carefully, followed

   All three verbs in the first part should be in the same tense. Since *used* is in the past tense and cannot be changed, (E) is the correct choice, since it uses two past tenses (*read, followed*).

Notice Parallelism

Another common error is faulty parallelism. Look for a series of items separated by commas and make sure each item has the same *form.*

3. <u>To strive, to seek, to find, and not yielding</u> are the heroic goals of Ulysses in Tennyson's famous poem.

   (A) To strive, to seek, to find, and not yielding
   (B) To strive, to seek, to find, and to yield
   (C) To strive, to seek, to find, and not to yield
   (D) To strive, to seek, to find, and yet to yield
   (E) Striving, seeking, finding, and yielding

Not yielding is incorrect. It should have the "to ___" form of the other items. Choice (C) is the best. (B), (D), and (E) are correct, but they change the meaning of the sentence.

Check the Adjectives and Adverbs

Adjective or adverb misuse constitutes another type of error.

4. <u>The tired mechanic, happily to be finished with a hard day's work,</u> closed the hood over the newly tuned engine.

   (A) The tired mechanic, happily to be finished with a hard day's work
   (B) Happily, the tired mechanic being finished with a hard day's work
   (C) Tired but happy with a hard day's work being done, the mechanic
   (D) The tired mechanic, happy to be finished with a hard day's work
   (E) With the pleasant fatigue of a job well done, the mechanic

Happily is used here to describe a person, the mechanic. The correct part of speech for describing a person or thing is an adjective, *happy.* (D) is the correct choice—grammatically correct, logical, economical, and clear without unnecessarily changing the intended meaning of the original sentence.

Consider Idioms

Sometimes a sentence contains an error in idiom—that is, it employs a word or phrase which is incorrect simply because it has not been established as standard usage. Such errors just don't "sound right."

5. <u>After waiting on the arrival of a washer repairman for hours</u>, the customer resigned himself to using the laundromat.

   (A) After waiting on the arrival of a washer repairman for hours
   (B) With no arrival of a washer repairman for hours
   (C) After hours of waiting for the arrival of a washer repairman
   (D) Waiting after hours for the arrival of a washer repairman
   (E) In the face of hours of waiting for a washer repairman

Waiting on is not idiomatic in this context, although a waiter may wait on a table. Here, the correct expression is *waiting for.* Choices (C), (D), and (E) employ this construction, but (D) and (E) significantly obscure and change the intended meaning of the original sentence.

Watch for Dangling Elements

A type of error that affects a whole phrase rather than just one word is a dangling element, or misplaced modifier.

6. <u>Looking through the lens of a camera</u>, Mount Rushmore seemed much smaller and farther away than it had only seconds before.

   (A) Looking through the lens of a camera
   (B) With camera in hand
   (C) Through the effects of the lens of a camera she looks through
   (D) When she looked through the camera lens
   (E) Against the camera

The sentence seems to say that Mount Rushmore is looking through the camera lens. Choice (D) makes it clear that a person is looking through the lens and does so without the excessive wordiness of choice (C).

Pay Attention to Comparisons

A sentence may contain a comparison error.

7. She wished that her career could be <u>as glamorous as the other women</u> but was not willing to work as hard as they had.

   (A) as glamorous as the other women
   (B) as glamorous as the other women's careers
   (C) with the glamour of other women
   (D) more glamorous than the careers of the other women
   (E) glamorous

   Here, two very different *in*comparable things are being compared. *Her career* is being compared to the *other women*. Choice (B), the most clear, complete, and sensible construction, compares *her career* to *the other women's careers.*

Summary

Generally, watch out for pronouns, verbs, and awkward larger structures (illustrated by errors like faulty parallelism). Other possible errors which have not been explained above are fully explained in the answer sections following the practice tests. Remember that, unlike these examples, the sentences on the test may contain more than one kind of error.

A PATTERNED PLAN OF ATTACK
Sentence Correction

READ the sentence, focusing on the underlined part.

If there is NO ERROR in the underlined section, choose answer (A).

If there is an error, try to IDENTIFY it. Look for these error types first: pronoun, verb, misplaced modifier, parallel construction.

ELIMINATE choices that retain these errors or introduce new ones.

CHOOSE the BEST rephrasing of the choices that remain, reading your selection into the sentence and MAKING SURE THE MEANING STAYS THE SAME.

Introduction to the Writing Test Essay Section

The essay section of the Writing Test is 30 minutes in length and contains one essay question. You are asked to draw upon your personal experience and observations for information, examples, and generalizations to be used in your writing. The essay question generates a raw score that ranges from 2 to 12. (This raw score is the sum of the scores of two readers who each assign a score of 1 to 6.)

ABILITY TESTED

The essay section of the exam tests your ability to read a topic carefully, to organize your ideas before you write, and to write with clarity and precision.

BASIC SKILLS NECESSARY

This section requires a basic college-level writing background. Papers are scored on the writer's ability to achieve the following: organization and development of ideas with supporting evidence of specific examples; understanding of the essay's intended audience (for example, a speech urging members of a city council to vote a certain way); comprehension of the assigned task; skillful use of language; and correctness of mechanics, usage, and paragraphing.

DIRECTIONS

In this section, you will have 30 minutes to plan and write one essay on the topic given. You may use the paper provided to plan your essay before you begin writing. You should plan your time wisely. Read the topic carefully to make sure that you are properly addressing the issue or situation. **You must write on the given topic. An essay on another topic will not be acceptable.**

The essay question is designed to give you an opportunity to write clearly and effectively. Use specific examples whenever appropriate to aid in supporting your ideas. Keep in mind that the quality of your writing is much more important than the quantity.

Your essay is to be written in the space provided. No other paper may be used. Your writing should be neat and legible. Because you have only a limited amount of space in which to write, please do **not** skip lines, do **not** write excessively large, and do **not** leave wide margins.

Remember, use the bottom of this page for any organizational notes you may wish to make.

ANALYSIS OF DIRECTIONS

1. On the essay part of the PPST, you will have 30 minutes to write on one assigned topic. You will have space for prewriting notes to help you organize your thoughts. (These notes will *not* be read by the persons grading your exam.)

2. It is recommended that you use this space to organize your thoughts. Double-check to determine how much space you have in which to write your essay. At present, the test provides two blank sides of lined 8½" by 11" paper.

GENERAL TIPS FOR WRITING THE ESSAY

1. Read the topic twice—three times if necessary—before writing. Circle or underline key words to help you focus on the assigned task.

2. Use a form of "prewriting" *before* you begin writing your actual essay. Prewriting may consist of outlining, brainstorming, clustering, etc. Spend about five minutes doing this "organizing" before you start writing. A poorly written essay is often the result of inadequate planning.

3. Don't let spelling slow down your writing. Keep the flow of your writing going; then come back later to correct spelling errors.

4. Try to leave several minutes at the end to reread and edit/correct your essay. At this time, don't make extensive changes. Simply correct spelling errors and other minor flaws.

5. Don't write excessively large. Don't leave wide margins. Don't skip any lines.

6. Double-check your time allotment and the amount of space you have in which to write your essay.

SAMPLE ESSAY TOPIC AND PREWRITING METHODS

TOPIC

Teachers can play an important part in our lives. Choose one particular teacher you had during your school years and discuss one of his or her personal qualities which contributed to that teacher's impact on you.

PREWRITING METHODS

Clustering

Use clustering as a way of organizing your thoughts before you write. After you choose the "subject" (in this case, person) for your essay, write it down on the prewriting area and draw a circle around it.

For a few moments, think of a few possible "personal qualities which contributed to that teacher's impact on you." Write them down and connect them to the central subject cluster.

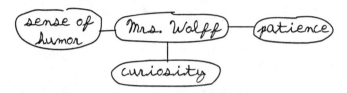

Now, from these qualities, select the one you can best develop into an essay. That is, choose the circle which you can support with *specific examples*.

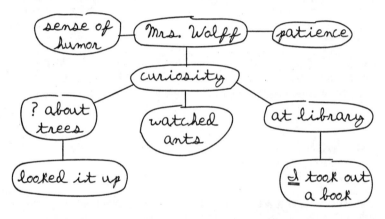

If you find that you can't come up with enough specific examples for the quality you initially chose, then choose another. You don't want to spend a great deal of time in clustering, however, just enough to give you a basic plan of how to write your essay. You can then number the parts of the cluster to give an order to your thoughts.

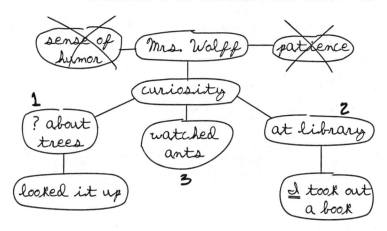

You don't have to use all of the elements of your cluster. (In fact, you'll be ignoring those headings for which you don't have support.) Clustering provides a way to put all of your thoughts down on paper before you write so that you can quickly see the structure of the whole paper.

Outlining

Another way of prewriting is outlining. A simple outline for this essay could go something like this.

Mrs. Wolff

  I. Sense of humor
 II. Patience
III. Curiosity
    A. Didn't know about trees
      1. Looked it up
      2. We were also excited
    B. Watched ants
    C. Saw her at library
      1. She studies Napoleon
      2. I took out a book

Organizing an outline like the one above (it need not be this formal) will help you write a well-structured, well-planned essay. You can readily see that constructing a good essay from the outline above would be much easier than writing it without any planning.

Whichever way you prewrite—cluster, outline, etc.—the important thing is that you think and plan before you actually begin to write the essay.

ESSAY SAMPLES

Here's the topic again and the finished essay, first written well and then poorly. Both essays are evaluated (comments run alongside each paragraph). Analyze each essay's strengths and weaknesses.

TOPIC

Teachers can play an important part in our lives. Choose one particular teacher you had during your school years and discuss one of his or her personal qualities which contributed to that teacher's impact on you.

WELL-WRITTEN ESSAY

Mrs. Wolff was my third-grade teacher more than ten years ago in upstate New York. Little did I know it then, but through one of her personal qualities—her curiosity—Mrs. Wolff helped to instill in me an enthusiasm for learning which I still have to this day.

Orienting reader to subject

Restating topic in thesis sentence

Mrs. Wolff had an enormous curiosity. In whatever we were studying, Mrs. Wolff wanted to find out "why?" Once when we were learning about trees, a student asked her a question she couldn't answer: Is the bark on a tree dead? Mrs. Wolff thought for a few seconds and then responded that she didn't know. But rather than move on to another question, Mrs. Wolff moved instead to the

Vivid specific details to support generalization

class encyclopedia and began searching. When she found the answer and read it aloud to the class, the excitement of her discovery was contagious. And this happened many, many times throughout the school year.

"Impact" of event noted

One Saturday my mother asked me to go to the town library to return some books. Whom did I see there but Mrs. Wolff, eagerly reading from a pile of books stacked in front of her. I said hello and asked what she was doing. Mrs. Wolff told me about the French history class she was taking at night and proceeded to describe what she was learning. Her enthusiasm for Napoleon kept me riveted for over an hour, until the library closed, but not before Mrs. Wolff encouraged me to take out a book for myself about Napoleon.

Another example with more specific details

Clear statement of significance of event

Another time I saw Mrs. Wolff lying on the lawn, face down. I thought she was hurt. But then I soon discovered that she had been watching an ant colony which had fascinated her for over an hour!

Another specific supporting detail

Mrs. Wolff's regard for her own education couldn't help but spread to her students. By her example, I came to love learning and to this day embrace it enthusiastically.

Summary sentence reinforcing overall point

WEAK ESSAY

Mrs. Wolff was a great teacher. She was good at helping us learn things and helping us like learning.

Incorrect restatement of topic

The factor why she had an impact on me was that she loved learning so much, she would always keep on trying to find things out if she didn't know them. Like whenever she didn't have an answer for something. Instead of forgetting it, she would always try to find it out. If you asked her a question or something, and she didn't know, then she would go and find it out. Or if she wanted to know something she would always try to look it up.

Sentence fragment

Vague reference, no specific example

So Mrs. Wolff helped me to like learning because I could watch her and see what she did, and then pretty soon I started to like learning. And so even now I like learning a lot because it's fun and because you found out a lot of things that you wouldn't ordinarily know which sometimes might come in handy.

Again, lack of specific detail

Off-topic conclusion

Mrs. Wolff is also a great swimmer. I have seen her at the beach many times and she just loves to swim. My father told me that Mrs. Wolff was once an Olympic swimmer and, in fact, that she won a medal in the Olympics but she has never showed it to us, so I can't be sure.

Irrelevant point
Off topic

So, in conclusion, Mrs. Wolff was a great teacher and made a big impact on me because of her liking to learn things so much that soon I began to like to learn things alot too.

Summary statement adds nothing new

In general, the response is disunified, lacks relevant and specific details, lacks planning and organization, and displays several mechanical errors.

Remember, a well-written essay will be on the assigned topic, address each of the points in the given topic, use supporting examples with detail, and be well organized, showing unity, coherence, and logical progression. It should be written in correct standard written English.

ESSAY SCORING GUIDE

The following guide should give you some indication of the reader's basis for scoring your paper. It should also assist you in evaluating or having someone else evaluate your practice essays.

SCORE 6

Score 6 for an essay that demonstrates a high degree of competency in writing while keeping minor errors to a minimum. This essay is well organized and well developed, using appropriate supporting examples and details. The essay uses language that is mature and varied and shows unity, coherence, and logical progression.

SCORE 5

Score 5 for an essay that demonstrates competence in writing, although it may have minor errors. As is an essay scoring 6, this essay is well organized and well developed, using appropriate supporting examples and details. (It may have fewer examples and details than a 6 paper.) The essay uses some variety in language and again shows unity, coherence, and logical progression. A 5 paper may not be as fluent as a 6 paper.

SCORE 4

Score 4 for an essay that demonstrates competence in writing, although it may have occasional errors. This essay is adequately organized and developed, using some supporting examples and details. The essay may contain some writing errors that are not serious and is fairly fluent.

SCORE 3

Score 3 for an essay that demonstrates some competence in writing but is clearly flawed. This essay is inadequately organized and lacks proper development. Supporting examples and detail are minimal. There is little or no variety in sentence structure, and there are obvious errors in mechanics and usage.

SCORE 2

Score 2 for an essay that demonstrates incompetence in writing. This essay is disorganized, with little or no development, and lacks examples and detail. Serious errors in mechanics, usage, or sentence structure are evident.

SCORE 1

Score 1 for an essay that demonstrates incompetence in writing. This essay is poorly organized, showing no development or logical progression. It contains many serious errors in writing.

SCORE 0

Score 0 for an essay that is off topic.

PRACTICE ESSAY TOPICS

Here are topics you may use for practice. Allow 30 minutes to plan and write each essay. Give yourself about a half page to organize your notes and two sides of lined 8½" by 11" paper to write the essay. Then, upon completion of each essay, evaluate (or have a friend evaluate) your writing using the criteria just mentioned and a checklist such as is provided in the scoring sections for each practice test in this book.

TOPIC 1

Suppose that the oldest building in your home town is to be torn down. In the space provided, write an essay in which you make a case to preserve the structure from demolition.

TOPIC 2

Choose a controversial film, novel, or play to which objections have been or might be raised. In the space provided, write an essay in which you argue either for or against exposing senior high school students to the work you have selected.

TOPIC 3

Many childhood experiences leave lifelong impressions on people. In the space provided, write an essay in which you describe a childhood experience and the effect it had on your life.

TOPIC 4

A local college is attempting to improve the college experience for its students by responding to suggestions for changes. If you could change one thing about the college experience in order to make it better, what would it be? Your answer may be based on your own experience or on the experience of others.

TOPIC 5

It is often said that we learn more from our mistakes than from our successes. Whether or not this is true, mistakes can play an important part in our lives. Think of a mistake you may have at one time made. In the space provided, write an essay discussing this mistake and its effect on you.

PART III

Mathematics Review

The following pages are designed to give you an intensive review of the basic skills used on the PPST Mathematics Test. Arithmetic, algebra, geometry, axioms, properties of numbers, terms, and simple statistics are covered. Before you begin the diagnostic review tests, it would be wise to become familiar with basic mathematics terminology, formulas, and general mathematical information, a review of which begins on the following page. Then proceed to the arithmetic diagnostic test, which you should take to spot your weak areas. Then use the arithmetic review that follows to strengthen those areas.

After reviewing the arithmetic, take the algebra diagnostic test and once again use the review that follows to strengthen your weak areas. Next, take the geometry diagnostic test and carefully read the complete geometry review.

Even if you are strong in arithmetic, algebra, and geometry, you may wish to skim the topic headings in each area to refresh your memory of important concepts. If you are weak in math, you should read through the complete review. *Note, however, that recent PPSTs have emphasized arithmetic more than they have algebra and geometry. Therefore, you should spend the major portion of your review time on sharpening your arithmetic skills and knowledge of terms and concepts.*

Symbols, Terminology, Formulas, and General Mathematical Information

COMMON MATH SYMBOLS AND TERMS

Symbol references:

$=$ is equal to	$\geq$ is greater than or equal to
$\neq$ is not equal to	$\leq$ is less than or equal to
$>$ is greater than	$\parallel$ is parallel to
$<$ is less than	$\perp$ is perpendicular to

Natural numbers—the counting numbers: 1, 2, 3, . . .

Whole numbers—the counting numbers beginning with zero: 0, 1, 2, 3, . . .

Integers—positive and negative whole numbers and zero: . . . −3, −2, −1, 0, 1, 2, . . .

Odd numbers—numbers not divisible by 2: 1, 3, 5, 7, . . .

Even numbers—numbers divisible by 2: 0, 2, 4, 6, . . .

Prime number—number divisible by only 1 and itself: 2, 3, 5, 7, 11, 13, . . .

Composite number—number divisible by more than just 1 and itself: 4, 6, 8, 9, 10, 12, 14, 15, . . .

Squares—the result when numbers are multiplied by themselves, $(2 \cdot 2 = 4)$, $(3 \cdot 3 = 9)$: 1, 4, 9, 16, 25, 36, . . .

Cubes—the result when numbers are multiplied by themselves twice, $(2 \cdot 2 \cdot 2 = 8)$, $(3 \cdot 3 \cdot 3 = 27)$: 1, 8, 27, . . .

MATH FORMULAS

Triangle	perimeter $= s_1 + s_2 + s_3$
	area $= \frac{1}{2}bh$
Square	perimeter $= 4s$
	area $= s \cdot s$, or s^2
Rectangle	perimeter $= 2(b + h)$, or $2b + 2h$
	area $= bh$, or lw
Parallelogram	perimeter $= 2(l + w)$, or $2l + 2w$
	area $= bh$
Trapezoid	perimeter $= b_1 + b_2 + s_1 + s_2$
	area $= \frac{1}{2}h(b_1 + b_2)$, or $h\left(\dfrac{b_1 + b_2}{2}\right)$
Circle	circumference $= 2\pi r$, or πd
	area $= \pi r^2$

Pythagorean theorem (for right triangles) $a^2 + b^2 = c^2$
  The sum of the square of the legs of a right triangle equals the
    square of the hypotenuse.

Cube	volume $= s \cdot s \cdot s = s^3$
	surface area $= s \cdot s \cdot 6$
Rectangular prism	volume $= l \cdot w \cdot h$
	surface area $= 2(lw) + 2(lh) + 2(wh)$

IMPORTANT EQUIVALENTS

$\frac{1}{100} = 0.01 = 1\%$

$\frac{1}{10} = 0.1 = 10\%$

$\frac{1}{5} = \frac{2}{10} = 0.2 = 0.20 = 20\%$

$\frac{3}{10} = 0.3 = 0.30 = 30\%$

$\frac{2}{5} = \frac{4}{10} = 0.4 = 0.40 = 40\%$

$\frac{1}{2} = \frac{5}{10} = 0.5 = 0.50 = 50\%$

$\frac{3}{5} = \frac{6}{10} = 0.6 = 0.60 = 60\%$

$\frac{7}{10} = 0.7 = 0.70 = 70\%$

$\frac{4}{5} = \frac{8}{10} = 0.8 = 0.80 = 80\%$

$\frac{9}{10} = 0.9 = 0.90 = 90\%$

$\frac{1}{4} = \frac{25}{100} = 0.25 = 25\%$

$\frac{3}{4} = \frac{75}{100} = 0.75 = 75\%$

$\frac{1}{3} = 0.33\frac{1}{3} = 33\frac{1}{3}\%$

$\frac{2}{3} = 0.66\frac{2}{3} = 66\frac{2}{3}\%$

$\frac{1}{8} = 0.125 = 0.12\frac{1}{2} = 12\frac{1}{2}\%$

$\frac{3}{8} = 0.375 = 0.37\frac{1}{2} = 37\frac{1}{2}\%$

$\frac{5}{8} = 0.625 = 0.62\frac{1}{2} = 62\frac{1}{2}\%$

$\frac{7}{8} = 0.875 = 0.87\frac{1}{2} = 87\frac{1}{2}\%$

$\frac{1}{6} = 0.16\frac{2}{3} = 16\frac{2}{3}\%$

$\frac{5}{6} = 0.83\frac{1}{3} = 83\frac{1}{3}\%$

$1 = 1.00 = 100\%$

$2 = 2.00 = 200\%$

$3\frac{1}{2} = 3.5 = 3.50 = 350\%$

MEASURES

CUSTOMARY SYSTEM, OR ENGLISH SYSTEM

Length

12 inches (in) = 1 foot (ft)
3 feet = 1 yard (yd)
36 inches = 1 yard
1760 yards = 1 mile (mi)
5280 feet = 1 mile

Area

144 square inches (sq in) = 1 square foot (sq ft)
9 square feet = 1 square yard (sq yd)

Weight

16 ounces (oz) = 1 pound (lb)
2000 pounds = 1 ton (T)

Capacity

2 cups = 1 pint (pt)
2 pints = 1 quart (qt)
4 quarts = 1 gallon (gal)
4 pecks = 1 bushel

Time

365 days = 1 year
52 weeks = 1 year
10 years = 1 decade
100 years = 1 century

METRIC SYSTEM,
OR THE INTERNATIONAL SYSTEM OF UNITS

Length—meter

Kilometer (km) = 1000 meters (m)
Hectometer (hm) = 100 meters
Dekameter (dam) = 10 meters

Meter

10 decimeters (dm) = 1 meter
100 centimeters (cm) = 1 meter
1000 millimeters (mm) = 1 meter

Volume—liter

Common measures

1000 milliliters (ml, or mL) = 1 liter (l, or L)
1000 liters = 1 kiloliter (kl, or kL)

Mass—gram

Common measures

1000 milligrams (mg) = 1 gram (g)
1000 grams = 1 kilogram (kg)
1000 kilograms = 1 metric ton (t)

Some Approximations

1 meter is a little more than a yard $3'' m\Lambda = 39''$
1 kilometer is about 0.6 mile
1 kilogram is about 2.2 pounds
1 liter is slightly more than 1 quart 33.7

MATH WORDS AND PHRASES

Words that signal an operation:

ADDITION

- Sum
- Total
- Plus
- Increase
- More than
- Greater than

MULTIPLICATION

- Of
- Product
- Times
- At (Sometimes)
- Total (Sometimes)

SUBTRACTION

- Difference
- Less
- Decreased
- Reduced
- Fewer
- Have left

DIVISION

- Quotient
- Divisor
- Dividend
- Ratio
- Parts

MATHEMATICAL PROPERTIES AND BASIC STATISTICS

SOME PROPERTIES (AXIOMS) OF ADDITION

Commutative means that the *order* does not make any difference.

$$2 + 3 = 3 + 2$$
$$a + b = b + a$$

Note: Commutative does *not* hold for subtraction.

$$3 - 1 \neq 1 - 3$$
$$a - b \neq b - a$$

Associative means that the *grouping* does not make any difference.

$$(2 + 3) + 4 = 2 + (3 + 4)$$
$$(a + b) + c = a + (b + c)$$

The grouping has changed (parentheses moved), but the sides are still equal.

Note: Associative does *not* hold for subtraction.

$$4 - (3 - 1) \neq (4 - 3) - 1$$
$$a - (b - c) \neq (a - b) - c$$

The **identity element** for addition is 0. Any number added to 0 gives the original number.

$$3 + 0 = 3$$
$$a + 0 = a$$

The **additive inverse** is the opposite (negative) of the number. Any number plus its additive inverse equals 0 (the identity).

$$3 + (-3) = 0; \text{therefore } 3 \text{ and } -3 \text{ are inverses}$$
$$-2 + 2 = 0; \text{therefore } -2 \text{ and } 2 \text{ are inverses}$$
$$a + (-a) = 0; \text{therefore } a \text{ and } -a \text{ are inverses}$$

SOME PROPERTIES (AXIOMS) OF MULTIPLICATION

Commutative means that the *order* does not make any difference.

$$2 \times 3 = 3 \times 2$$
$$a \times b = b \times a$$

Note: Commutative does not hold for division.

$$2 \div 4 \neq 4 \div 2$$

Associative means that the *grouping* does not make any difference.

$$(2 \times 3) \times 4 = 2 \times (3 \times 4)$$
$$(a \times b) \times c = a \times (b \times c)$$

The grouping has changed (parentheses moved), but the sides are still equal.

Note: Associative does *not* hold for division.

$$(8 \div 4) \div 2 \neq 8 \div (4 \div 2)$$

The **identity element** for multiplication is 1. Any number multiplied by 1 gives the original number.

$$3 \times 1 = 3$$
$$a \times 1 = a$$

The **multiplicative inverse** is the reciprocal of the number. Any number multiplied by its reciprocal equals 1.

$$2 \times \tfrac{1}{2} = 1; \text{ therefore 2 and } \tfrac{1}{2} \text{ are inverses}$$
$$a \times \frac{1}{a} = 1; \text{ therefore } a \text{ and } \frac{1}{a} \text{ are inverses}$$

A PROPERTY OF TWO OPERATIONS

The **distributive property** is the process of distributing the number on the outside of the parentheses to each number on the inside.

$$2(3 + 4) = 2(3) + 2(4)$$
$$a(b + c) = a(b) + a(c)$$

Note: You cannot use the distributive property with only one operation.

$$3(4 \times 5 \times 6) \neq 3(4) \times 3(5) \times 3(6)$$
$$a(bcd) \neq a(b) \times a(c) \times a(d) \text{ or } (ab)(ac)(ad)$$

SOME BASIC TERMS IN STATISTICS

To find the arithmetic **mean,** or average, simply total the numbers and divide by the number of numbers.

Find the arithmetic mean of 3, 5, 6, 7, and 9. The toal is $3 + 5 + 6 + 7 + 9 = 30$. Then divide 30 by 5, giving a mean, or average, of 6.

To find the **mode,** look for the most frequently occurring score or measure.

Find the mode of these scores: 3, 5, 5, 5, 6, 7. The mode is 5, since it appears most. If there are two modes, distribution of scores is called **bimodal.**

To find the **median,** arrange the scores or numbers in order by size. Then find the middle score or number.

Find the median of these scores: 2, 5, 7, 3, 6. First arrange them in order by size: 7, 6, 5, 3, 2. The middle score is 5; therefore the median is 5.

If the number of scores is even, take the average of the two middle scores. Find the median of these scores: 2, 5, 7, 4, 3, 6. First arrange them in order by size: 7, 6, 5, 4, 3, 2. The two middle numbers are 4 and 5; therefore the median is 4.5.

The **range** of a group of scores or numbers is calculated by subtracting the smallest from the largest.

Find the range of the scores 3, 2, 7, 9, 12. The range is $12 - 2 = 10$.

Arithmetic

ARITHMETIC DIAGNOSTIC TEST

1. $6 = ?/4$

2. Change $5\frac{3}{4}$ to an improper fraction.

3. Change $\frac{32}{6}$ to a whole number or mixed number in lowest terms.

4. $\frac{2}{5} + \frac{3}{5} =$

5. $\frac{1}{3} + \frac{1}{4} + \frac{1}{2} =$

6. $1\frac{3}{8} + 2\frac{5}{6} =$

7. $\frac{7}{9} - \frac{5}{9} =$

8. $11 - \frac{2}{3} =$

9. $6\frac{1}{4} - 3\frac{3}{4} =$

10. $\frac{1}{6} \times \frac{1}{6} =$

11. $2\frac{3}{8} \times 1\frac{5}{6} =$

12. $\frac{1}{4} \div \frac{3}{2} =$

13. $2\frac{3}{7} \div 1\frac{1}{4} =$

14. $0.07 + 1.2 + 0.471 =$

15. $0.45 - 0.003 =$

16. $\$78.24 - \$31.68 =$

17. $0.5 \times 0.5 =$

18. $8.001 \times 2.3 =$

19. $0.7\overline{)0.147}$

20. $0.002\overline{)12}$

21. $\frac{1}{3}$ of $7.20 =

22. Circle the larger number: 7.9 or 4.35

23. 39 out of 100 means _____.

24. Change 4% to a decimal.

25. 46% of 58 =

26. Change 0.009 to a percent.

27. Change 12.5% to a fraction.

28. Change $\frac{3}{8}$ to a percent.

29. Is 93 prime?

30. What is the percent increase of a rise in temperature from 80° to 100°?

31. Average 0, 8, and 10.

32. $8^2 =$

33. Approximate $\sqrt{30}$.

Answers

1. 24
2. $\frac{23}{4}$
3. $5\frac{2}{6}$ or $5\frac{1}{3}$
4. $\frac{5}{5}$ or 1
5. $\frac{13}{12}$ or $1\frac{1}{12}$
6. $4\frac{5}{24}$
7. $\frac{2}{9}$
8. $10\frac{1}{3}$
9. $2\frac{2}{4}$ or $2\frac{1}{2}$
10. $\frac{1}{36}$
11. $\frac{209}{48}$ or $4\frac{17}{48}$

12. $\frac{1}{6}$
13. $\frac{68}{35}$ or $1\frac{33}{35}$
14. 1.741
15. 0.447
16. $46.56
17. 0.25
18. 18.4023
19. 0.21
20. 6,000
21. $2.40
22. 7.9

23. 39% or $\frac{39}{100}$
24. 0.04
25. 26.68
26. 0.9% or $\frac{9}{10}$%
27. $\frac{125}{1000}$ or $\frac{1}{8}$
28. 37.5% or $37\frac{1}{2}$%
29. No
30. 25%
31. 6
32. 64
33. 5.5 or $5\frac{1}{2}$

ARITHMETIC REVIEW

ROUNDING OFF

To **round off** any number,

1. Underline the place value to which you're rounding off.
2. Look to the immediate right (one place) of your underlined place value.
3. Identify the numbr (the one to the right). If it is 5 or higher, round your underlined place value up 1. If the number (the one to the right) is 4 or less, leave your underlined place value as it is and change all the other numbers to its right to zeros.

Round to the nearest thousands.

345,678 becomes 346,000
928,499 becomes 928,000

This works with decimals as well. Round to the nearest hundredth.

3.4678 becomes 3.47
298,435.083 becomes 298,435.08

PLACE VALUE

Each position in any number has **place value.** For instance, in the number 485, 4 is in the hundreds place, 8 is in the tens place, and 5 is in the ones place. Thus, place value is as follows.

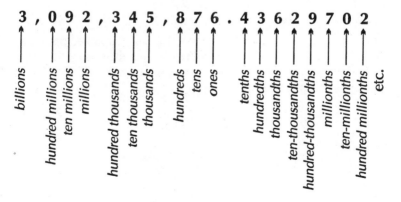

FRACTIONS AND MIXED NUMBERS

Fractions

Fractions consist of two numbers: a **numerator** (which is above the line) and a **denominator** (which is below the line).

$$\frac{1}{2} \begin{array}{l} \text{numerator} \\ \text{denominator} \end{array} \quad \text{or} \quad \text{numerator} \; {}^{1}\!/_{2} \; \text{denominator}$$

The denominator lets us know the number of equal parts into which something is divided. The numerator tells us how many of these equal parts are contained in the fraction. Thus, if the fraction is $\frac{3}{5}$ of a pie, then the denominator 5 tells us that the pie has been divided into 5 equal parts, of which 3 (numerator) are in the fraction.

Sometimes it helps to think of the dividing line (in the middle of the fraction) as meaning *out of*. In other words, $\frac{3}{5}$ would also mean 3 *out of* 5 equal pieces from the whole pie.

Common Fractions and Improper Fractions

A fraction like $\frac{3}{5}$, where the numerator is smaller than the denominator, is less than 1. This kind of fraction is called a **common fraction.**

But sometimes a fraction may be more than 1 (when the numerator is larger than the denominator). Thus, $\frac{12}{7}$ is more than 1. This kind of fraction is called an **improper fraction.**

Mixed Numbers

When a term contains both a whole number (such as 3, 8, 25, etc.) and a fraction (such as $\frac{1}{2}$, $\frac{1}{4}$, $\frac{3}{4}$, etc.), it is called a **mixed number.** For instance, $5\frac{1}{4}$ and $290\frac{3}{4}$ are both mixed numbers.

To **change an improper fraction to a mixed number,** you divide the denominator into the numerator.

$$\frac{18}{5} = 3\frac{3}{5} \qquad 5{\overline{\smash{)}18}}$$
$$\begin{array}{r} 3 \\ 5{\overline{\smash{)}18}} \\ \underline{15} \\ 3 \end{array}$$

To **change a mixed number to an improper fraction,** you multiply the denominator times the whole number, add in the numerator, and put the total over the original denominator.

$$4\tfrac{1}{2} = \tfrac{9}{2} \qquad 2 \times 4 + 1 = 9$$

Reducing Fractions

A fraction must be **reduced to lowest terms,** which is done by dividing both the numerator and denominator by the largest number that will divide evenly into both. For example, $\tfrac{14}{16}$ is reduced by dividing both terms by 2, thus giving us $\tfrac{7}{8}$. Likewise, $\tfrac{20}{25}$ is reduced to $\tfrac{4}{5}$ by dividing both numerator and denominator by 5.

Adding Fractions

To **add fractions,** you must first change all denominators to their *lowest common denominator* (LCD)—the lowest number that can be divided evenly by all the denominators in the problem. When you have all the denominators the same, you may add fractions by simply adding the numerators (the denominator remains the same).

$$\begin{array}{l} \dfrac{3}{8} = \dfrac{3}{8} \\[2mm] +\ \dfrac{1}{2} = \dfrac{4}{8} \\[1mm] \hline \quad\ \dfrac{7}{8} \end{array} \leftarrow \left\{ \begin{array}{l} \tfrac{1}{2} \text{ is} \\ \text{changed to } \tfrac{4}{8} \end{array} \right. \qquad \begin{array}{l} \dfrac{1}{4} = \dfrac{3}{12} \\[2mm] +\ \dfrac{1}{3} = \dfrac{4}{12} \\[1mm] \hline \quad\ \dfrac{7}{12} \end{array} \bigg\rangle \left\{ \begin{array}{l} \text{change both} \\ \text{fractions to} \\ \text{LCD of 12} \end{array} \right.$$

In the first example, we changed the $\tfrac{1}{2}$ to $\tfrac{4}{8}$ because 8 is the lowest common denominator, and then we added the numerators 3 and 4 to get $\tfrac{7}{8}$.

In the second example, we had to change both fractions to get the lowest common demominator of 12, and then we added the numerators to get $\tfrac{7}{12}$. Of course, if the denominators are already the same, just add the numerators.

$$\tfrac{6}{11} + \tfrac{3}{11} = \tfrac{9}{11}$$

Adding Mixed Numbers

To **add mixed numbers,** the same rule (find the LCD) applies, but make sure that you always add the whole numbers to get your final answer.

$$2\tfrac{1}{2} = 2\tfrac{2}{4} \leftarrow \{\tfrac{1}{2} \text{ is changed to } \tfrac{2}{4}$$
$$+\ 3\tfrac{1}{4} = 3\tfrac{1}{4}$$
$$\overline{\qquad 5\tfrac{3}{4}} \leftarrow \{\text{remember to add the whole numbers}$$

Subtracting Fractions

To **subtract fractions,** the same rule (find the LCD) applies, except that you subtract the numerators.

$$\begin{array}{r} \tfrac{7}{8} = \tfrac{7}{8} \\ -\ \tfrac{1}{4} = \tfrac{2}{8} \\ \hline \tfrac{5}{8} \end{array} \qquad \begin{array}{r} \tfrac{3}{4} = \tfrac{9}{12} \\ -\ \tfrac{1}{3} = \tfrac{4}{12} \\ \hline \tfrac{5}{12} \end{array}$$

Subtracting Mixed Numbers

When you **subtract mixed numbers,** sometimes you may have to *borrow* from the whole number, just like you sometimes borrow from the next column when subtracting ordinary numbers.

$$\begin{array}{r} 6\overset{4}{\cancel{5}}\overset{11}{\cancel{1}} \\ -\ 129 \\ \hline 522 \end{array} \qquad \begin{array}{r} \overset{3}{4}\overset{7}{\cancel{1}\tfrac{}{6}} \\ -\ 2\tfrac{5}{6} \\ \hline 1\tfrac{2}{6} = 1\tfrac{1}{3} \end{array}$$

you borrowed 1 from the 10s column

you borrowed 1 in the form of $\tfrac{6}{6}$ from the 1's column

To **subtract a mixed number from a whole number,** you have to *borrow* from the whole number.

$$6 = 5\tfrac{5}{5} \leftarrow \begin{cases} \text{borrow 1 in the form of} \\ \tfrac{5}{5} \text{ from the 6} \end{cases}$$

$$\frac{-3\tfrac{1}{5} = 3\tfrac{1}{5}}{2\tfrac{4}{5}} \leftarrow \begin{cases} \text{remember to subtract the} \\ \text{remaining whole numbers} \end{cases}$$

Multiplying Fractions

To **multiply fractions,** simply multiply the numerators; then multiply the denominators. Reduce to lowest terms if necessary.

$$\frac{2}{3} \times \frac{5}{12} = \frac{10}{36} \qquad \text{reduce } \frac{10}{36} \text{ to } \frac{5}{18}$$

This answer had to be reduced as it wasn't in lowest terms.

Canceling when multiplying fractions: You could first have *canceled*. That would have eliminated the need to reduce your answer. To cancel, find a number that divides evenly into one numerator and one denominator. In this case, 2 will divide evenly into 2 in the numerator (it goes 1 time) and 12 in the denominator (it goes in 6 times).

$$\frac{\overset{1}{\cancel{2}}}{3} \times \frac{5}{\underset{6}{\cancel{12}}} =$$

Now that you've canceled, you can multiply out as you did before.

$$\frac{\overset{1}{\cancel{2}}}{3} \times \frac{5}{\underset{6}{\cancel{12}}} = \frac{5}{18}$$

Remember, you may cancel only when *multiplying* fractions.

Multiplying Mixed Numbers

To **multiply mixed numbers,** first change any mixed number to an improper fraction. Then multiply as previously shown. To change mixed numbers to improper fractions,

1. Multiply the whole number by the denominator of the fraction.
2. Add this to the numerator of the fraction.
3. This is now your numerator.

4. The denominator remains the same.

$$3\frac{1}{3} \times 2\frac{1}{4} = \frac{10}{3} \times \frac{9}{4} = \frac{90}{12} = 7\frac{6}{12} = 7\frac{1}{2}$$

Then change the answer, if in improper fraction form, back to a mixed number and reduce if necessary.

Dividing Fractions

To **divide fractions,** invert (turn upside down) the second fraction and multiply. Then reduce if necessary.

$$\frac{1}{6} \div \frac{1}{5} = \frac{1}{6} \times \frac{5}{1} = \frac{5}{6} \qquad \frac{1}{6} \div \frac{1}{3} = \frac{1}{6} \times \frac{3}{1} = \frac{3}{6} = \frac{1}{2}$$

Simplifying Fractions

If either numerator or denominator consists of several numbers, these numbers must be combined into one number. Then reduce if necessary.

$$\frac{28+14}{26+17} = \frac{42}{43}$$

or

$$\frac{\frac{1}{4}+\frac{1}{2}}{\frac{1}{3}+\frac{1}{4}} = \frac{\frac{1}{4}+\frac{2}{4}}{\frac{4}{12}+\frac{3}{12}} = \frac{\frac{3}{4}}{\frac{7}{12}} = \frac{3}{4} \times \frac{12}{7} = \frac{36}{28} = \frac{9}{7} = 1\frac{2}{7}$$

DECIMALS

Fractions may also be written **in decimal form** by using a symbol called a **decimal point.** All numbers to the left of the decimal point are whole numbers. All numbers to the right of the decimal point are fractions with denominators of only 10, 100, 1000, 10,000, etc., as follows.

$$0.6 = \frac{6}{10} = \frac{3}{5} \qquad 0.0007 = \frac{7}{10,000}$$
$$0.7 = \frac{7}{10} \qquad 0.00007 = \frac{7}{100,000}$$
$$0.07 = \frac{7}{100} \qquad 0.25 = \frac{25}{100} = \frac{1}{4}$$
$$0.007 = \frac{7}{1000}$$

Adding and Subtracting Decimals

To **add or subtract decimals,** just line up the decimal points and then add or subtract in the same manner you would add or subtract regular numbers.

$$23.6 + 1.75 + 300.002 = \begin{array}{r} 23.6 \\ 1.75 \\ \underline{300.002} \\ 325.352 \end{array}$$

Adding in zeros can make the problem easier to work.

$$\begin{array}{r} 23.600 \\ 1.750 \\ \underline{300.002} \\ 325.352 \end{array}$$

and

$$54.26 - 1.1 = \begin{array}{r} 54.26 \\ \underline{-1.10} \\ 53.16 \end{array}$$

and

$$78.9 - 37.43 = \begin{array}{r} 78.\overset{8}{9}\overset{1}{0} \\ \underline{-37.43} \\ 41.47 \end{array}$$

Whole numbers can have decimal points to their right.

$$17 - 8.43 = \begin{array}{r} 1\overset{6}{7}.\overset{9}{0}\overset{1}{0} \\ \underline{-8.43} \\ 8.57 \end{array}$$

Multiplying Decimals

To **multiply decimals,** just multiply as usual. Then count the total number of digits above the line which are to the right of all decimal points. Place your decimal point in your answer so there are the same number of digits to the right of it as there are above the line.

$$
\begin{array}{r}
40.012 \leftarrow 3 \text{ digits} \\
\times \quad 3.1 \leftarrow 1 \text{ digit} \\
\hline
40012 \\
120036 \\
\hline
124.0372 \leftarrow 4 \text{ digits}
\end{array}
$$

$\left\{\begin{array}{l}\text{total of 4 digits above the line}\\ \text{that are to the right of the decimal point}\end{array}\right.$

$\left\{\begin{array}{l}\text{decimal point placed so there is}\\ \text{same number of digits to the right}\\ \text{of the decimal point}\end{array}\right.$

Dividing Decimals

Dividing decimals is the same as dividing other numbers, except that if the divisor (the number you're dividing by) has a decimal, move it to the right as many places as necessary until it is a whole number. Then move the decimal point in the dividend (the number being divided into) the same number of places. Sometimes you may have to add zeros to the dividend (the number inside the division sign).

$$
1.25\overline{)5.} = 125\overline{)500.}^{\,4.}
$$

or

$$
0.002\overline{)26.} = 2\overline{)26,000.}^{\,13,000.}
$$

CHANGING FORM

Changing Decimals to Percents

To **change decimals to percents,**

1. Move the decimal point two places to the right.
2. Insert a percent sign.

$$0.75 = 75\% \qquad 0.05 = 5\%$$

Changing Percents to Decimals

To **change percents to decimals,**

1. Eliminate the percent sign.
2. Move the decimal point two places to the left (sometimes adding zeros will be necessary).

$$75\% = 0.75 \qquad 5\% = 0.05$$
$$23\% = 0.23 \qquad 0.2\% = 0.002$$

Changing Fractions to Percents

To **change a fraction to a percent,**

1. Multiply by 100.
2. Insert a percent sign.

$$\tfrac{1}{2}: \quad \tfrac{1}{2} \times 100 = \tfrac{100}{2} = 50\%$$
$$\tfrac{2}{5}: \quad \tfrac{2}{5} \times 100 = \tfrac{200}{5} = 40\%$$

Changing Percents to Fractions

To **change percents to fractions,**

1. Divide the percent by 100.
2. Eliminate the percent sign.
3. Reduce if necessary.

$$60\% = \tfrac{60}{100} = \tfrac{3}{5} \qquad 13\% = \tfrac{13}{100}$$

Changing Fractions to Decimals

To **change a fraction to a decimal,** simply do what the operation says. In other words, $\tfrac{13}{20}$ means 13 divided by 20. So do just that (insert decimal points and zeros accordingly):

$$20\overline{)13.00}^{\,.65} = 0.65 \qquad \tfrac{5}{8} = 8\overline{)5.000}^{\,.625} = 0.625$$

Changing Decimals to Fractions

To **change a decimal to a fraction,**

1. Move the decimal point two places to the right.
2. Put that number over 100.
3. Reduce if necessary.

$$0.65 = \frac{65}{100} = \frac{13}{20}$$
$$0.05 = \frac{5}{100} = \frac{1}{20}$$
$$0.75 = \frac{75}{100} = \frac{3}{4}$$

Read it:　　0.8

Write it:　　$\frac{8}{10}$

Reduce it:　　$\frac{4}{5}$

PERCENT

Finding Percent of a Number

To **determine percent of a number,** change the percent to a fraction or decimal (whichever is easier for you) and multiply. Remember, the word *of* means multiply.

What is 20% of 80?

$$\frac{20}{100} \times 80 = \frac{1600}{100} = 16$$
or
$$0.20 \times 80 = 16.00 = 16$$

What is 12% of 50?

$$\frac{12}{100} \times 50 = \frac{600}{100} = 6$$
or
$$0.12 \times 50 = 6.00 = 6$$

What is $\frac{1}{2}$% of 18?

$$\frac{\frac{1}{2}}{100} \times 18 = \frac{1}{200} \times 18 = \frac{18}{200} = \frac{9}{100}$$
or
$$0.005 \times 18 = 0.09$$

Other Applications of Percent

Turn the question word-for-word into an **equation.** For *what* substitute the letter *x;* for *is* substitute an *equal sign;* for *of* substitute a *multiplication sign*. Change percents to decimals or fractions, whichever you find easier. Then solve the equation.

18 is what percent of 90?

$$18 = x(90)$$
$$\frac{18}{90} = x$$
$$\frac{1}{5} = x$$
$$20\% = x$$

10 is 50% of what number?

$$10 = 0.50(x)$$
$$\frac{10}{0.50} = x$$
$$20 = x$$

What is 15% of 60?

$$x = \frac{15}{100} \times 60 = \frac{90}{10} = 9$$
$$\text{or}$$
$$0.15(60) = 9$$

Finding Percentage Increase or Percentage Decrease

To **find the percentage change** (increase or decrease), use this formula:

$$\frac{\text{change}}{\text{starting point}} \times 100 = \text{ percentage change}$$

What is the percentage decrease of a $500 item on sale for $400?

$$\text{Change: } 500 - 400 = 100$$

$$\frac{\text{change}}{\text{starting point}} \times 100 = \frac{100}{500} \times 100 = \frac{1}{5} \times 100 = 20\% \text{ decrease}$$

What is the percentage increase of Jon's salary if it went from $150 a week to $200 a week?

$$\text{Change: } 200 - 150 = 50$$

$$\frac{\text{change}}{\text{starting point}} \times 100 = \frac{50}{150} \times 100 = \frac{1}{3} \times 100 = 33\frac{1}{3}\% \text{ increase}$$

PRIME NUMBERS

A **prime number** is a number that can be evenly divided by only itself and 1. For example, 19 is a prime number because it can be evenly divided only by 19 and 1, but 21 is not a prime number because 21 can be evenly divided by other numbers (3 and 7).

The only even prime number is 2; thereafter, any even number may be divided evenly by 2. Zero and 1 are *not* prime numbers. The first ten prime numbers are 2, 3, 5, 7, 11, 13, 17, 19, 23, and 29.

MEAN, MEDIAN, AND MODE

Arithmetic Mean, or Average

To find the **mean,** or average, of a group of numbers,

1. Add them.
2. Divide by the number of items you added.

What is the mean of 10, 20, 35, 40, and 45?

$$10 + 20 + 35 + 40 + 45 = 150$$
$$150 \div 5 = 30$$

The mean is 30.

What is the mean of 0, 12, 18, 20, 31, and 45?

$$0 + 12 + 18 + 20 + 31 + 45 = 126$$
$$126 \div 6 = 21$$

The mean is 21.

What is the mean of 25, 27, 27, and 27?

$$25 + 27 + 27 + 27 = 106$$
$$106 \div 4 = 26\tfrac{1}{2}$$

The mean is $26\tfrac{1}{2}$.

Median

A **median** is simply the middle number of a list of numbers after it has been written in order. (If the list contains an even number of items, average the two middle numbers to get the median.) For example, in the following list—3, 4, 6, *9*, 21, 24, 56—the number 9 is the median.

Mode

The **mode** is simply the number most frequently listed in a group of numbers. For example, in the following group—5, 9, 7, 3, 9, 4, 6, 9, 7, 9, 2—the mode is 9 because it appears more often than any other number.

SQUARES AND SQUARE ROOTS

To **square a number** just multiply it by itself. For example, 6 squared (written 6^2) is 6×6 or 36. 36 is called a perfect square (the square of a whole number). Any exponent means multiply the number by itself that many times.

$$8^2 = 8 \times 8 = 64$$
$$5^3 = 5 \times 5 \times 5 = 125$$

Remember, $x^1 = x$ and $x^0 = 1$ when x is any number (other than 0).

Following is a list of **perfect squares.**

$$0^2 = 0 \qquad 5^2 = 25 \qquad 9^2 = 81$$
$$1^2 = 1 \qquad 6^2 = 36 \qquad 10^2 = 100$$
$$2^2 = 4 \qquad 7^2 = 49 \qquad 11^2 = 121$$
$$3^2 = 9 \qquad 8^2 = 64 \qquad 12^2 = 144 \quad \text{etc.}$$
$$4^2 = 16$$

To find the **square root** of a number, you want to find some number that when multiplied by itself gives you the original number. In other words, to find the square root of 25, you want to find the number that when multiplied by itself gives you 25. The square root of 25, then, is 5. The symbol for square root is $\sqrt{}$. Following is a list of **perfect (whole number) square roots:**

$$\sqrt{0} = 0 \quad \sqrt{16} = 4 \quad \sqrt{64} = 8$$
$$\sqrt{1} = 1 \quad \sqrt{25} = 5 \quad \sqrt{81} = 9$$
$$\sqrt{4} = 2 \quad \sqrt{36} = 6 \quad \sqrt{100} = 10 \quad \text{etc.}$$
$$\sqrt{9} = 3 \quad \sqrt{49} = 7$$

Square roots of **nonperfect squares** can be approximated. Two approximations you may wish to remember are

$$\sqrt{2} \approx 1.4$$
$$\sqrt{3} \approx 1.7$$

Square Root Rules

Two numbers multiplied under a radical (square root) sign equal the product of the two square roots.

$$\sqrt{(4)(25)} = \sqrt{4} \times \sqrt{25} = 2 \times 5 = 10 \quad \text{or} \quad \sqrt{100} = 10$$

And likewise with division,

$$\sqrt{\frac{64}{4}} = \frac{\sqrt{64}}{\sqrt{4}} = \frac{8}{2} = 4 \quad \text{or} \quad \sqrt{16} = 4$$

Addition and subtraction, however, are different. The numbers must be combined under the radical before any computation of square roots may be done.

$$\sqrt{10+6} = \sqrt{16} = 4 \quad (\sqrt{10+6} \text{ does } \textit{not} \text{ equal } [\neq] \sqrt{10} + \sqrt{6})$$
$$\text{or}$$
$$\sqrt{93-12} = \sqrt{81} = 9$$

Approximating Square Roots

To **find a square root which will not be a whole number,** you should approximate.

Approximate $\sqrt{57}$.

Because $\sqrt{57}$ is between $\sqrt{49}$ and $\sqrt{64}$, it will fall somewhere between 7 and 8. And because 57 is just about halfway between 49 and 64, $\sqrt{57}$ is therefore approximately $7\frac{1}{2}$.

Approximate $\sqrt{83}$.

$$\sqrt{81} < \sqrt{83} < \sqrt{100}$$
$$9 \qquad\qquad 10$$

Since $\sqrt{83}$ is slightly more than $\sqrt{81}$ (whose square root is 9), then $\sqrt{83}$ is a little more than 9. Since 83 is only 2 steps up from the nearest perfect square (81) and 17 steps to the next perfect square (100), then 83 is $\frac{2}{19}$ of the way to 100.

$$\frac{2}{19} \approx \frac{2}{20} = \frac{1}{10} = 0.1$$

Therefore, $\sqrt{83} \approx 9.1$

Simplifying Square Roots

To **simplify numbers under a radical** (square root sign),

1. Factor the number to two numbers, one (or more) of which is a perfect square.
2. Then take the square root of the perfect square(s).
3. Leave the other under the $\sqrt{\ }$.

Simplify $\sqrt{75}$.

$$\sqrt{75} = \sqrt{25 \times 3} = \sqrt{25} \times \sqrt{3} = 5\sqrt{3}$$

Simplify $\sqrt{200}$.

$$\sqrt{200} = \sqrt{100 \times 2} = \sqrt{100} \times \sqrt{2} = 10\sqrt{2}$$

Simplify $\sqrt{900}$.

$$\sqrt{900} = \sqrt{100 \times 9} = \sqrt{100} \times \sqrt{9} = 10 \times 3 = 30$$

SIGNED NUMBERS
(POSITIVE NUMBERS AND NEGATIVE NUMBERS)

On a **number line,** numbers to the right of 0 are positive. Numbers to the left of 0 are negative, as follows.

etc. —————————————— etc.
-3 -2 -1 0 $+1$ $+2$ $+3$

Given any two numbers on a number line, the one on the right is always larger, regardless of its sign (positive or negative).

Addition of Signed Numbers

When **adding two numbers with the same sign** (either both positive or both negative), add the numbers and keep the same sign.

$$
\begin{array}{r} +5 \\ + +7 \\ \hline +12 \end{array}
\qquad
\begin{array}{r} -8 \\ + -3 \\ \hline -11 \end{array}
$$

When **adding two numbers with different signs** (one positive and one negative), subtract the numbers and keep the sign from the larger one.

$$
\begin{array}{r} +5 \\ + -7 \\ \hline -2 \end{array}
\qquad
\begin{array}{r} -59 \\ + +72 \\ \hline +13 \end{array}
$$

Subtraction of Signed Numbers

To **subtract positive and/or negative numbers,** just change the sign of the number being subtracted and then add.

$$
\begin{array}{cc}
+12 & +12 \\
-+4 & +-4 \\
\hline
 & +8
\end{array}
$$

$$
\begin{array}{cc}
-14 & -14 \\
--4 & ++4 \\
\hline
 & -10
\end{array}
$$

$$
\begin{array}{cc}
-19 & -19 \\
-+6 & +-6 \\
\hline
 & -25
\end{array}
$$

$$
\begin{array}{cc}
+20 & +20 \\
--3 & ++3 \\
\hline
 & +23
\end{array}
$$

Multiplying and Dividing Signed Numbers

To **multiply or divide signed numbers,** treat them just like regular numbers but remember this rule: An odd number of negative signs will produce a negative answer. An even number of negative signs will produce a positive answer.

$$(-3)(+8)(-5)(-1)(-2) = +240$$
$$(-3)(+8)(-1)(-2) = -48$$
$$\frac{-64}{-2} = +32$$
$$\frac{-64}{2} = -32$$

PARENTHESES

Parentheses are used to group numbers. Everything inside parentheses must be done before any other operations.

$$50(2 + 6) = 50(8) = 400$$

When a **parenthesis is preceded by a minus sign,** change the minus to a plus by changing all the signs in front of each term inside the parentheses. Then remove the parentheses.

$$6 - (-3 + a - 2b + c)$$
$$= 6 + (+3 - a + 2b - c)$$
$$= 6 + 3 - a + 2b - c$$
$$= 9 - a + 2b - c$$

ORDER OF OPERATIONS

If multiplication, division, powers, addition, parentheses, etc., are all contained in one problem, the **order of operations** is as follows:

1. parentheses
2. powers and square roots
3. multiplication ⎫
   $\quad$ whichever comes first, left to right
4. division ⎭
5. addition ⎫
   $\quad$ whichever comes first, left to right
6. subtraction ⎭

For example:

$$10 - 3 \times 6 + 10^2 + (6 + 1) \times 4$$
$$= 10 - 3 \times 6 + 10^2 + (7) \times 4 \quad \text{(parentheses first)}$$
$$= 10 - 3 \times 6 + 100 + (7) \times 4 \quad \text{(powers next)}$$
$$= 10 - 18 + 100 + 28 \quad \text{(multiplication)}$$
$$= -8 + 100 + 28 \quad \text{(addition / subtraction, left to right)}$$
$$= 92 + 28$$
$$= 120$$

An easy way to remember the order of operations *after parentheses* is: **P**lease **M**y **D**ear **A**unt **S**arah (**P**owers, **M**ultiplication, **D**ivision, **A**ddition, **S**ubtraction).

Algebra

ALGEBRA DIAGNOSTIC TEST

1. Solve for x: $x + 5 = 17$

2. Solve for x: $4x + 9 = 21$

3. Solve for x: $5x + 7 = 3x - 9$

4. Solve for x: $mx - n = y$

5. Solve for x: $\dfrac{r}{x} = \dfrac{s}{t}$

6. Solve for y: $\dfrac{3}{7} = \dfrac{y}{8}$

7. Evaluate: $3x^2 + 5y + 7$ if $x = -2$ and $y = 3$

8. Simplify: $8xy^2 + 3xy + 4xy^2 - 2xy =$

9. Simplify: $6x^2(4x^3y) =$

10. Simplify: $(5x + 2z) + (3x - 4z) =$

11. Simplify: $(4x - 7z) - (3x - 4z) =$

12. Factor: $ab + ac$

13. Solve for x: $2x + 3 \leq 11$

14. Solve for x: $3x + 4 \geq 5x - 8$

Answers

1. $x = 12$

2. $x = 3$

3. $x = -8$

4. $x = \dfrac{(y + n)}{m}$

5. $x = \dfrac{rt}{s}$

6. $y = \frac{24}{7}$ or $3\frac{3}{7}$

7. 34

8. $12xy^2 + xy$

9. $24x^5 y$

10. $8x - 2z$

11. $x - 3z$

12. $a(b + c)$

13. $x \le 4$

14. $x \le 6$

ALGEBRA REVIEW

EQUATIONS

An **equation** is a relationship between numbers and/or symbols. It helps to remember that an equation is like a balance scale, with the equal sign (=) being the fulcrum, or center. Thus, if you do the *same thing to both sides* of the equal sign (say, add 5 to each side), the equation will still be balanced. To solve the equation $x - 5 = 23$, you must get x by itself on one side; therefore, add 5 to both sides.

$$\begin{aligned} x - 5 &= 23 \\ +5 \quad &+5 \\ \hline x \quad &= 28 \end{aligned}$$

In the same manner, you may subtract, multiply, or divide *both* sides of an equation by the same (nonzero) number, and the equation will not change. Sometimes you may have to use more than one step to solve for an unknown.

$$3x + 4 = 19$$

Subtract 4 from both sides to get the 3x by itself on one side:

$$3x + 4 = 19$$
$$\underline{-4 \quad -4}$$
$$3x \quad\quad = 15$$

Then divide both sides by 3 to get x:

$$\frac{3x}{3} = \frac{15}{3}$$
$$x = 5$$

Remember: Solving an equation is using **opposite operations,** until the letter is on a side by itself (for addition, subtract; for multiplication, divide; etc.).

UNDERSTOOD MULTIPLYING

When two or more letters, or a number and letters, are written next to each other, they are **understood to be multiplied.** Thus, $8x$ means 8 times x. Or ab means a times b. Or $18ab$ means 18 times a times b.

Parentheses also represent multiplication. Thus, $(a)b$ means a times b. A raised dot also means multiplication. Thus, $6 \cdot 5$ means 6 times 5.

LITERAL EQUATIONS

Literal equations have no numbers, only symbols (letters).

Solve for Q: $QP - X = Y$

First add X to both sides.

$$QP - X = Y$$
$$\underline{+X \quad +X}$$
$$QP \quad\quad = Y + X$$

Then divide both sides by P.

$$\frac{QP}{P} = \frac{Y + X}{P}$$
$$Q = \frac{Y + X}{P}$$

Again, opposite operations are used to isolate Q.

CROSS MULTIPLYING

$$\text{Solve for } x: \quad \frac{b}{x} = \frac{p}{q}$$

To solve this equation quickly, you **cross multiply.** To cross multiply,

1. Bring the denominators up next to the opposite side numerators.
2. Multiply.

$$\frac{b}{x} = \frac{p}{q}$$
$$bq = px$$

Then divide both sides by p to get x alone.

$$\frac{bq}{p} = \frac{px}{p}$$
$$\frac{bq}{p} = x \quad \text{or} \quad x = \frac{bq}{p}$$

Cross multiplying can be used only when the format is two fractions separated by an equal sign.

PROPORTIONS

Proportions are written as two fractions equal to each other.

$$\text{Solve this proportion for } x: \quad \frac{p}{q} = \frac{x}{y}$$

This is read "p is to q as x is to y." Cross multiply and solve:

$$py = xq$$
$$\frac{py}{q} = \frac{xq}{q}$$
$$\frac{py}{q} = x \quad \text{or} \quad x = \frac{py}{q}$$

EVALUATING EXPRESSIONS

To **evaluate an expression,** just insert the value for the unknowns and do the arithmetic.

Evaluate: $2x^2 + 3y + 6$ if $x = 2$ and $y = 9$

$$2(2^2) + 3(9) + 6$$
$$= 2(4) + 27 + 6$$
$$= 8 + 27 + 6$$
$$= 41$$

MONOMIALS AND POLYNOMIALS

A **monomial** is an algebraic expression that consists of only one term. For instance, $9x$, $4a^2$, and $3mpxz^2$ are all monomials.

A **polynomial** consists of two or more terms; $x + y$, $y^2 - x^2$, and $x^2 + 3x + 5y^2$ are all polynomials.

Adding and Subtracting Monomials

To **add or subtract monomials,** follow the same rules as with regular signed numbers, provided that the *terms are alike.*

$$15x^2yz$$
$$-18x^2yz$$
$$\overline{-3x^2yz}$$

$$3x + 2x = 5x$$

Multiplying and Dividing Monomials

To **multiply monomials,** add the exponents of the same terms.

$$(x^3)(x^4) = x^7$$

$$(x^2y)(x^3y^2) = x^5y^3$$

$$-4(m^2n)(-3m^4n^3) = 12m^6n^4 \text{ (multiply numbers)}$$

To **divide monomials,** subtract the exponents of the like terms.

$$\frac{y^{15}}{y^4} = y^{11} \qquad \frac{x^5 y^2}{x^3 y} = x^2 y \qquad \frac{36a^4 b^6}{-9ab} = -4a^3 b^5$$

Remember: x is the same as x^1.

Adding and Subtracting Polynomials

To **add or subtract polynomials,** just arrange like terms in columns and then add or subtract:

Add:
$$\begin{array}{l} a^2 + ab + b^2 \\ \underline{3a^2 + 4ab - 2b^2} \\ 4a^2 + 5ab - b^2 \end{array}$$

Subtract:
$$\begin{array}{cc} a^2 + b^2 & a^2 + b^2 \\ \underline{-2a^2 - b^2} \rightarrow & \underline{+ -2a^2 + b^2} \\ & -a^2 + 2b^2 \end{array}$$

Multiplying Polynomials

To **multiply polynomials,** multiply each term in one polynomial by each term in the other polynomial. Then simplify if necessary.

$$(3x + a)(2x - 2a) = \begin{array}{r} 2x - 2a \\ \times 3x + a \\ \hline +2ax - 2a^2 \\ 6x^2 - 6ax \\ \hline 6x^2 - 4ax - 2a^2 \end{array} \quad \text{similar to} \quad \begin{array}{r} 23 \\ \times 19 \\ \hline 207 \\ 23 \\ \hline 437 \end{array}$$

FACTORING

To **factor** means to find two or more quantities whose product equals the original quantity. To **factor out a common factor,**

1. Find the largest common monomial factor of each term.
2. Divide the original polynomial by this factor to obtain the second factor. The second factor will be a polynomial.

$$2y^3 - 6y = 2y(y^2 - 3)$$

$$x^5 - 4x^3 + x^2 = x^2(x^3 - 4x + 1)$$

To **factor the difference between two squares,**

1. Find the square root of the first term and the square root of the second term.
2. Express your answer as the product of the sum of the quantities from step 1 times the difference of those quantities.

$$x^2 - 144 = (x + 12)(x - 12)$$

$$a^2 - b^2 = (a + b)(a - b)$$

INEQUALITIES

An **inequality** is a statement in which the relationships are not equal. Instead of using an equal sign (=) as in an equation, we use > (greater than) and < (less than) or ≥ (greater than or equal to) and ≤ (less than or equal to).

When working with inequalities, treat them exactly like equations, *except* if you multiply or divide both sides by a negative number, you must *reverse* the direction of the sign.

Solve for x: $2x + 4 > 6$

$$
\begin{array}{r}
2x + 4 > 6 \\
-4 - 4 \\
\hline
2x \quad\ > 2
\end{array}
$$

$$\frac{2x}{2} > \frac{2}{2}$$
$$x > 1$$

Solve for x: $-7x > 14$ (divide by -7 and reverse the sign)

$$\frac{-7x}{-7} < \frac{14}{-7}$$
$$x < -2$$

$3x + 2 \geq 5x - 10$ becomes $-2x \geq -12$ by opposite operations. Divide both sides by -2 and reverse the sign.

$$\frac{-2x}{-2} \leq \frac{-12}{-2}$$
$$x \leq 6$$

Geometry

GEOMETRY DIAGNOSTIC TEST

1. Name any angle of this triangle three different ways.

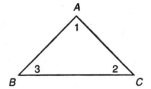

2. A(n) _____ angle measures less than 90 degrees.

3. A(n) _____ angle measures 90 degrees.

4. A(n) _____ angle measures more than 90 degrees.

5. A(n) _____ angle measures 180 degrees.

6. Two angles are complementary when their sum is _____.

7. Two angles are supplementary when their sum is _____.

8. In the diagram, find the measures of $\angle a$, $\angle b$, and $\angle c$.

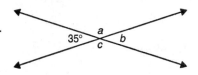

9. Lines that stay the same distance apart and never meet are called _____ lines.

10. Lines that meet to form 90 degree angles are called _____ lines.

11. A(n) _____ triangle has three equal sides. Therefore, each interior angle measures _____.

Questions 12 and 13

12. In the triangle, $\overline{AC}$ must be shorter than _____ inches.

13. In the triangle, which angle is smaller, ∠A or ∠C?

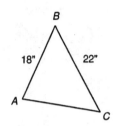

14. What is the measure of ∠ACD?

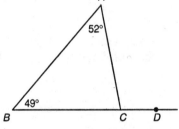

15. What is the length of $\overline{AC}$?

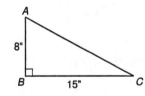

16. What is the length of $\overline{BC}$?

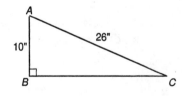

17. Name each of the following polygons.

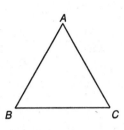

(A) $\overline{AB} = \overline{BC} = \overline{AC}$
     $\angle A = \angle B = \angle C = 60°$

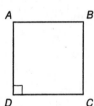

(B) $\overline{AB} = \overline{BC} = \overline{CD} = \overline{AD}$
     $\angle A = \angle B = \angle C = \angle D = 90°$

(C) $\overline{AB} \parallel \overline{DC}$
     $\overline{AB} = \overline{DC}$
     $\overline{AD} \parallel \overline{BC}$
     $\overline{AD} = \overline{BC}$
     $\angle A = \angle C$

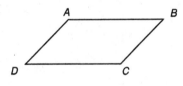

(D) $\overline{AB} = \overline{DC}$
     $\overline{AD} = \overline{BC}$
     $\angle A = \angle B = \angle C = \angle D = 90°$

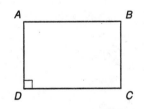

(E) $\overline{AB} \parallel \overline{DC}$

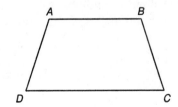

18. Fill in the blanks for circle R.

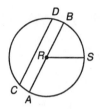

    (A) $\overline{RS}$ is called the _____.
    (B) $\overline{AB}$ is called the _____.
    (C) $\overline{CD}$ is called a _____.

19. Find the area and circumference for the
    circle ($\pi \approx \frac{22}{7}$).

    (A) area =
    (B) circumference =

20. Find the area and perimeter of the
    figure.

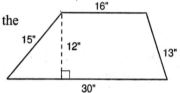

    (A) area =
    (B) perimeter =

21. Find the area and perim-
    eter of the figure (*ABCD*
    is a parallelogram).

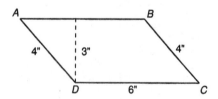

    (A) area =
    (B) perimeter =

22. Find the volume of the
    figure if $V = (\pi r^2)h$ (use
    3.14 for π).

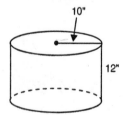

    (A) volume =

23. What is the surface area and volume of the cube?

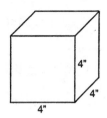

    (A) surface area =
    (B) volume =

Answers

1. $\angle 3$, $\angle CBA$, $\angle ABC$, $\angle B$
   $\angle 1$, $\angle BAC$, $\angle CAB$, $\angle A$
   $\angle 2$, $\angle ACB$, $\angle BCA$, $\angle C$

2. acute

3. right

4. obtuse

5. straight

6. $90°$

7. $180°$

8. $a = 145°$
   $b = 35°$
   $c = 145°$

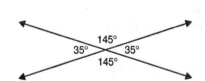

9. parallel

10. perpendicular

11. equilateral, $60°$

12. 40 inches   Since $\overline{AB} + \overline{BC} = 40$ inches
   then $\overline{AC} < \overline{AB} + \overline{BC}$
   and $\overline{AC} < 40$

13. $\angle C$ must be the smaller angle, since it is opposite the shorter side $\overline{AB}$.

14. $\angle ACD = 101°$

15. $\overline{AC} = 17$ inches

16. Since $\triangle ABC$ is a right triangle, use the Pythagorean theorem.

$$a^2 + b^2 = c^2$$
$$10^2 + b^2 = 26^2$$
$$100 + b^2 = 676$$
$$b^2 = 576$$
$$b = 24''$$

17. (A) equilateral triangle
    (B) square
    (C) parallelogram
    (D) rectangle
    (E) trapezoid

18. (A) radius
    (B) diameter
    (C) chord

19. (A) area = πr^2
    $$= \pi(7^2)$$
    $$= \tfrac{22}{7}(7)(7)$$
    $$= 154 \text{ square inches}$$

    (B) circumference = πd
    $$= \pi(14) \quad (d = 14'' \text{ since } r = 7'')$$
    $$= \tfrac{22}{7}(14)$$
    $$= 22(2)$$
    $$= 44 \text{ inches}$$

20. (A) area $= \frac{1}{2}(a+b)h$
$= \frac{1}{2}(16+30)12$
$= \frac{1}{2}(46)12$
$= 23(12)$
$= 276$ square inches

(B) perimeter $= 16 + 13 + 30 + 15 = 74$ inches

21. (A) area $= bh$
$= 6(3)$
$= 18$ square inches

(B) perimeter $= 6 + 4 + 6 + 4$
$= 20$ inches

22. volume $= (\pi r^2)h$
$= (\pi \cdot 10^2)(12)$
$= 3.14(100)(12)$
$= 314(12)$
$= 3768$ cubic inches

23. (A) All six surfaces have an area of 4×4, or 16 square inches, since each surface is a square. Therefore, $16(6) = 96$ square inches in the surface area.

(B) Volume $=$ side $\times$ side $\times$ side, or $4^3 = 64$ cubic inches.

GEOMETRY REVIEW

Plane geometry is the study of shapes and figures in two dimensions (the plane).

Solid geometry is the study of shapes and figures in three dimensions.

A *point* is the must fundamental idea in geometry. It is represented by a dot and named by a capital letter.

LINES

Straight Lines

A **straight line** is the shortest distance between two points. It continues forever in both directions. A line consists of an infinite number of points. It is named by any two points on the line. The symbol ⟷ written on top of the two letters is used to denote that line.

This is line *AB*.

It is written $\overleftrightarrow{AB}$.

A line may also be named by one small letter. The symbol would not be used.

This is line *l*.

Line Segments

A **line segment** is a piece of a line. A line segment has two endpoints. It is named by its two endpoints. The symbol — written on top of the two letters is used to denote that line segment.

This is line segment CD.

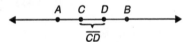

It is written $\overline{CD}$.
Note that it is a piece of $\overleftrightarrow{AB}$.

Rays

A **ray** has only one endpoint and continues forever in one direction. A ray can be thought of as a half-line. It is named by the letter of its endpoint and any other point on the ray. The symbol ⟶ written on top of the two letters is used to denote that ray.

This is ray *AB*.

It is written $\overrightarrow{AB}$.

This is ray *BC*.

It is written $\overrightarrow{BC}$ or $\overleftarrow{CB}$.
Note that the direction of the symbol is the direction of the ray.

ANGLES

An **angle** is formed by two rays that start from the same point. That point is called the **vertex;** the rays are called the **sides** of the angle. An angle is measured in **degrees.** The degrees indicate the size of the angle, from one side to the other.

In the diagram, the angle is formed by rays $\overrightarrow{AB}$ and $\overrightarrow{AC}$. *A* is the vertex. $\overrightarrow{AB}$ and $\overrightarrow{AC}$ are the sides of the angle.

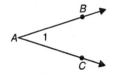

The symbol $\angle$ is used to denote an angle. An angle can be named in various ways.

1. By the letter of the vertex—therefore, the angle above could be named $\angle A$.
2. By the number (or small letter) in its interior—therefore, the angle above could be named $\angle 1$.
3. By the letters of the three points that form it—therefore, the angle above could be named $\angle BAC$, or $\angle CAB$. The center letter is always the letter of the vertex.

TYPES OF ANGLES

Adjacent Angles

Adjacent angles are any angles that share a common side and a common vertex.

In the diagram, $\angle 1$ and $\angle 2$ are adjacent angles.

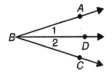

Right Angles

A **right angle** has a measure of 90°. The symbol ⌐ in the interior of an angle designates the fact that a right angle is formed.

In the diagram, ∠ABC is a right angle.

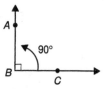

Acute Angles

Any angle whose measure is less than 90° is called an **acute angle.**

In the diagram, ∠b is acute.

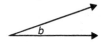

Obtuse Angles

Any angle whose measure is larger than 90°, but smaller than 180°, is called an **obtuse angle.**

In the diagram, ∠4 is an obtuse angle.

Straight Angles

A **straight angle** has a measure of 180°.

In the diagram, ∠BAC is a straight angle (also called a line).

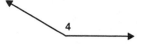

Complementary Angles

Two angles whose sum is 90° are called **complementary angles.**

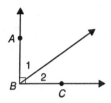

In the diagram, since ∠*ABC* is a right angle,
∠1 + ∠2 = 90°.

Therefore, ∠1 and ∠2 are complementary angles. If ∠1 = 55°, its
complement, ∠2, would be 90° − 55° = 35°.

Supplementary Angles

Two angles whose sum is 180° are called **supplementary angles.**
Two adjacent angles that form a straight line are supplementary.

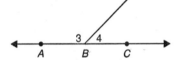

In the diagram, since ∠*ABC* is a
straight angle, ∠3 + ∠4 = 180°.

Therefore, ∠3 and ∠4 are supplementary angles. If ∠3 = 122°, its
supplement, ∠4, would be 180° − 122° = 58°.

Angle Bisectors

A ray from the vertex of an angle that divides the angle into two
equal pieces is called an **angle bisector.**

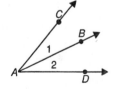

In the diagram, $\overrightarrow{AB}$ is the angle bisector of
∠*CAD*.

Therefore, ∠1 = ∠2.

Vertical and Adjacent Angles

If two straight lines intersect, they do so at a point. Four angles are formed. Those angles opposite each other are called **vertical angles.** Those angles sharing a common side and a common vertex are, again, **adjacent angles.** Vertical angles are always equal.

In the diagram, line *l* and line *m* intersect at point *Q*. ∠1, ∠2, ∠3, and ∠4 are formed.

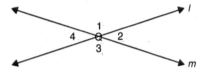

$$\left.\begin{array}{l} \angle 1 \text{ and } \angle 3 \\ \angle 2 \text{ and } \angle 4 \end{array}\right\} \text{ are vertical angles}$$

$$\left.\begin{array}{l} \angle 1 \text{ and } \angle 2 \\ \angle 2 \text{ and } \angle 3 \\ \angle 3 \text{ and } \angle 4 \\ \angle 1 \text{ and } \angle 4 \end{array}\right\} \text{ are adjacent angles}$$

Therefore, ∠1 = ∠3 and ∠2 = ∠4.

TYPES OF LINES

Intersecting Lines

Two or more lines that cross each other at a point are called **intersecting lines.** That point is on each of those lines.

In the diagram, lines *l* and *m* intersect at *Q*.

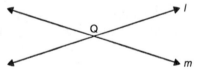

Perpendicular Lines

Two lines that meet to form right angles (90°) are called **perpendicular lines.** The symbol ⊥ is used to denote perpendicular lines.

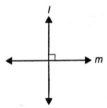

In the diagram, line $l \perp$ line m.

Parallel Lines

Two or more lines that remain the same distance apart at all times are called **parallel lines.** Parallel lines never meet. The symbol ∥ is used to denote parallel lines.

In the diagram, $l \parallel m$.

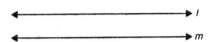

Polygons

Closed shapes or figures with three or more sides are called **polygons.** (*Poly* means "many"; *gon* means "sides"; thus, *polygon* means "many sides.")

TRIANGLES

This section deals with those polygons having the fewest number of sides. A **triangle** is a three-sided polygon. It has three angles in its interior. The sum of these angles is *always* 180°. The symbol for triangle is △. A triangle is named by all three letters of its vertices.

This is △*ABC*.

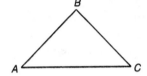

Types of Triangles

1. A triangle having all three sides equal (meaning all three sides have the same length) is called an **equilateral triangle.**

2. A triangle having two sides equal is called an **isosceles triangle.**

3. A triangle having none of its sides equal is called a **scalene triangle.**

4. A triangle having a right (90°) angle in its interior is called a **right triangle.**

Facts About Triangles

Every triangle has a **base** (bottom side) and a **height** (altitude). Every height is the **perpendicular** (forms right angles) distance from a vertex to its opposite side (the base).

In this diagram of $\triangle ABC$, $\overline{BC}$ is the base, and $\overline{AE}$ is the height. $\overline{AE} \perp \overline{BC}$.

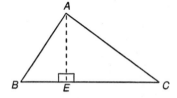

Every triangle has a **median.** The median is the line segment drawn from a vertex to the midpoint of the opposite side.

In this diagram of $\triangle ABC$, E is the midpoint of $\overline{BC}$.

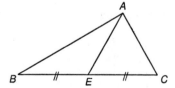

Therefore, $\overline{BE} = \overline{EC}$. $\overline{AE}$ is the median of $\triangle ABC$.

In an equilateral triangle, all three sides are equal, and all three angles are equal. If all three angles are equal and their sum is 180°, the following must be true:

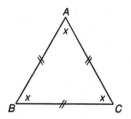

$$x + x + x = 180°$$
$$3x = 180°$$
$$x = 60°$$

Every angle of an equilateral triangle always has a measure of 60°.

In any triangle, the longest side is always opposite from the largest angle. Likewise, the shortest side is always opposite from the smallest angle. In a right triangle, the longest side is always opposite from the right angle, as the right angle is the largest angle in the triangle.

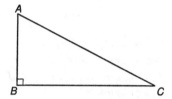

$\overline{AC}$ is the longest side of right $\triangle ABC$.

The sum of the lengths of any two sides of a triangle must be larger than the length of the third side.

In the diagram of $\triangle ABC$,

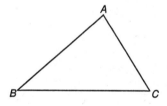

$$\overline{AB} + \overline{BC} > \overline{AC}$$
$$\overline{AB} + \overline{AC} > \overline{BC}$$
$$\overline{AC} + \overline{BC} > \overline{AB}$$

If one side of a triangle is extended, the exterior angle formed by that extension is equal to the sum of the other two interior angles.

In the diagram of $\triangle ABC$, side BC is extended to D.

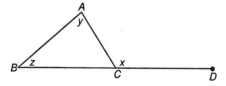

$\angle ACD$ is the exterior angle formed.
$\angle x = \angle y + \angle z$

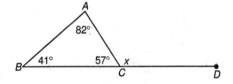

$x = 82° + 41°$
  $= 123°$

Pythagorean Theorem

In any right triangle, the relationship between the lengths of the sides is stated by the **Pythagorean theorem.** The parts of a right triangle are as follows.

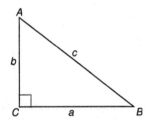

$\angle C$ is the right angle.

The side opposite the right angle is called the **hypotenuse** (side c). (The hypotenuse is always the longest side.)

The other two sides are called the **legs** (sides a and b).

The three lengths a, b, and c are always numbers such that
$$a^2 + b^2 = c^2$$

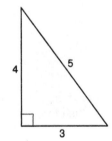

If $a = 3$, $b = 4$, and $c = 5$,
$$a^2 + b^2 = c^2$$
$$3^2 + 4^2 = 5^2$$
$$9 + 16 = 25$$
$$25 = 25$$

Therefore, 3-4-5 is called a **Pythagorean triple.** There are other values for *a, b,* and *c* that always work. Some are: 1-1-$\sqrt{2}$, 5-12-13, and 8-15-17. Any multiple of one of these triples also works. For example, using the 3-4-5 triple, 6-8-10, 9-12-15, and 15-20-25 are also Pythagorean triples.

If perfect squares are known, the lengths of these sides can be determined easily. A knowledge of the use of algebraic equations can also be used to determine the lengths of the sides.

$$a^2 + b^2 = c^2$$
$$x^2 + 10^2 = 15^2$$
$$x^2 + 100 = 225$$
$$x^2 = 125$$
$$x = \sqrt{125}$$
$$= \sqrt{25} \times \sqrt{5}$$
$$= 5\sqrt{5}$$

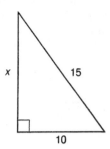

QUADRILATERALS

A polygon having four sides is called a **quadrilateral.** There are four angles in its interior. The sum of these interior angles is always 360°. A quadrilateral is named by using the four letters of its vertices.

This is quadrilateral *ABCD*.

Types of Quadrilaterals

The **square** has four equal sides and four right angles.

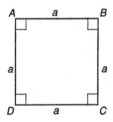

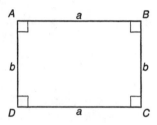

The **rectangle** has opposite sides equal and four right angles.

The **parallelogram** has opposite sides equal and parallel, opposite angles equal, and consecutive angles supplementary. Every parallelogram has a height.

$\angle A = \angle C$
$\angle B = \angle D$
$\angle A + \angle B = 180°$
$\angle A + \angle D = 180°$
$\angle B + \angle C = 180°$
$\angle C + \angle D = 180°$

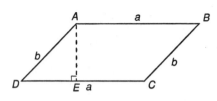

AE is the height of the parallelogram, $\overline{AB} \parallel \overline{CD}$, and $\overline{AD} \parallel \overline{BC}$.

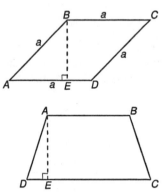

The **rhombus** is a parallelogram with four equal sides. A rhombus has a height. BE is the height.

The **trapezoid** has only one pair of parallel sides. A trapezoid has a height. AE is the height. $\overline{AB} \parallel \overline{DC}$.

OTHER POLYGONS

1. The **pentagon** is a five-sided polygon.
2. The **hexagon** is a six-sided polygon.
3. The **octagon** is an eight-sided polygon.
4. The **nonagon** is a nine-sided polygon.
5. The **decagon** is a ten-sided polygon.

FACTS ABOUT POLYGONS

Regular Polygons

Regular means all sides have the same length and all angles have the same measure. A regular three-sided polygon is the equilateral triangle. A regular four-sided polygon is the square. There are no other special names. Other polygons will simply be described as regular, if they are. For example, a regular five-sided polygon is called a regular pentagon. A regular six-sided polygon is called a regular hexagon.

Perimeter

Perimeter means the total distance all the way around the outside of any polygon. The perimeter of any polygon can be determined by adding up the lengths of all the sides. The total distance around will be the sum of all sides of the polygon. No special formulas are necessary.

Area

Area (A) means the amount of space inside the polygon. The formulas for each area are as follows:

Triangle: $A = \frac{1}{2}bh$

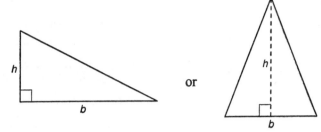

or

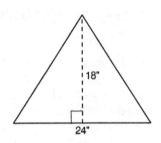

$A = \frac{1}{2}bh$
$ = \frac{1}{2}(24)(18)$
$ = 216$ sq in

Square or rectangle: A = *lw*

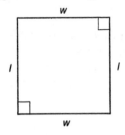   or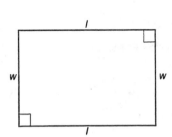

$A = l(w) = 4(4) = 16$ sq in

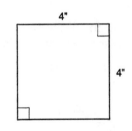

$A = l(w) = 12(5) = 60$ sq in

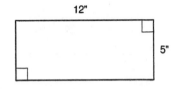

Parallelogram: A = *bh*

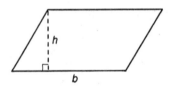

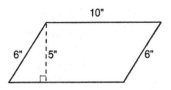

$A = b(h)$
  $= 10(5) = 50$ sq in

Trapezoid: $A = \frac{1}{2}(a+b)h$

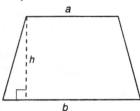

$A = \frac{1}{2}(a+b)h$
  $= \frac{1}{2}(8+12)7$
  $= \frac{1}{2}(20)7$
  $= 70$ sq in

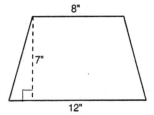

CIRCLES

A closed shape whose side is formed by one curved line, all points of which are equidistant from the center point, is called a **circle.** Circles are named by the letter of their center point.

This is circle M.

M is the center point, since it is the same distance away from any point on the circle.

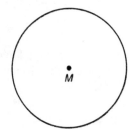

Parts of a Circle

The **radius** is the distance from the center to any point on the circle.

$\overline{MA}$ is a radius.
$\overline{MB}$ is a radius.

In any circle, all radii (plural) are the same length.

The **diameter** of a circle is the distance across the circle, through the center.

$\overline{AB}$ is a diameter.
$\overline{CD}$ is a diameter.

In any circle, all diameters are the same length. Each diameter is two radii.

A **chord** of a circle is a line segment whose endpoints lie on the circle itself.

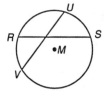

$\overline{RS}$ is a chord.
$\overline{UV}$ is a chord.

The diameter is the longest chord in any circle.

An **arc** is the distance between any two points *on* the circle itself. An arc is a piece of the circle. The symbol ⌢ is used to denote an arc. It is written on top of the two endpoints that form the arc. Arcs are measured in degrees. There are 360° around the circle.

This is $\overset{\frown}{EF}$.

Minor $\overset{\frown}{EF}$ is the shorter distance between E and F.
Major $\overset{\frown}{EF}$ is the longer distance between E and F.
When $\overset{\frown}{EF}$ is written, the minor arc is assumed.

Area and Circumference

Circumference is the distance around the circle. Since there are no sides to add up, a formula is needed. π (pi) is a Greek letter that represents a specific number. In fractional or decimal form, the commonly used approximations are $\pi \approx 3.14$ or $\pi \approx \frac{22}{7}$. The formula for circumference is $C = \pi d$ or $C = 2\pi r$.

In circle M, $d = 8$, since $r = 4$.

$C = \pi d$
$\quad = \pi(8)$
$\quad = 3.14(8)$
$\quad = 25.12$ in

The **area** of a circle can be determined by: $A = \pi(r^2)$

In circle M, $r = 5$, since $d = 10$.

$A = \pi(r^2)$
$\quad = \pi(5^2)$
$\quad = 3.14(25)$
$\quad = 78.5$ sq in

VOLUME

In three dimensions, there are different facts that can be determined about shapes. **Volume** is the capacity to hold. The formula for volume of each shape is different. The volume of any **prism** (a three-dimensional shape having many sides, but two bases) can be determined by: volume (V) = (area of base)(height of prism).

Specifically for a **rectangular solid,**

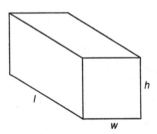

$V = (lw)(h)$
  $= lwh$

Specifically for a **cylinder** (circular bases),

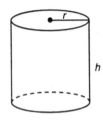

$V = (\pi r^2)h$
  $= \pi r^2 h$

Volume is labeled "cubic" units.

SURFACE AREA

The **surface area** of a three-dimensional solid is the area of all of the surfaces that form the solid. Find the area of each surface, and then add up those areas. The surface area of a rectangular solid can be found by adding up the areas of all six surfaces.

The surface area of this prism is

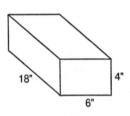

top	$18 \times 6 = 108$
bottom	$18 \times 6 = 108$
left side	$6 \times 4 = 24$
right side	$6 \times 4 = 24$
front	$18 \times 4 = 72$
back	$18 \times 4 = \underline{72}$
	408 sq in

PART IV

Selective Review of Grammar and Usage

The subjects in this section are arranged alphabetically, as follows:

Adjectives and Adverbs
Comparisons
Dangling Modifiers
Double Negatives
Either . . . Or and
   Neither . . . Nor
Exact Word Choice
Fewer and *Less*
Fragment Sentences
Idiom
Many and *Much*

Misplaced Modifiers
Parallelism
Pronouns
Punctuation: the Comma
Punctuation: the Semicolon
Punctuation: the Colon
Squinting Modifiers
Subject-Verb Agreement
Verb Tense
Wordiness

Selective Review of Grammar and Usage

ADJECTIVES AND ADVERBS

Both adjectives and adverbs are modifiers; they give additional information.

Adjectives give additional information about nouns.

The *coastal* region is known for its *foggy* nights.

Coastal gives additional information about *region*, and *foggy* gives additional information about *nights*.

Adverbs give additional information about verbs.

Acting *quickly*, Superman prevented an earthquake from *completely* destroying the state of California.

Quickly gives additional information about *acting*, and *completely* gives additional information about *destroying*.

COMPARISONS

Sentence clarity suffers if the items being compared are not alike.

His iridescent *jogging suit* was much more distracting than the other *athletes*.

In this case, a *jogging suit* is compared to *athletes*. These items are not alike. A clear and correct comparison compares the *jogging suit* to *other jogging suits*.

His iridescent *jogging suit* was much more distracting than *those of* the other athletes.

The words **as** *and* **than** *are often part of the structure of comparison sentences. A clear and correct comparison structure may employ either an* **as** . . . **as** *phrase or an* **as** . . . **as** . . . **than** *phrase but never an* **as** . . . **than** *phrase.*

Correct: Kurt is *as* talented *as* the other musicians.
Correct: Kurt is *as* talented *as* but not more talented *than* the other musicians.
Incorrect: Kurt is *as* talented *than* the other musicians.

DANGLING MODIFIERS

A modifier "dangles" when it does not clearly or logically refer to the statement immediately following it.

Strolling along the beach, a wave suddenly drenched us.

This sentence seems to say that the *wave* is doing the *strolling*. A correct sentence clarifies the modifier as follows:

While we were strolling along the beach, a wave suddenly drenched us.

In short, a dangling modifier is an introductory phrase that does not refer clearly or logically to a subsequent element (usually the subject) in a sentence.

DOUBLE NEGATIVES

A double negative occurs when one negative word or phrase is used along with another.

Fred could *not hardly* remember when he had enjoyed himself so much.

Not and *hardly* are both negative words, and when two negatives are used to modify the same term (in this case, *remember*), the result is a double negative. A correct expression requires only a single negative.

Fred could *not* remember when he had enjoyed himself so much.

EITHER . . . OR AND NEITHER . . . NOR

When comparing two items, you may use either *with* or.

Either rain *or* snow is likely to spoil our vacation.

You may also use neither *with* nor.

Neither rain *nor* snow will spoil our vacation.

Remember never *to use* nor *without* neither, *as in*

No rain *nor* snow will spoil our vacation.

EXACT WORD CHOICE

Sometimes, words that sound alike are confused with one another. Checking their dictionary meanings will help you to avoid their misuse.

COMMONLY CONFUSED WORDS

adapt/adept	lay/lie
capital/capitol	persecute/prosecute
compile/comply	precede/proceed
detain/retain	raise/rise
elicit/illicit	set/sit
foreword/forward	their/there/they're
human/humane	weather/whether
incite/insight	

FEWER AND *LESS*

When describing countable *items,* use fewer.

There are *fewer teachers* in the job market this year.

When describing uncountable *items,* use less.

Keeping one's car properly tuned means *less engine trouble* and *less gasoline consumption.*

Note that an uncountable item is not necessarily an immeasurable item. For example, *gasoline* may be measured but not counted.

FRAGMENT SENTENCES

A fragment sentence is one which is incomplete, one in which crucial information is missing.

Here are some types of fragment sentences.

Fragment: After the movie is over.
Missing information: What happens after the movie is over.
Complete sentence: After the movie is over, *we will enjoy a late supper.*

Fragment: Central air conditioning, a heated pool, and a view of the valley.
Missing information: A subject and a verb.
Complete sentence: Their new *home featured* central air conditioning, a heated pool, and a view of the valley.

Fragment: Books with large, colorful pictures.
Missing information: A verb.
Complete sentence: Books with large, colorful pictures *are* rare.

IDIOM

To native English speakers, certain expressions "sound right" because they are so commonly used. Such expressions are called "idiomatic" and are correct simply because they are so widely accepted.

Here is a list of examples.

Idiomatic	Unidiomatic
addicted *to*	addicted *from*
angry *with*	angry *at*
capable *of*	capable *to*
different *from*	different *than*
forbid *to*	forbid *from*
obedient *to*	obedient *in*
on *the* whole	on *a* whole

Remember that the standard of correctness is standard written English. Be alert to idiomatic expressions not acceptable in or characteristic of standard *written* English.

MANY AND MUCH

Many and *much* follow the same rules as do *fewer* and *less*.

Many *is used with* countable *items.*

Many trees filled the landscape that now contains townhouses.

Much *is used with* uncountable *items.*

Much happiness filled the house whenever the family gathered to celebrate.

MISPLACED MODIFIERS

A misplaced modifier is one that is placed too close to a word that it could but should not modify.

Camille prepared a roast for the family that was served burned.

In this case, because *that was served burned* is so close to *family,* the sentence seems to say that the *family* was *burned.* Here is a corrected version.

Camille served a burned roast to the family.

Note that this correction also eliminates excess words.

PARALLELISM

Phrases in a sentence are parallel when they have the same grammatical structure.

Here are three examples of parallel phrases.

to stay happy, to keep fit, and to prosper
staying happy, keeping fit, and prospering
happiness, fitness, and prosperity

Mixing structures in the following sentence results in *faulty* parallelism.

Faulty: The young college graduate listed her goals as *staying happy, keeping fit,* and *prosperity.*
Correct: The young college graduate listed her goals as *happiness, fitness,* and *prosperity.*

Sometimes, faulty parallelism occurs relative to only two items.

Faulty: Enjoying the concert and *to meet* some of the performers delighted Fred.
Correct: Enjoying the concert and *meeting* some of the performers delighted Fred.

PRONOUNS

Use **I, he, she, we,** *and* **they** *in place of the* **subject** *of a sentence.* (*The subject is the* **doer.**)

Bill wrote a sentence.
He wrote a sentence.
I wrote a sentence.
Susan was late for work.
She was late for work.
My family always takes a summer vacation.
We always take a summer vacation.
Jerry's family always takes a summer vacation.
They always take a summer vacation.

Use me, him, her, us, *and* them *in place of the* object *of a sentence.* (*The object is the* receiver.)

Bill greeted *Jerry.*
Bill greeted *him.*
Bill greeted *me.*
The boss fired *Susan.*
The boss fired *her.*
Camille helped *Christopher and me* pack our suitcases.
Camille helped *us* pack our suitcases.
The lifeguard saved *three people* from drowning.
The lifeguard saved *them* from drowning.

Use who *as a* subject (*a* doer).

Who knocked at the door?
Do you know *who knocked* at the door?
No doubt, it was a neighbor *who,* a few minutes ago, *knocked* at the door.

Use whom *as an* object (*a* receiver).

To *whom* were you *speaking*?
Your line was busy, and I wondered to *whom* you were *speaking.*
I'm the person *whom* you *telephoned* yesterday.

PERSONAL PRONOUNS

	Nominative (subject)		Objective (object)		Possessive (ownership)	
	singular	*plural*	*singular*	*plural*	*singular*	*plural*
First Person	I	we	me	us	my mine	our ours
Second Person	you	you	you	you	your yours	yours yours
Third Person	he she it	they	him her it	them	his her, hers its	their theirs

RELATIVE PRONOUNS

Nominative (subject)	Objective (object)	Possessive (ownership)
who (persons)	whom	whose*
which (things)	which	
that (things and persons)	that	

*The possessive *whose* is often also used for animals and things, as in "That's the dog whose foot was sore."

PUNCTUATION: THE COMMA

Certain parts of sentences *cannot* be separated from one another. Therefore, commas should **not** be used in the following cases.

Do* not *use a comma to separate a subject from its verb.

The enclosed forms from our office, are to be filled out now.

(There should be no comma after *office.*)

Do* not *use a comma to separate a verb from its object.

Tell me before noon, if you are going to come.

(There should be no comma after *noon.*)

Do* not *use a comma to separate an adjective from its noun.

It was an old, rusty, car.

(There should be no comma after *rusty.*)

Do* not *use a comma to separate a preposition from its object.

It was a question of, what to do now.

(There should be no comma after *of.*)

Do* not *use a comma to separate a prepositional phrase from the word it modifies when it immediately follows the modified word.

The boat floated, in the lake.

(There should be no comma after *floated.*)

Do* not *use a comma to separate a coordinating conjunction from the word, phrase, or clause that it joins to the sentence.

Studying is easy for most, but, for me it is hard.

(There should be no comma after *but.*)

Do* not *use a comma to separate compound verbs from one another.

The cat played with the catnip mouse for hours, and then hid it under the sofa.

(There should be no comma after *hours.*)

The following sentences illustrate situations in which a comma **should** be used.

Use a comma before a coordinating conjunction in a compound sentence.

I felt happy about my new job, *but* the pay was not quite enough.

Use a comma to set off interrupting or introductory words or phrases.

Safe in the house, we watched the rain fall outside.

Tom, *after all,* is one of twelve children.

Use a comma to separate a series of words or word groups.

Diet, exercise, and *rest* all contribute to good health.

The threat of runaway inflation, the heightened tension regarding foreign affairs, and *the lack of quality education in many schools* are issues that will be addressed.

Use a comma to set off nonessential clauses and phrases that are descriptive but not needed to get across the basic meaning of the sentence. Such phrases are termed **nonrestrictive.**

Maria, *who dislikes school,* is failing English.

Remember, though, that a phrase necessary to the basic meaning of the sentence, a *restrictive* phrase, must *not* be set apart by commas.

The Maria *who dislikes school* is failing English.

The meaning here is that there are two or more Marias and that the one who dislikes school is the one who is failing English.

Use a comma to set off appositives (second noun or noun equivalents that give additional information about a preceding noun).

Mr. Johnson, *a teacher,* ran for chairman of the school board.

Use a comma to separate the elements of dates, places, addresses, degrees, and titles.

Dates: Tuesday, September 16, 2001, will be my twenty-ninth birthday.

Places: Stamford, Connecticut, is my home town.

Addresses: He has lived for years at *12345 Somewhere St., Anytown, Florida.*

Degrees: John Boswell, *M.A.,* is soon to become John Boswell, *Ph.D.*

Titles: Sam Owens, *Jr.,* owns a clothing store in the center of town.

Use a comma after introductory clauses or verb phrases.

Although I had six years of sewing experience, I still had difficulty making my first wool blazer.

By jogging two miles a day, Jack lost twenty pounds during the summer.

PUNCTUATION: THE SEMICOLON

The semicolon is like a balance. It always separates elements of equal power of meaning: two or more words, phrases, or sentences. *It should never separate a main clause from a subordinate clause or a word or phrase from a clause.*

Use a semicolon to separate main clauses when the separation is not done by a coordinating conjunction (**and, but, or, nor, for**).

Ask Joe for the book; he still has it.

Use a semicolon to separate main clauses joined by a coordinating conjunction when there are commas in any of the clauses.

Although it is dark, we should start now; for we must finish on time.

Use a semicolon to separate main clauses joined by a conjunctive adverb (**therefore, however, moreover, nevertheless, etc.**).

We didn't have much time; nevertheless, we felt we should begin.

Use a semicolon to separate items in a series when there are commas within the items.

Nora's dress was red, blue, and green; Lucy's was lilac and white; and Helen's was black, turquoise, and white.

PUNCTUATION: THE COLON

The colon is a formal introducer. It is usually translated to mean *as follows.* The colon should be employed sparingly and never after *is, are, was,* or *were* when presenting a series.

The major use of the colon is to introduce a formal appositive, list, summary, quotation, example, or other explanatory material whether or not the words as follows *or* the following *are used.*

The following attended (*or,* Those who attended are as follows): Bob, Mary, Jack, and Sue.

Patrick Henry's words were the rallying cry of the revolt: "Give me liberty or give me death!"

SQUINTING MODIFIERS

A squinting modifier is sometimes called an ambiguous modifier and consists of a modifier that could equally well modify **either** *of two words or phrases.*

The executive entering the office *hurriedly* made the decision.

It is not clear whether *hurriedly* refers to the executive's entrance or the speed at which he or she made the decision. Here is a clearer version.

Entering the office, the executive *hurriedly* made the decision.

SUBJECT-VERB AGREEMENT

A plural subject goes with a plural verb; a singular subject goes with a singular verb.

The following sentence is *incorrect* because the subject is plural and the verb is singular.

The *crate* of nails, bolts, and hinges *were* delivered to the factory on Tuesday.

The correct form of this sentence is

The *crate* of nails, bolts, and hinges *was* delivered to the factory on Tuesday.

The matter of subject-verb agreement becomes a bit more trouble-some when the sentence begins with **here** *or* **there.**

The following sentence shows *incorrect* usage.

There *is* a *dusty old trunk* and *some boxes* in the attic.

Whenever a sentence begins with *here* or *there*, the subject *follows* the verb. In this case, the subject is plural, so the verb must also be plural, *are* instead of *is.*

VERB TENSE

Most verbs are regular. For these verbs, add -ed *to talk about the past and* **will** *or* **shall** *to talk about the future.*

Past: I *walked* yesterday.
Present: I *walk* today.
Future: I *will walk* tomorrow.

One way to practice the basic forms of regular verbs is to recite the *past tense* and *past participle* when you are given only the *present tense.* Here are some examples.

Present	Past (-ed)
I *talk* today.	I *talked* yesterday.
I *help* you today.	I *helped* you yesterday.
I *close* shop early today.	I *closed* shop early yesterday.

Past Participle (-ed)
I have *talked* on many occasions.
I have *helped* you often.
I have *closed* shop early for a week.

Some verbs are **irregular** *and require special constructions to express the past and past participle.*

Here are some of the most troublesome irregular verbs.

Present	Past	Past Participle
begin	began	begun
burst	burst	burst
do	did	done
drown	drowned	drowned
go	went	gone
hang (to execute)	hanged	hanged
hang (to suspend)	hung	hung
lay (to put in place)	laid	laid
lie (to rest)	lay	lain
set (to place in position)	set	set
sit (to be seated)	sat	sat
shine (to provide light)	shone	shone
shine (to polish)	shined	shined
raise (to lift up)	raised	raised
rise (to get up)	rose	risen
swim	swam	swum
swing	swung	swung

WORDINESS

For the PPST, the type of wordiness you should learn to recognize is **repetition,** *or* **redundancy.**

Here are some examples.

> Several *new initiatives* were opposed by the panel, but the *final outcome* has not been announced.

> *Currently,* there is *now* no doubt that the panel will *positively approve* the initiatives.

> After *hearing* of the panel's decision, those *listening* to the announcement called it *important* and *significant.*

A FINAL NOTE

This review is intended to familiarize you with those common rules and conventions that seem most applicable to PPST questions. The explanations following each practice test provide further information about matters discussed here and some new information as well.

PART V

Two Full-Length Practice Tests

This section contains two full-length practice simulation PPSTs. The practice tests are followed by complete answers, explanations, and analysis. The format, levels of difficulty, question structure, and number of questions are similar to those on the actual PPST. The actual PPST is copyrighted and may not be duplicated, and these questions are not taken directly from the actual tests.

When taking these tests, try to simulate the test conditions by following the time allotments carefully.

ANSWER SHEET FOR PRACTICE TEST 1

(Remove This Sheet and Use It to Mark Your Answers)

CUT HERE

READING TEST

1	Ⓐ Ⓑ Ⓒ Ⓓ Ⓔ	21	Ⓐ Ⓑ Ⓒ Ⓓ Ⓔ
2	Ⓐ Ⓑ Ⓒ Ⓓ Ⓔ	22	Ⓐ Ⓑ Ⓒ Ⓓ Ⓔ
3	Ⓐ Ⓑ Ⓒ Ⓓ Ⓔ	23	Ⓐ Ⓑ Ⓒ Ⓓ Ⓔ
4	Ⓐ Ⓑ Ⓒ Ⓓ Ⓔ	24	Ⓐ Ⓑ Ⓒ Ⓓ Ⓔ
5	Ⓐ Ⓑ Ⓒ Ⓓ Ⓔ	25	Ⓐ Ⓑ Ⓒ Ⓓ Ⓔ
6	Ⓐ Ⓑ Ⓒ Ⓓ Ⓔ	26	Ⓐ Ⓑ Ⓒ Ⓓ Ⓔ
7	Ⓐ Ⓑ Ⓒ Ⓓ Ⓔ	27	Ⓐ Ⓑ Ⓒ Ⓓ Ⓔ
8	Ⓐ Ⓑ Ⓒ Ⓓ Ⓔ	28	Ⓐ Ⓑ Ⓒ Ⓓ Ⓔ
9	Ⓐ Ⓑ Ⓒ Ⓓ Ⓔ	29	Ⓐ Ⓑ Ⓒ Ⓓ Ⓔ
10	Ⓐ Ⓑ Ⓒ Ⓓ Ⓔ	30	Ⓐ Ⓑ Ⓒ Ⓓ Ⓔ
11	Ⓐ Ⓑ Ⓒ Ⓓ Ⓔ	31	Ⓐ Ⓑ Ⓒ Ⓓ Ⓔ
12	Ⓐ Ⓑ Ⓒ Ⓓ Ⓔ	32	Ⓐ Ⓑ Ⓒ Ⓓ Ⓔ
13	Ⓐ Ⓑ Ⓒ Ⓓ Ⓔ	33	Ⓐ Ⓑ Ⓒ Ⓓ Ⓔ
14	Ⓐ Ⓑ Ⓒ Ⓓ Ⓔ	34	Ⓐ Ⓑ Ⓒ Ⓓ Ⓔ
15	Ⓐ Ⓑ Ⓒ Ⓓ Ⓔ	35	Ⓐ Ⓑ Ⓒ Ⓓ Ⓔ
16	Ⓐ Ⓑ Ⓒ Ⓓ Ⓔ	36	Ⓐ Ⓑ Ⓒ Ⓓ Ⓔ
17	Ⓐ Ⓑ Ⓒ Ⓓ Ⓔ	37	Ⓐ Ⓑ Ⓒ Ⓓ Ⓔ
18	Ⓐ Ⓑ Ⓒ Ⓓ Ⓔ	38	Ⓐ Ⓑ Ⓒ Ⓓ Ⓔ
19	Ⓐ Ⓑ Ⓒ Ⓓ Ⓔ	39	Ⓐ Ⓑ Ⓒ Ⓓ Ⓔ
20	Ⓐ Ⓑ Ⓒ Ⓓ Ⓔ	40	Ⓐ Ⓑ Ⓒ Ⓓ Ⓔ

MATHEMATICS TEST

1	Ⓐ Ⓑ Ⓒ Ⓓ Ⓔ	21	Ⓐ Ⓑ Ⓒ Ⓓ Ⓔ
2	Ⓐ Ⓑ Ⓒ Ⓓ Ⓔ	22	Ⓐ Ⓑ Ⓒ Ⓓ Ⓔ
3	Ⓐ Ⓑ Ⓒ Ⓓ Ⓔ	23	Ⓐ Ⓑ Ⓒ Ⓓ Ⓔ
4	Ⓐ Ⓑ Ⓒ Ⓓ Ⓔ	24	Ⓐ Ⓑ Ⓒ Ⓓ Ⓔ
5	Ⓐ Ⓑ Ⓒ Ⓓ Ⓔ	25	Ⓐ Ⓑ Ⓒ Ⓓ Ⓔ
6	Ⓐ Ⓑ Ⓒ Ⓓ Ⓔ	26	Ⓐ Ⓑ Ⓒ Ⓓ Ⓔ
7	Ⓐ Ⓑ Ⓒ Ⓓ Ⓔ	27	Ⓐ Ⓑ Ⓒ Ⓓ Ⓔ
8	Ⓐ Ⓑ Ⓒ Ⓓ Ⓔ	28	Ⓐ Ⓑ Ⓒ Ⓓ Ⓔ
9	Ⓐ Ⓑ Ⓒ Ⓓ Ⓔ	29	Ⓐ Ⓑ Ⓒ Ⓓ Ⓔ
10	Ⓐ Ⓑ Ⓒ Ⓓ Ⓔ	30	Ⓐ Ⓑ Ⓒ Ⓓ Ⓔ
11	Ⓐ Ⓑ Ⓒ Ⓓ Ⓔ	31	Ⓐ Ⓑ Ⓒ Ⓓ Ⓔ
12	Ⓐ Ⓑ Ⓒ Ⓓ Ⓔ	32	Ⓐ Ⓑ Ⓒ Ⓓ Ⓔ
13	Ⓐ Ⓑ Ⓒ Ⓓ Ⓔ	33	Ⓐ Ⓑ Ⓒ Ⓓ Ⓔ
14	Ⓐ Ⓑ Ⓒ Ⓓ Ⓔ	34	Ⓐ Ⓑ Ⓒ Ⓓ Ⓔ
15	Ⓐ Ⓑ Ⓒ Ⓓ Ⓔ	35	Ⓐ Ⓑ Ⓒ Ⓓ Ⓔ
16	Ⓐ Ⓑ Ⓒ Ⓓ Ⓔ	36	Ⓐ Ⓑ Ⓒ Ⓓ Ⓔ
17	Ⓐ Ⓑ Ⓒ Ⓓ Ⓔ	37	Ⓐ Ⓑ Ⓒ Ⓓ Ⓔ
18	Ⓐ Ⓑ Ⓒ Ⓓ Ⓔ	38	Ⓐ Ⓑ Ⓒ Ⓓ Ⓔ
19	Ⓐ Ⓑ Ⓒ Ⓓ Ⓔ	39	Ⓐ Ⓑ Ⓒ Ⓓ Ⓔ
20	Ⓐ Ⓑ Ⓒ Ⓓ Ⓔ	40	Ⓐ Ⓑ Ⓒ Ⓓ Ⓔ

ANSWER SHEET FOR PRACTICE TEST 1

(Remove This Sheet and Use It to Mark Your Answers)

WRITING TEST: MULTIPLE CHOICE

Part A

1 Ⓐ Ⓑ Ⓒ Ⓓ Ⓔ
2 Ⓐ Ⓑ Ⓒ Ⓓ Ⓔ
3 Ⓐ Ⓑ Ⓒ Ⓓ Ⓔ
4 Ⓐ Ⓑ Ⓒ Ⓓ Ⓔ
5 Ⓐ Ⓑ Ⓒ Ⓓ Ⓔ

6 Ⓐ Ⓑ Ⓒ Ⓓ Ⓔ
7 Ⓐ Ⓑ Ⓒ Ⓓ Ⓔ
8 Ⓐ Ⓑ Ⓒ Ⓓ Ⓔ
9 Ⓐ Ⓑ Ⓒ Ⓓ Ⓔ
10 Ⓐ Ⓑ Ⓒ Ⓓ Ⓔ

11 Ⓐ Ⓑ Ⓒ Ⓓ Ⓔ
12 Ⓐ Ⓑ Ⓒ Ⓓ Ⓔ
13 Ⓐ Ⓑ Ⓒ Ⓓ Ⓔ
14 Ⓐ Ⓑ Ⓒ Ⓓ Ⓔ
15 Ⓐ Ⓑ Ⓒ Ⓓ Ⓔ

16 Ⓐ Ⓑ Ⓒ Ⓓ Ⓔ
17 Ⓐ Ⓑ Ⓒ Ⓓ Ⓔ
18 Ⓐ Ⓑ Ⓒ Ⓓ Ⓔ
19 Ⓐ Ⓑ Ⓒ Ⓓ Ⓔ
20 Ⓐ Ⓑ Ⓒ Ⓓ Ⓔ

21 Ⓐ Ⓑ Ⓒ Ⓓ Ⓔ
22 Ⓐ Ⓑ Ⓒ Ⓓ Ⓔ
23 Ⓐ Ⓑ Ⓒ Ⓓ Ⓔ
24 Ⓐ Ⓑ Ⓒ Ⓓ Ⓔ
25 Ⓐ Ⓑ Ⓒ Ⓓ Ⓔ

Part B

26 Ⓐ Ⓑ Ⓒ Ⓓ Ⓔ
27 Ⓐ Ⓑ Ⓒ Ⓓ Ⓔ
28 Ⓐ Ⓑ Ⓒ Ⓓ Ⓔ
29 Ⓐ Ⓑ Ⓒ Ⓓ Ⓔ
30 Ⓐ Ⓑ Ⓒ Ⓓ Ⓔ

31 Ⓐ Ⓑ Ⓒ Ⓓ Ⓔ
32 Ⓐ Ⓑ Ⓒ Ⓓ Ⓔ
33 Ⓐ Ⓑ Ⓒ Ⓓ Ⓔ
34 Ⓐ Ⓑ Ⓒ Ⓓ Ⓔ
35 Ⓐ Ⓑ Ⓒ Ⓓ Ⓔ

36 Ⓐ Ⓑ Ⓒ Ⓓ Ⓔ
37 Ⓐ Ⓑ Ⓒ Ⓓ Ⓔ
38 Ⓐ Ⓑ Ⓒ Ⓓ Ⓔ
39 Ⓐ Ⓑ Ⓒ Ⓓ Ⓔ
40 Ⓐ Ⓑ Ⓒ Ⓓ Ⓔ

41 Ⓐ Ⓑ Ⓒ Ⓓ Ⓔ
42 Ⓐ Ⓑ Ⓒ Ⓓ Ⓔ
43 Ⓐ Ⓑ Ⓒ Ⓓ Ⓔ
44 Ⓐ Ⓑ Ⓒ Ⓓ Ⓔ
45 Ⓐ Ⓑ Ⓒ Ⓓ Ⓔ

Practice Test 1

READING TEST

TIME: 60 Minutes
40 Questions

<u>Directions</u>: A question or number of questions follow each of the statements or passages in this section. Using only the *stated* or *implied* information given in the statement or passage, answer the question or questions by choosing the *best* answer from among the five choices given.

1. The major function of social psychology as a behavioral science, and therefore as a discipline which can contribute to the solution of many social problems, is its investigation of the psychology of the individual in society. Thus, the scientist's main objective is to attempt to determine the influences of the social environment upon the personal behavior of individuals.

   Which of the following best summarizes the passage?

   (A) Social psychology is a science in which the behavior of the scientist in the social environment is a major function.
   (B) The social environment influences the behavior of individuals.
   (C) Social psychology studies the ways in which people in society are affected by their surroundings.
   (D) Understanding human behavior, through the help of social psychology, leads to the eventual betterment of society.
   (E) A minor objective of social psychology is the solution of social problems.

2. The quiet child is one of our concerns today. Our philosophy about children and speaking in the classroom has flip-flopped. Today we are interested in what Ruth Strickland implies when she refers to the idea of "freeing the child to talk."

Which of the following is implied by this passage?

(A) Teachers in the past have preferred quiet and reticent students.
(B) The behavior of children in the classroom is a trivial concern that can change abruptly.
(C) Whether or not a child is quiet determines the quality of his or her education.
(D) Ruth Strickland never explicitly stated her opinions about children and speaking in the classroom.
(E) There are fewer quiet children today than in the past.

3. For some, the term *creative writing* seems to imply precious writing, useless writing, flowery writing, writing that is a luxury rather than a necessity, something that is produced under the influence of drugs or leisure, a hobby.

By "precious," the author of this passage means

(A) beloved
(B) costly
(C) desirable
(D) valuable
(E) affected

4. No matter how significant the speaker's message, and no matter how strongly he or she feels about it, it will be lost unless the listeners attend to it. Attention and perception are key concepts in communication.

The primary purpose of the statement is to

(A) imply that some speakers without strong feelings find an attentive audience
(B) note that some very important messages fall on deaf ears
(C) stress the critical role of listening in oral communication
(D) urge readers to listen more carefully to spoken language
(E) argue that attention and perception are unimportant concepts in communication

5. Many of today's secondary school students will retire (either voluntarily or by coercion) from their careers or professions between the ages of forty and fifty. Indeed, by 2015, the problems of today's elderly are going to be the problems of the middle-aged.

If the above statement is true, then which of the following must also be true?

(A) People are beginning to age more quickly.
(B) There will be more leisure time available for more people in the future.
(C) Today's secondary school students will be entering careers which require youthful stamina.
(D) No one in the future will want to work during the second half of their lives.
(E) Retirement will become a more attractive possibility in the future.

Questions 6 and 7 refer to the following passage.

In future decades, what is actually required is the development of a new type of citizen—an individual who possesses confidence in his or her own potential, a person who is not intimidated by the prospect of not actively pursuing a career after the age of forty-five, and an individual who comprehends that technology can produce an easier world but only humans can produce a better one.

6. Which of the following is an unstated assumption made by the author of this passage?

(A) Technology is the unrecognized key to a better future.
(B) Present citizens are intimidated by the prospect of ending their careers in middle age.
(C) Present citizens do not have limitless potentials.
(D) Many people in the future will pursue at least two careers in the course of a lifetime.
(E) An easier world is not necessarily a safer one.

7. The author of the passage would disagree with which of the following statements?

   (A) The new type of citizen described in the passage does not presently exist.
   (B) Future decades may bring about a change in the existing types of citizens.
   (C) A new type of citizen will become necessary in future decades.
   (D) Technology should be regarded as a source of a better life.
   (E) Human potential is not limited, and we should be especially careful not to think of our potential as limited.

Questions 8, 9, and 10 refer to the following passage.

The arts have been dismissed by some legislators as mere entertainment. As we strive not merely to amuse, but to reveal the great truths of human nature, we must remember that some regard our performances as "sound and fury, signifying nothing."

8. The author of this passage is probably

   (A) a citizen writing to a legislator
   (B) an actor writing to other actors
   (C) an actor playing a part
   (D) a painter writing to other painters
   (E) a philosopher writing to political scientists

9. The passage supports a concept of art as

   (A) a political activity
   (B) more than entertainment
   (C) empty of entertainment value
   (D) generously subsidized by the government
   (E) of no use to a serious audience

10. The author repeats "some" in order to indicate that

   (A) the problem described is a relatively small one
   (B) the legislators may be in the same group that regards perfor-
       mances as signifying nothing
   (C) the actor will never meet with a wholly sympathetic audi-
       ence
   (D) the "sound and fury" on stage is paralleled in the legislature
   (E) most members of the audience are merely amused

Questions 11, 12, and 13 are based on the following passage.

If we must have evaluation, at least do it without grades. Grades
are not good indicators of intellectual ability; we must abolish them.
Then we will have students who are motivated by factors such as
interest, factors more important than a letter on a transcript. And
the abolition of grades will encourage us to concentrate less on
evaluation and more on instruction.

11. In order to agree with this author's argument, we must presume
    that

   (A) wherever grades exist, instruction is poor
   (B) there are indicators of intellectual ability that are better than
       grades
   (C) graded students are not good students
   (D) intellectual ability can be measured only in a school situa-
       tion
   (E) grades are the remaining hindrance to effective education

12. A reader of this passage might conclude that the author feels that
    graded students are not motivated by

   (A) the prospect of a high grade point average
   (B) interest in the subject matter of their course
   (C) the evaluation criteria established by their instructors
   (D) a thoroughly prepared instructor
   (E) the practicality of academic disciplines

13. This passage is most probably directed at which of the following audiences?

   (A) Politicians
   (B) Parents
   (C) Students
   (D) Teachers
   (E) Civic leaders

Questions 14, 15, and 16 refer to the following passage.

   We should spend more time enjoying life than preparing for its challenges, but sometimes we don't. For example, toward the end of every semester, all students at the university are tired and grumpy because they have spent long nights preparing for final exams. Consequently, they rarely look back on college as a time spent enjoying good fellowship and fine entertainment.

14. To agree with this author, we must accept which of the following implications of his or her argument?

   (A) It is worthwhile to prepare only for enjoyment.
   (B) School examinations do not require preparation.
   (C) Preparation is inappropriate only toward the end of the semester.
   (D) The result of preparation for exams is fatigue.
   (E) College students study too much.

15. According to this writer, the most memorable characteristic of college life should be

   (A) social interaction
   (B) academic fastidiousness
   (C) the value of sleep
   (D) more efficient exam preparation
   (E) a pleasant attitude

16. The author might have strengthened the argument without abandoning it by

(A) changing "all" to "some"
(B) advancing arguments in favor of studying all night
(C) acknowledging that grumpiness is not necessarily related to fatigue
(D) choosing a different example to illustrate the initial point
(E) focusing the argument more explicitly on a particular audience

17. When asked by his students to comment on the value of steroids for increasing muscle size, the physical education teacher said, "Steroids can be very dangerous. Many bodybuilders use them for a short period before a contest. However, the long-term use of steroids might possibly cause severe damage to the reproductive system while it helps to build a beautiful body."

In this statement, the teacher is

(A) categorically against the use of steroids
(B) an advocate of steroids but not of reproduction
(C) recommending the short-term use of steroids
(D) trying not to condemn steroid users
(E) preferring muscle definition to muscle size

Questions 18 and 19 refer to the following passage.

In modern society, those who are most adaptable to both an inflating economy and the decreasing value of the individual will survive in comfort. It is these survivors who will have the most value in the future.

18. The kind of value that the survivors possess is

(A) inflating
(B) decreasing
(C) individual
(D) comfortable
(E) unstated

19. What conclusion about value must we accept if we accept the author's statement?

    (A) Value transcends the factors of time and place.
    (B) Survival is its own value.
    (C) Decreasing value must be tolerated.
    (D) Socioeconomic factors affect the definition of value.
    (E) Value is inversely proportional to the economy.

Questions 20 through 24 refer to the following passage.

Creative writing may serve many purposes for the writer. Above all, it is a means of self-expression. It is the individual's way of saying, "These are my thoughts, and they are uniquely experienced
LINE by me." But creative writing can also serve as a safety valve for
(5)   dormant tensions. This implies that a period of time has evolved in which the child gave an idea some deep thought and that the message on paper is revealing of this deep, inner thought. Finally, a worthwhile by-product of creative writing is the stimulus it gives students to do further reading and experimentation in their areas
(10)   of interest. A child might become an ardent reader of good literature in order to satisfy an appetite whetted by a creative writing endeavor.

20. The primary purpose of the author of this passage is to

    (A) call attention to a widespread lack of self-expression
    (B) address the increasing anxiety that plagues many individuals
    (C) stress the value of good literature, both amateur and professional
    (D) encourage the reader to try some creative writing
    (E) discuss some positive purposes and effects of creative writing

21. The content of the passage indicates that the passage would be least likely to appear in which of the following?

    (A) *Journal of English Teaching Techniques*
    (B) *Psychology Today*
    (C) *Journal of Technical Writing*
    (D) *Teaching English Today*
    (E) *The Creative Writer*

22. According to the passage, creative writing can help release dormant tensions because

    (A) the writer will usually write something autobiographical
    (B) understanding literature means understanding the tensions of the characters
    (C) creative writing can express what the writer has long held within
    (D) tensions are a by-product of writer's block
    (E) self-expression is never tense

23. All of the following are probably important to the ability to write creatively EXCEPT

    (A) deep thought
    (B) time to think and ponder
    (C) spelling
    (D) reading
    (E) good literature

24. According to the passage, creative writing is most of all a

    (A) stimulus for further reading
    (B) release valve for dormant tensions
    (C) way of expressing one's feelings and thoughts
    (D) chance to let off steam
    (E) by-product of reading

Questions 25 through 30 are based on the following passage.

Throughout human history, predictions of future events have found receptive audiences: during the thirteenth century, the English scientist Roger Bacon discussed the development of such things as optical instruments and motor boats; in the fifteenth century, Leonardo da Vinci wrote about tanks and helicopters; in the nineteenth century, Jules Verne described trips to the moon. Humans have always been interested in where they are going. Since humanity's continued existence is dependent upon its making intelligent decisions about the future, such fascination has taken on a very practical dimension. Along with the changes in social mores and attitudes, greater numbers of people are demanding a role

in planning the future. The social studies curriculum must provide students with an understanding of how significant future challenges will be with regard to our national survival, social problems, reli-
(15)   gion, marriage and family life, and political processes.

It is vital that social studies teachers immerse themselves in the new field of futuristics—the study of future prospects and possibilities affecting the human condition. Futuristics, as an academic area, is already being taught at many major universities for the
(20)   purpose of encouraging students to achieve an awareness that they can contribute to the development of a much better national and global society than they ever dreamed of. The perspective of futurism is very important for today's students, since they know they can do nothing about the past.

25. Which of the following is the intended audience for the passage?

   (A) Students planning which courses to take in high school
   (B) Teachers considering changing or enriching the curriculum
   (C) Historians interested in the ways that the past reflects the future
   (D) Politicians drafting future legislation that addresses present social problems
   (E) Parents concerned about what their children should be learning

26. In order to show that "humans have always been interested in where they are going," the author provides which of the following types of facts?

   (A) Unfounded
   (B) Extraterrestrial
   (C) Political
   (D) Historical
   (E) Scientific

27. Which of the following is an assumption of the passage but is not explicitly stated?

    (A) Futuristic studies should take precedence over all other social studies.
    (B) Today's students know little about the past and less about the future.
    (C) Many social studies curriculums do not adequately acknowledge the importance of futurism.
    (D) Some figures in the past have been the equivalent of modern fortunetellers.
    (E) Social studies gives little thought to the future.

28. In the passage, the intended meaning of "global society" is which of the following?

    (A) A society well aware of the contributions of Bacon, da Vinci, and Verne
    (B) A society whose students have had courses in international relations
    (C) A society able to communicate with other societies around the globe
    (D) A society including the globes of other solar systems
    (E) A society including all the nations of the earth

29. Which of the following statements, if true, would most weaken the author's argument?

    (A) Figures other than Bacon, da Vinci, and Verne might have been mentioned as well.
    (B) Apart from Bacon, da Vinci, and Verne, many others who have tried to "see into" the future have voiced prospects and possibilities that did not come true.
    (C) Those major universities not offering courses in futuristics are considering them.
    (D) Futuristics has been the nonacademic interest of great numbers of people for many centuries.
    (E) Futuristic predictions are the stock-in-trade of many sincere politicians trying to urge the passage of significant legislation.

30. The author of this passage is most likely

    (A) a historian
    (B) a traditionalist
    (C) a high school teacher
    (D) an educator
    (E) a pacifist

Questions 31 through 35 refer to the following passage.

Possibly everyone at some point has been in a classroom where he or she didn't dare express an idea for fear that it would be chopped off. And if it was expressed, it was chopped off and no further
LINE ideas came forth. Perhaps everyone at some time has been in a
(5) student group where a participant started to express an insight but was nipped in the bud by a teacher who corrected the student's usage. Perhaps some have been in a classroom where a child was groping for just the right way to express a thought only to have the teacher or another child supply the words. And some have won-
(10) dered why a certain child was so talkative at age five and so reticent at sixteen.

31. The author implies which of the following in the passage?

    (A) Wondering about human inhibitions will do little to solve the problem.
    (B) Only certain children are either uninhibited at age five or inhibited at age sixteen.
    (C) Sixteen-year-olds should spend more time in the classroom with five-year-olds.
    (D) Attending school may cause children to become inhibited.
    (E) Inhibitions go along with maturity.

32. Which of the following terms is an appropriate substitute for "chopped off"?

    (A) put out
    (B) removed
    (C) severely criticized
    (D) misunderstood
    (E) cut back

33. Which of the following techniques is the author using to make the point that classroom situations can be very undesirable?

   (A) An appeal to the personal experiences of the readers
   (B) Disguised references to recent educational theory
   (C) Unsubstantiated and illogical anecdotes
   (D) A story
   (E) References to his or her own experiences as a teacher

34. The author's attitude may be described as being

   (A) supportive
   (B) critical
   (C) skeptical
   (D) favorable
   (E) affected

35. The author would probably most strongly agree with which of the following statements?

   (A) Students should think carefully before expressing ideas in class.
   (B) Teachers should be critical of students' expressions.
   (C) Talkative students should be tactfully silenced.
   (D) Teachers should be careful not to inhibit students' expressions.
   (E) Teachers should assist students in completing their expressions.

36. Over the last decade, teachers in elementary schools have received modest pay raises regularly, but considering inflation, their salaries have decreased twenty-three percent.

   Which of the following best expresses the point of the statement above?

   (A) Being a teacher means living at or below the poverty line.
   (B) Many teachers must hold second jobs.
   (C) The effects of inflation can negate the benefits of a pay raise.
   (D) Teachers' salaries are not adequate.
   (E) Those who teach in elementary schools can live on less than those who teach in high schools.

37. For preschool children, television cartoons could serve to stimulate them to create their own drawings if their parents provided them with the graphic materials and the indispensable encouragement.

    The author of the statement would probably agree with which of the following?

    (A) A decision to ban television cartoons as useless is not wise.
    (B) Television cartoons are the preschooler's primary source of creative inspiration.
    (C) For older children, cartoons have no educational value.
    (D) Cartoons are a viable substitute for parents when they are not available.
    (E) Cartoons accelerate a young child's learning of new words.

38. There are many people who, after experiencing severe disappointments, lose every vestige of self-esteem; they view themselves as failures in every respect; there is no more to do or to attempt.

    The author stresses which of the following responses to disappointment?

    (A) Rehabilitation
    (B) Hopelessness
    (C) Optimism
    (D) Happiness
    (E) Courage

39. It is clear that the first four or five years of a child's life are the period of most rapid change in physical and mental characteristics and greatest susceptibility to environmental influences. Attitudes are formed, values are learned, habits are developed, and innate abilities are fostered or retarded by conditions the child encounters during these early years.

Which of the following, if true, would most weaken the author's argument?

(A) Many young children possess attitudes and habits similar to those of their peers.
(B) There are significant, basic differences between a five-year-old from Samoa and one from New York.
(C) "Midlife crisis" provokes many adults to change their entire personality structures within only a few months.
(D) The environment continues to influence personal characteristics in adolescents.
(E) Environmental influences can have either positive or negative effects on human development.

40. In order for an individual to judge whether two or more speech sounds are alike or different or to make more difficult judgments, the sounds must be kept in memory and retrieved for comparison.

The passage supports which of the following conclusions?

(A) Most speech sounds are more different than they are alike.
(B) Visual discrimination is easier than auditory discrimination.
(C) A number of individuals cannot discriminate between different sounds.
(D) People with good memories are also good listeners.
(E) A person cannot compare two sounds at precisely the same time.

STOP: IF YOU FINISH BEFORE TIME IS CALLED, CHECK YOUR WORK ON THIS SECTION ONLY. DO NOT WORK ON ANY OTHER SECTION IN THE TEST.

MATHEMATICS TEST

TIME: 60 Minutes
    40 Questions

<u>Directions</u>: Each of the questions or incomplete statements below is followed by five suggested answers or completions. Select the best answer or completion of the five choices given and fill in the corresponding lettered space on the answer sheet.

1. If 10 kilometers equal 6.2 miles, then how many miles are in 45 kilometers?
   (A) 4.5
   (B) 7.25
   (C) 27.9
   (D) 29.7
   (E) 62

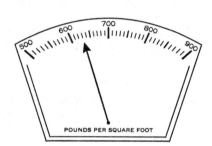

2. A gauge, pictured above, measures pressure. The reading on the gauge in pounds per square foot is

   (A) 600.3
   (B) 603
   (C) 630
   (D) 730
   (E) 770

BILL FOR PURCHASES

Science Textbooks	$840
Lab Equipment	460
Formaldehyde	320
Teacher's Manuals	120
TOTAL	$2220

3. Scholastic Supplies, Inc., sends the above bill to Zither Junior High School. Although the bill includes the cost of science lab workbooks, Scholastic Supplies forgot to list them on the bill. How much did the science lab workbooks cost Zither Junior High School?

(A) $480   (D) $560
(B) $500   (E) $620
(C) $520

4. Springfield High School's average SAT scores over a five-year period were

	Math	Verbal
1991	520	540
1992	515	532
1993	518	528
1994	510	525
1995	507	510

What was the mean (average) of the verbal SAT scores for the five-year period 1991 through 1995?

(A) 512   (B) 514   (C) 521   (D) 527   (E) 528

> Rossanna knows that a geometric figure is a
> rectangle and that it has sides of 18 and 22.

5. How can Rossanna compute the area of a square that has the same *perimeter* as the rectangle discussed above?

   (A) Add 18 and 22, double this sum, divide by 4, then multiply by 2.
   (B) Add 18 and 22, double this sum, divide by 4, then multiply by 4.
   (C) Add 18 and 22, double this sum, divide by 4, then square the quotient.
   (D) Add 18 and 22, double this sum, then multiply by 4.
   (E) Add twice 18 to twice 22, divide by 2, then square the quotient.

6. Arnold purchases one pair of slacks, a dress shirt, a tie, and a sports coat. The shirt and slacks each cost three times what the tie cost. The sports coat cost twice what the shirt cost. If Arnold paid a total of $156 for all four items, what was the price of the pair of slacks?

   (A) $12   (B) $36   (C) $48   (D) $78   (E) $84

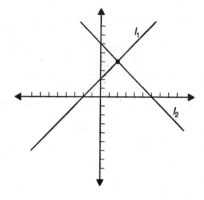

7. In the graph above, what is the solution of the equations of the two lines l_1 and l_2?

(A) $x = 4, y = 2$
(B) $x = 0, y = 2$
(C) $x = 2, y = 0$
(D) $x = 2, y = 4$
(E) The solution cannot be determined from the information given.

Questions 8 and 9 refer to the following graph.

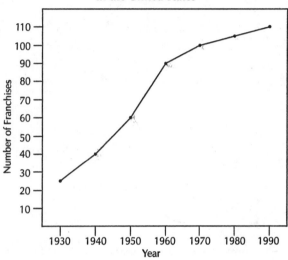

Growth of Major League Sports Franchises in the United States

8. From 1940 to 1950, the number of major league sports franchises in the United States increased by what percentage?

   (A) 20%   (D) 60%
   (B) 40%   (E) 100%
   (C) 50%

9. For which 10-year periods did the number of franchises increase by less than 10?

    I. 1930–1940
   II. 1950–1960
  III. 1970–1980
  IV. 1980–1990

   (A) I and II only
   (B) II and III only
   (C) III and IV only
   (D) I, III, and IV only
   (E) I, II, III, and IV

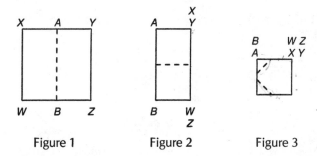

Figure 1   Figure 2   Figure 3

10. In Figure 1 above, a square piece of paper is folded along dotted line AB so that X is on top of Y and W is on top of Z (Figure 2). The paper is then folded again so that B is on top of A and WZ is on top of XY (Figure 3). Two small corners are cut out of the folded paper as shown in Figure 3. If the paper is unfolded, which of the following could be the result?

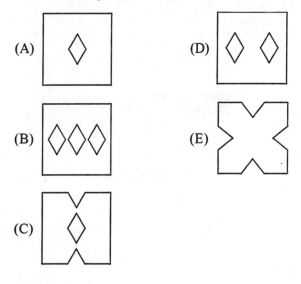

11. If cassette tapes cost $2.98 for a package of two tapes, how much change will Roy receive from a twenty dollar bill if he purchases twelve tapes?

(A) $2.02   (B) $2.12   (C) $2.18   (D) $2.22   (E) $3.02

12. All of the following are equal to the equation $2x + 4 = 3x + 3$ EXCEPT

(A) $4 = x + 3$
(B) $-x + 4 = 3$
(C) $2x + 1 = 3x$
(D) $x = -1$
(E) $2x = 3x - 1$

13. Which of the following is the smallest?

(A) $\frac{3}{5}$ (B) $\frac{4}{9}$ (C) $\frac{7}{13}$ (D) $\frac{23}{44}$ (E) $\frac{2}{3}$

14. 210,000 equals

(A) $(2 \times 10^4) + (1 \times 10^3)$
(B) $(2 \times 10^5) + (1 \times 10^4)$
(C) $(2 \times 10^6) + (1 \times 10^5)$
(D) $(2 \times 10^7) + (1 \times 10^6)$
(E) $(2 \times 10^8) + (1 \times 10^7)$

HOUSES SOLD IN ONE YEAR

Age	Number
1–2	1200
3–4	1570
5–6	1630
7–8	1440
9–10	1720

15. According to the chart above, how many more houses from 5 to 10 years old were sold than those from 4 to 8 years old?

(A) 2455
(B) 1570
(C) 150
(D) 130
(E) The number cannot be determined from the information given.

16. The product of two numbers is greater than 0 and equals one of the numbers. Which of the following must be one of the numbers?

(A) −1
(B) 0
(C) 1

(D) A prime number
(E) A reciprocal

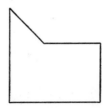

17. The best way to compute the area of the figure above would be to break it in which of the following ways?

(A)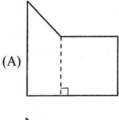

(D)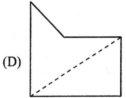

(B)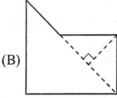

(E)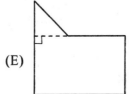

(C)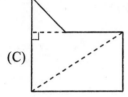

18. If $10m - 50 + 20p = 0$, what is the value of $m + 2p$?

    (A) 2   (B) 5   (C) 10   (D) 20   (E) 500

19. Round off 0.14739 to the nearest thousandth.

    (A) 0.1473   (D) 0.148
    (B) 0.1474   (E) 0.15
    (C) 0.147

20. Given that $a\#b\#c = 2a - 3b + 5c$, what is the value of $3\#(-2)\#4$?

    (A) 20   (B) 24   (C) 26   (D) 28   (E) 32

21. The large square above consists of squares and isosceles right triangles. If the large square has side 4 cm, then the area of the shaded portion in square cm is

    (A) 2   (B) 4   (C) 6   (D) 8   (E) 12

22. Juan approximated 35×45 as 40×50, but the answer was much too high. To get a better approximation, he should multiply

    (A) 50×50 (D) 30×40
    (B) 45×50 (E) 20×30
    (C) 30×50

23. If 16 out of 400 dentists polled recommended Popsodint toothpaste, what percent recommended Popsodint?

    (A) 4   (B) 8   (C) 16   (D) 25   (E) 40

24. Teachers will be assigned special camp duty one day of the week during a seven-day camping trip. If all the days of the week (Monday through Sunday) are tossed into a cap and each teacher chooses one day of the week, what is the probability that the first teacher will randomly select a weekday (Monday through Friday)?

(A) 1/7   (B) 2/7   (C) 1/5   (D) 5/7   (E) 5/2

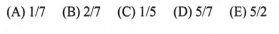

25. On the number line above, what is the point 15 units to the left of point Q?

(A) 10   (B) 5   (C) 0   (D) –9   (E) –10

26. If the product of two numbers is five more than the sum of the two numbers, which of the following equations could represent the relationship?

(A) $AB + 5 = A + B$ (D) $A/B = 5 + A + B$
(B) $5AB = A + B$ (E) $A(B) + 5 = A + B + 5$
(C) $AB = A + B + 5$

27. Which of the following is determined by division?

   I. The price of car A if it costs six times the price of car B
  II. The difference in temperature between two cities
 III. The number of yards in 39 feet

(A) I only   (D) I and II only
(B) II only   (E) I and III only
(C) III only

HOURLY SNOWFALL RATE

Temperature in Degrees	Average Snowfall in Inches
−10	2
−15	2.5
−20	3
−25	3.5
−30	4

28. The chart above shows the temperature and snowfall during one day in Moose Jaw, Saskatchewan. Which of the following is true about the data published in the chart?

(A) As the temperature increased, the amount of snowfall decreased.
(B) As the temperature decreased, the amount of snowfall decreased.
(C) As the temperature increased, the amount of snowfall remained the same.
(D) As the temperature decreased, the amount of snowfall increased.
(E) As the temperature decreased, the amount of snowfall remained the same.

29. A Spifmobile is selling at a 30% discount off its sticker price. Its sticker price is $8000. What is its new selling price?

(A) $2400   (D) $7970
(B) $5600   (E) $7976
(C) $6600

30. Harmon's new sports car averages 35 miles per each gallon of gasoline. Assuming Harmon is able to maintain his average miles per gallon, how far can he drive on 12 gallons of gas?

(A) Almost 3 miles   (D) 420 miles
(B) 42 miles   (E) 700 miles
(C) 350 miles

31. A parallelogram has two sides of dimensions 9 and 7. What would be the side of a square with the same perimeter?

    (A) 32   (B) 18   (C) 14   (D) 8   (E) 4

32. It is estimated that at a picnic each adult will drink $\frac{1}{5}$ of a gallon of lemonade. How many gallons of lemonade should be brought to the picnic if 28 people, all adults, are expected to attend?

    (A) 3   (D) Between 5 and 6
    (B) Between 3 and 4   (E) More than 6
    (C) 5

33. If John can type twenty pages in four hours, how many hours will it take him to type fifty pages?

    (A) 5   (B) 6   (C) 8   (D) 9   (E) 10

34. Thomas purchased 20 goldfish at 85¢ each and then bought 8 bags of goldfish food, also at 85¢ each. What would be the simplest way to compute his total amount spent?

    (A) $20 \times 85¢ + 4 \times 85¢ + 2 \times 85¢ + 2 \times 85¢$
    (B) $28 \times 85¢$
    (C) $8 \times 20 \times 85¢$
    (D) $20 \times 85¢$
    (E) $850¢ \times 2$

35. In Hicksville's Little League, team A has twice as many victories as team B, team C has 5 fewer victories than team A, and team D has 4 more victories than team B. If total victories of all four teams equal 29, how many victories does team D have?

    (A) 5   (B) 9   (C) 10   (D) 12   (E) 14

> All dogs are green.
> Bowser is a dog.

36. If the statements above are true, which of the following must also be true?

   (A) Bowser can be blue.
   (B) No cats are green.
   (C) Some cats are green.
   (D) Bowser is green.
   (E) Bowser is not a dog.

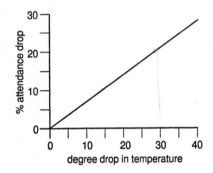

37. According to the graph above, if the temperature falls 30 degrees, what percentage will school attendance drop?

   (A) 10   (B) 20   (C) 30   (D) 40   (E) 50

38. Maria needs to compute 30% of 50. To get a correct answer, all of the following will work EXCEPT

   (A) 0.30×50 (D) $50 \div \frac{10}{3}$
   (B) 0.50×30 (E) $50 \div \frac{3}{10}$
   (C) $\frac{3}{10} \times 50$

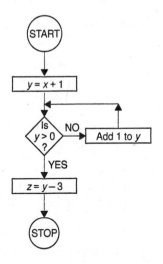

39. In the flow chart above, if $x = 3$, then what is the value of z?

    (A) -1 (B) 0   (C) 1   (D) 3   (E) 6

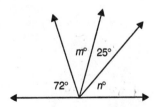

40. In the figure above, what is the number of degrees in the sum of $m + n$?

    (A) 83
    (B) 93
    (C) 97
    (D) 103
    (E) The number of degrees cannot be determined from the information given.

STOP: IF YOU FINISH BEFORE TIME IS CALLED, CHECK YOUR WORK ON THIS SECTION ONLY. DO NOT WORK ON ANY OTHER SECTION IN THE TEST.

WRITING TEST: MULTIPLE-CHOICE SECTION

TIME: 30 Minutes
45 Questions

PART A

SUGGESTED TIME: 10 Minutes
25 Questions

Directions: Some of the following sentences are correct. Others contain problems in grammar, usage, idiom, diction, punctuation, and capitalization.

If there is an error, it will be underlined and lettered. Find the one underlined part that must be changed to make the sentence correct and choose the corresponding letter on your answer sheet. Mark (E) if the sentence contains no error.

1. The <u>remarks of the</u> Prime Minister <u>not only</u> embarrass the gov-
        A   B
   ernment but also <u>made</u> the settlement of the border dispute
                C
   <u>impossible.</u> <u>No error</u>
      D   E

2. <u>By dividing</u> the responsibility for the project <u>between you and I,</u>
       A   B
   we should be able to complete <u>it</u> before Saturday. <u>No error</u>
   <u>C</u>   D   E

3. In 1919, the publication of Sir Walter Scott's

   <u>Ivanhoe</u> <u>has consolidated</u> <u>his</u> position as the <u>leading</u> historical
            A   B   C
   novelist <u>in Europe.</u> <u>No error</u>
           D   E

4. The <u>witnesses'</u> testimony <u>does</u> not differ significantly <u>to</u> the de-
        A   B   C

   fense lawyer's opening statement <u>about</u> the robbery. <u>No error</u>
                                       D   E

5. Though the two teams <u>scored only</u> one goal in the three games
                         A

   <u>they</u> played, the fine defensive play seems <u>satisfying</u> the large
    B   C

   crowds <u>that</u> attended the matches. <u>No error</u>
          D   E

6. Albertville, <u>nestling</u> on the northwest fringe of the French Alps,
               A

   <u>will be</u> the <u>site</u> of the meetings <u>in</u> 2002. <u>No error</u>
     B   C   D   E

7. After the first ten moves of the chess match, <u>it</u> <u>appeared</u> that the
                                                A   B

   Hungarian champion <u>had fell</u> so far behind that she
                      C

   <u>could not possibly recover.</u> <u>No error</u>
             D   E

8. Although you <u>have filled out</u> all the forms and <u>paid</u> the fees, <u>one</u>
                      A   B   C

   still must supply the consulate with a <u>recently taken</u> photograph.
                                             D

   <u>No error</u>
    E

9. <u>A number</u> of conscripts, <u>who</u> <u>would later join</u> the Intelligence
      A   B   C

   Service, <u>were given</u> intensive classes in Russian and Chinese.
            D

   <u>No error</u>
    E

10. Hurrying to reach the bank before it closed, I left my attention
       A   B   C
    wander and scraped the door of the car on the gate. No error
               D   E

11. In eighteenth-century New England, children as young as five

    work beside their parents in the fields to make certain the crops
     A   B
    were harvested before the onset of winter. No error
         C   D   E

12. Bellini's opera, a very forceful adaptation of Shakespeare's play,
                          A
    does not provide hardly any of the rich characterization we find
          B   C   D
    in the drama. No error
             E

13. In the interviews conducted by Mary Lee Johnson, an experi-
                       A
    enced journalist, and her husband, men who would not answer
                                         B
    her questions gladly replied to his. No error
              C   D   E

14. There is, according to today's *Times,* two races in the state Re-
       A   B   C
    publican primary that are too close to predict. No error
                       D   E

15. Given the rise in the number of propaganda broadcasts, it is no
     A   B
    wonder that the public responds more skeptical to the latest claim
                                  C   D
    by the opposition party. No error
                         E

16. If <u>anyone</u> wants to <u>appreciate</u> both the inherent folly and the dan-
        A   B
gerous implications of this weapons project, <u>he</u> has
                                   C
<u>only to read</u> Dr. Tellus's article. <u>No error</u>
    D   E

17. Most of the runners finished before noon with no ill <u>effects</u> <u>from</u>
                                          A   B
the smog, <u>and</u> a few were <u>seriously</u> unwell and unable to com-
          C   D
plete the race. <u>No error</u>
                    E

18. The population of New Hampshire, though <u>increasing rapidly</u>
                                            A
since 1990, <u>are</u> still <u>far smaller</u> than <u>that of</u> Rhode Island or Con-
            B   C   D
necticut. <u>No error</u>
         E

19. Plays <u>like</u> Ibsen's *Ghosts* or *St. Joan*, though often <u>performed</u> in
        A   B
London's West End, <u>seen</u> rarely <u>in</u> professional productions on
                      C   D
Broadway. <u>No error</u>
          E

20. <u>In regards to</u> the sudden decline <u>in</u> the price of gasoline, six of
        A   B
the OPEC nations <u>have sent</u> representatives <u>to meet</u> in Geneva.
                    C   D
<u>No error</u>
  E

21. In the early seventeenth century, young boys sung the soprano
                                                    A

    parts that are now sung by women. No error
     B   C   D   E

22. The rising crime rate, in addition to border control and drug smug-
                                       A

    gling, are to be discussed on the next broadcast of *Meet the Press.*
            B   C   D

    No error
      E

23. If a person concentrates on getting his work done on time, you
                    A   B   C

    will enjoy recreational activities all the more. No error
     D   E

24. Ideas, that seemed shocking to theatergoers in 1910 now seem
     A   B   C

    commonplace to us. No error
                 D   E

25. As the two previous messages, the latest communication from
     A

    the terrorists insists upon a safe passage out of the country before
                   B   C

    any hostage is released. No error
                 D   E

PART B

SUGGESTED TIME: 20 Minutes
                 20 Questions

Directions: Some part of each sentence below is underlined; some-times the whole sentence is underlined. Five choices for rephrasing the underlined part follow each sentence. The first choice (A) repeats the original, and the other four are different. If choice (A) seems bet-ter than the alternatives, choose answer (A); if not, choose one of the others.

For each sentence, consider the requirements of standard written English. Your choice should be a correct, concise, and effective ex-pression, not awkward or ambiguous. Focus on grammar, word choice, sentence construction, and punctuation. If a choice changes the mean-ing of the original sentence, do not select it.

26. Despite the dangers of the journey, all of the men selected for the expedition had an eagerness to set out at once.

    (A) had an eagerness to set out
    (B) were eager for setting out
    (C) had eagerness for setting out
    (D) wished eagerly for setting out
    (E) were eager to set out

27. The state elections have not turned out as expected, there is no change in the number of Republican senators.

    (A) as expected, there is
    (B) as people expected, there is
    (C) as expected; there is
    (D) as expected, but there is
    (E) as expected; there being

28. In modern Africa, some <u>regimes which ignore</u> the conventions on which modern diplomacy rests, Libya or South Africa, for example.

    (A) regimes which ignore
    (B) regimes ignore
    (C) regimes that ignore
    (D) regimes, which ignore
    (E) regimes ignoring

29. <u>When Smithers agreed to run</u> for mayor, she knew she faced an uphill battle.

    (A) When Smithers agreed to run
    (B) When Smithers agrees to run
    (C) After the agreement was made by Smithers to run
    (D) When Smithers agreed about running
    (E) After Smithers's agreement about running

30. At midnight, the election results were <u>uncertain, it was after three when they were conclusive</u>.

    (A) uncertain, it was after three when they were conclusive
    (B) uncertain, it was after three when it was conclusive
    (C) uncertain; it was after three when they were conclusive
    (D) uncertain; it was after three when it was conclusive
    (E) uncertain; being concluded after three

31. <u>Many songs were recorded by the rock group that</u> covertly hinted of devil worship, according to the critics.

    (A) Many songs were recorded by the rock group that
    (B) Many songs were recorded by the rock group who
    (C) The rock group that recorded many songs
    (D) The recording of many songs by the rock group
    (E) The rock group recorded many songs that

32. The unexplained surcharge of eighty-five dollars <u>surprised and angered the customers</u>.

    (A) surprised and angered the customers
    (B) surprised the customers, and angered them
    (C) surprised the customers, angering them
    (D) was surprising to the customers, and it angered them
    (E) was a surprise and a source of anger to the customers

33. The position requires a worker who can <u>use the law library, the computer, and write fluently</u>.

    (A) use the law library, the computer, and write fluently
    (B) use the law library and the computer and write fluently
    (C) use the law library and use the computer and write fluently
    (D) use the law library, the computer, and fluent writing
    (E) use the law library and the computer; and write fluently

34. <u>Because the sales of cigarettes declined was why Joseph Cruz, the vice-president, believed the company lost money.</u>

    (A) Because the sales of cigarettes declined was why Joseph Cruz, the vice-president, believed the company lost money.
    (B) Because the sales of cigarettes declined, the vice-president, Joseph Cruz, believed was why the company lost money.
    (C) The vice-president, Joseph Cruz, believed why the company lost money was because the sales of cigarettes declined.
    (D) The vice-president, Joseph Cruz, believed the company lost money because the sales of cigarettes declined.
    (E) Joseph Cruz, the vice-president, believed the reason the company lost money was because the sales of cigarettes declining.

35. We ought to have two levels of diplomatic <u>immunity; one would allow</u> only favored nations to retain freedom from search.

    (A) immunity; one would allow
    (B) immunity, one would allow
    (C) immunity, allowing
    (D) immunity, one will allow
    (E) immunity, which would allow

36. Some reptiles <u>living in the deserts</u> of New Mexico and Arizona were there centuries before the continent was discovered.

   (A) living in the deserts
   (B) which living in the deserts
   (C) that are living in the deserts
   (D) who live in the deserts
   (E) who live in the desert

37. The cafes of Budapest are as busy <u>as ever, they are the</u> meeting places of writers and artists.

   (A) as ever, they are the
   (B) as ever, being they are
   (C) as ever; they are
   (D) as ever; being they are
   (E) as ever; being

38. <u>Rostov was born and trained in Russia, and she performed</u> only in the United States.

   (A) Rostov was born and trained in Russia, and she performed
   (B) Although having been born and trained in Russia, Rostov performed
   (C) Although Rostov was born and trained in Russia, she performed
   (D) Born and trained in Russia was Rostov, and she performed
   (E) Rostov, being born and trained in Russia, performed

39. The president, as well as senators from four states, <u>have enthusiastically supported</u> the referendum.

   (A) have enthusiastically supported
   (B) enthusiastically support
   (C) having enthusiastically supported
   (D) has enthusiastically supported
   (E) are enthusiastically supporting

40. Carefully watching the highway patrolman parked by the road-side, <u>my car nearly ran into</u> a slow-moving van.

    (A) my car nearly ran into
    (B) I nearly ran my car into
    (C) my car was nearly run into
    (D) my car nearly running into
    (E) I ran my car nearly into

41. Gerrymandering <u>is when a voting area is unfairly divided</u> so that one political party gains advantage.

    (A) is when a voting area is unfairly divided
    (B) divides a voting area unfairly
    (C) makes fair voting unfair
    (D) occurs when a voting area is unfairly divided
    (E) is when a voting area is divided unfairly

42. Frank Buck, "the great white hunter," was always portrayed on film as <u>fearless and having great skill against dangerous animals.</u>

    (A) fearless and having great skill against dangerous animals
    (B) fearless and skillful against dangerous animals
    (C) having no fear and having great skill against dangerous animals
    (D) fearless and with skill against dangerous animals
    (E) facing dangerous animals with fear and with skill

43. <u>After having finished the marathon</u>, both the winner and the losers felt proud of their achievement.

    (A) After having finished the marathon
    (B) Having finished the marathon
    (C) Having been finished after the marathon
    (D) Finishing the marathon
    (E) The marathon finished

44. <u>The actor, along with his butler, bodyguard, chauffeur, two maids, and four dogs, are on board</u> the train bound for Cannes.

    (A) The actor, along with his butler, bodyguard, chauffeur, two maids, and four dogs, are on board

    (B) The actor and his butler and also his chauffeur, together with two maids and including four dogs, are on board

    (C) The actor, along with his butler, bodyguard, chauffeur, two maids, and four dogs, is on board

    (D) The actor, along with his butler, bodyguard, chauffeur, two maids, and four dogs, are climbing onto

    (E) The actor's butler, bodyguard, chauffeur, two maids, and four dogs are on board

45. <u>Neither the director nor the investors in the sequel predicts</u> that it will earn less money than the original film.

    (A) Neither the director nor the investors in the sequel predicts

    (B) Neither the investors in the sequel nor its director predicts

    (C) The director of the sequel, along with its investors, predicts

    (D) Neither the investors nor the directors of the sequel predicts

    (E) About the sequel, neither the director nor the investors predict

STOP: IF YOU FINISH BEFORE TIME IS CALLED, CHECK YOUR WORK ON THIS SECTION ONLY. DO NOT WORK ON ANY OTHER SECTION IN THE TEST.

WRITING TEST: ESSAY SECTION

TIME: 30 Minutes
     1 Essay

Directions: In this section, you will have 30 minutes to plan and write one essay on the topic given. You may use the paper provided to plan your essay before you begin writing. You should plan your time wisely. Read the topic carefully to make sure that you are properly addressing the issue or situation. **You must write on the given topic. An essay on another topic will not be acceptable.**

The essay question is designed to give you an opportunity to write clearly and effectively. Use specific examples whenever appropriate to aid in supporting your ideas. Keep in mind that the quality of your writing is much more important than the quantity.

Your essay is to be written in the space provided. No other paper may be used. Your writing should be neat and legible. Because you have only a limited amount of space in which to write, please do **not** skip lines, do **not** write excessively large, and do **not** leave wide margins.

Remember, use the bottom of this page for any organizational notes you may wish to make.

TOPIC

Different sports appeal to different people. Think of one sport that you enjoy, either as a spectator or as a participant. In the space provided, write an essay explaining why that particular sport appeals to you.

ANSWER KEY FOR PRACTICE TEST 1

	Reading Test		Mathematics Test		Writing Test Multiple-Choice
1. C	21. C	1. C	21. D	1. C	24. A
2. A	22. C	2. C	22. C	2. B	25. A
3. E	23. C	3. A	23. A	3. A	26. E
4. C	24. C	4. D	24. D	4. C	27. C
5. B	25. B	5. C	25. E	5. C	28. B
6. B	26. D	6. B	26. C	6. E	29. A
7. D	27. C	7. D	27. C	7. C	30. C
8. B	28. E	8. C	28. D	8. C	31. E
9. B	29. B	9. C	29. B	9. E	32. A
10. B	30. D	10. C	30. D	10. C	33. B
11. B	31. D	11. B	31. D	11. A	34. D
12. B	32. C	12. D	32. D	12. B	35. A
13. D	33. A	13. B	33. E	13. E	36. A
14. E	34. B	14. B	34. B	14. A	37. C
15. A	35. D	15. E	35. B	15. C	38. C
16. D	36. C	16. C	36. D	16. E	39. D
17. D	37. A	17. E	37. B	17. C	40. B
18. E	38. B	18. B	38. E	18. B	41. B
19. D	39. C	19. C	39. C	19. C	42. B
20. E	40. E	20. E	40. A	20. A	43. B
				21. A	44. C
				22. B	45. B
				23. C	

SCORING YOUR PPST PRACTICE TEST 1

To score your PPST Practice Test 1, total the number of correct responses for each test. Do not subtract any points for questions attempted but missed, as there is no penalty for guessing. The scores for each section range from 150 to 190. Because the Writing Test contains multiple-choice questions and an essay, that score is a composite score adjusted to give approximately equal weight to the number right on the multiple-choice section and to the essay score. The essay is scored holistically (a single score for overall quality) from 1 (low) to 6 (high). Each of two readers gives a 1 to 6 score. The score that the essay receives is the sum of these two readers' scores.

ANALYZING YOUR TEST RESULTS

The following charts should be used to carefully analyze your results and spot your strengths and weaknesses. The complete process of analyzing each subject area and each individual question should be completed for this Practice Test. These results should be reexamined for trends in types of error (repeated errors) or poor results in specific subject areas. **This reexamination and analysis is of tremendous importance for effective test preparation.**

PRACTICE TEST 1: SUBJECT AREA ANALYSIS SHEET

	Possible	Completed	Right	Wrong
Reading Test	40			
Mathematics Test	40			
Writing Test	45			
TOTAL	125			

ANALYSIS—TALLY SHEET FOR QUESTIONS MISSED

One of the most important parts of test preparation is analyzing **why** you missed a question so that you can reduce the number of mistakes. Now that you have taken Practice Test 1 and corrected your answers, carefully tally your mistakes by marking each of them in the proper column.

	Total Missed	Simple Mistake	Misread Problem	Lack of Knowlege
Reading Test				
Mathematics Test				
Writing Test				
TOTAL				

Reviewing the above data should help you determine **why** you are missing certain questions. Now that you have pinpointed types of errors, when you take Practice Test 2, focus on avoiding your most common type.

SCORE APPROXIMATORS

Reading Test

To approximate your reading score:
1. Count the number of questions you answered correctly.
2. Use the following table to match the number of correct answers and the corresponding approximate score range.

Number Right	Approximate Score Range
10–19	160–169
20–29	170–179
30–40	180–189

Remember, this is only an approximate score range. When you take the PPST, you will have questions that are similar to those in this book, however some questions may be slightly easier or more difficult.

Mathematics Test

To approximate your mathematics score:
1. Count the number of questions you answered correctly.
2. Use the following table to match the number of correct answers and the corresponding approximate score range.

Number Right	Approximate Score Range
0–10	150–160
11–20	161–170
21–30	171–180
31–40	181–190

Remember, this is an approximate score range.

Writing Test

These scores are difficult to approximate because the multiple-choice section score and the essay score are combined to give a total score.

Essay Checklist

Use this checklist to evaluate your essay.

Diagnosis/Prescription for Timed Writing Exercise

A good essay will:

_____ Address the assignment
      Be well focused
_____ Be well organized
      Have smooth transitions between paragraphs
      Be coherent, unified
_____ Be well developed
      Contain specific examples to support points
_____ Be grammatically sound (only minor flaws)
      Use correct sentence structure
      Use correct punctuation
      Use standard written English
_____ Use language skillfully
      Use a variety of sentence types
      Use a variety of words
_____ Be legible
      Have clear handwriting
      Be neat

ANSWERS AND EXPLANATIONS FOR PRACTICE TEST 1

READING TEST

1. (C) Choices (D) and (E) address subsidiary points only. Choice (A) mentions the behavior of the scientist rather than the behavior of individuals, and (B) does not even mention social psychology. Only (C) is both comprehensive and accurate.

2. (A) The final sentence expresses an interest in and appreciation for *talking* children, thus implying that the *flip-flop* is a change from the past preference for quiet children.

3. (E) All of the other terms stress negative attitudes toward creative writing, and choice (E) maintains this emphasis on the negative at the same time as it expresses one meaning of *precious*.

4. (C) Each of the other choices either describes a secondary rather than primary point or assigns a purpose (to urge) that is beyond the scope of the passage. And choice (E) is obviously incorrect.

5. (B) The passage portrays early retirement as an unattractive, problematic occurrence that will affect many but not all; (D) and (E) contradict the unattractive connotations of early retirement; and (A) and (C) state conclusions which are neither expressed nor implied in the passage.

6. (B) By saying that the *new* type of citizen will not be intimidated by ending careers, the author assumes that *present* citizens *are* intimidated. Incorrect choices either state an implication rather than an assumption (D) or draw conclusions beyond the scope of the passage as in (A), (C), and (E).

7. (D) Toward the end of the passage, the author expresses a skeptical, qualified view of the value of technology. Each of the other choices is consistent with the author's views.

8. (B) The *we* in the passage tells us that the author counts himself or herself among those who give performances.

9. (B) As the author says, art is *not merely to amuse*.

10. (B) The repeat of *some* recalls the earlier mention of *some legislators* and indicates that the legislators may be part of those who do not appreciate the full value of art.

11. (B) In order to accept an argument abolishing grades, we must presume that there are viable alternatives. None of the other choices is a necessary condition for agreement with the argument.

12. (B) By saying that the abolition of grades will increase student interest in subject matter, the author implies that graded students are less interested in and motivated by subject matter.

13. (D) The words *we will have students* indicate that the author is a teacher talking to teachers; so does *us* in the third sentence.

14. (E) Although choice (D) is part of the author's argument, acknowledging that exams cause fatigue will not make us accept the overall argument stressing fun over study. To accept that argument, we must accept the fact that students study too much (E).

15. (A) The author stresses the value of *good fellowship and fine entertainment*, both social characteristics.

16. (D) Taking a negative view of studying, the author does not pick as strong and generally acceptable an example of enjoying life as might have been presented. Choices (A) and (C) would weaken rather than strengthen the argument, and (B) contradicts the argument. Choice (E) is too vague, not specifying *which* audience, so we cannot tell what effect such a change would have.

17. (D) The teacher does not advocate, recommend, or prefer anything in particular; nor is the teacher categorically for or against steroids. Therefore, (A), (B), (C), and (E) should be eliminated because they assign an *absolute* point of view that is not expressed.

18. (E) The author says that survivors will be adaptable but does not specify the way in which adaptability will be a value.

19. (D) Each of the other choices goes beyond the scope of the passage. Choice (D) is directly relevant to the author's assertion that the economy is a significant factor.

20. (E) This is the most comprehensive choice, describing the overall purpose of the passage rather than secondary purposes and implications.

21. (C) A discussion of creative writing is relevant to English and psychology but not to technical writing.

22. (C) The passage states that dormant tensions may be released through the revealing of a *deep, inner thought*. Choice (C) refers to this idea.

23. (C) Spelling is the one characteristic that the author neither expresses nor implies as relevant to creative writing.

24. (C) The passage explicitly states that creative writing is, *above all, . . . a means of self-expression.*

25. (B) The passage stresses ways of changing the social studies curriculum, thus designating its audience as those who can effect such changes—teachers.

26. (D) *Humans have always been interested in where they are going* is preceded by a series of historical facts, that is, facts about occurrences of the past.

27. (C) By advocating the addition of futurism to the social studies curriculum, the author assumes that futurism is not adequately acknowledged. Without that assumption, the author would have no reason to make the argument.

28. (E) By distinguishing *global* from *national* in the passage, the author suggests that a global society is larger and more inclusive than a national one but does not go so far as to suggest that such a society necessarily includes outer space.

29. (B) Choices (C) and (D) would strengthen the argument of the value of futurism. Choices (A) and (E) are irrelevant to the strength or weakness of the argument. Choice (B) weakens the passage by calling into question those futurists of the past.

30. (D) The overall stress on changes in education indicates that the author is an educator.

31. (D) Through presenting a series of school situations in which students are discouraged from expressing themselves, the author implies that attending school may cause children to become inhibited.

32. (C) The passage overall suggests that students are inhibited by being severely criticized or corrected. The meaning of *chopped off* given by (C) is consistent with this overall view.

33. (A) The author repeatedly addresses the common experiences of *everyone*.

34. (B) By citing a number of negative situations, the author leaves no question that he or she is critical of the practices described.

35. (D) Choices (A), (B), and (C) contradict the implied argument of the passage, and (E) *may* contradict the implied argument because the meaning of *assist* is not made clear and possibly suggests that the teacher should supply words for the student. Choice (D) repeats the author's overall point.

36. (C) Each of the other choices is beyond the scope of the passage.

37. (A) Choices (C) and (E) make statements beyond the scope of the passage; (D) contradicts the passage (the parents' contribution is said to be *indispensable*); and (B) makes cartoons a *primary* source of inspiration. The author would agree that cartoons have some value and should not be banned.

38. (B) The author stresses a severely negative response to disappointment, and only (B) supplies a negative term.

39. (C) Choice (C) weakens the stress on early childhood as a time of rapid change by saying that midlife may be a time of rapid change as well.

40. (E) By stressing the separateness of speech sounds in memory, the author supports the conclusion of (E). Each of the other conclusions is beyond the scope of the passage.

MATHEMATICS TEST

1. (C) One way to solve this problem is to set up a ratio: 10 kilometers is to 6.2 miles as 45 kilometers is to how many miles? This ratio is expressed in mathematical terms as

$$\frac{10 \text{ km}}{6.2 \text{ m}} = \frac{45 \text{ km}}{x}$$

Cross multiplying gives
$$10x = 6.2 \times 45$$
$$10x = 279$$

Dividing both sides by 10 gives
$$\frac{10x}{10} = \frac{279}{10}$$
$$x = 27.9$$

Another method is to realize that 45 kilometers is exactly $4\frac{1}{2}$ times 10 kilometers. Therefore, the number of miles in 45 kilometers must be $4\frac{1}{2}$ times the number of miles in 10 kilometers, or $4\frac{1}{2}$ times 6.2. Thus, $4.5 \times 6.2 = 27.9$.

2. (C) The gauge indicator is slightly over 600, which eliminates choices (D) and (E), each of which is over 700. The space between 600 and 700 is divided into 10 equal sections. Since the total between 600 and 700 is 100 pounds per square foot, each of these 10 sections equals 10 lbs/sq ft. The indicator is exactly three sections beyond 600, so $600 + 3(10) = 630$ lbs/sq ft.

3. (A) The four listed items total $1740. Therefore, by subtracting from the listed total of $2200, we can see that the missing item must have cost $480. $2200 − $1740 = $480.

4. (D) The total of the five verbal SAT scores is 2635. Dividing that total by 5 (the number of scores) gives 527 as the average.

5. (C) Since the figure is a rectangle, its opposite sides are equal. To find its perimeter, first add the two sides, and then double the sum (or double each of the sides and add the results).

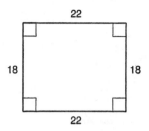

Now, to determine the side of a square with the same perimeter, simply divide by 4, since the side of a square is $\frac{1}{4}$ its perimeter. Finally, to find the area of the square, multiply its side times itself (square it).

6. (B) If we call the price of the tie x, then the price of the shirt is $3x$, the price of the slacks is $3x$, and the price of the coat is twice the shirt, or $6x$. Totaling the x's, we get $13x$. Since the total spent was $156, $13x = \$156$. Dividing both sides by 13 gives

$$\frac{13x}{13} = \frac{\$156}{13}$$
$$x = \$12$$

Therefore, the price of the pair of slacks, $3x$, is $3(\$12) = \$36$.

7. (D) The solution of two lines can be determined by the coordinates of the point at which the lines intersect. Lines l_1 and l_2 intersect at $(2, 4)$. Therefore, $x = 2$ and $y = 4$.

8. (C) In 1940, there were 40 sports franchises in the United States. By 1950, there were 60 sports franchises. So in 1950, there were "half again as many" as in 1940 $(40 + 20 = 60)$. This is a 50% increase. Another way of computing percent change is by using the formula "change divided by starting point."

$$\frac{\text{change}}{\text{starting point}} = \frac{20}{40} = 0.50 = 50\%$$

9. (C) For only two 10-year periods did the number of franchises increase by fewer than 10: from 1970 to 1980 (an increase of about 5) and from 1980 to 1990 (another increase of about 5). In each of the other 10-year periods shown on the chart, the number of sports franchises increased by more than 10.

10. (C) Take some scissors and a piece of paper and try it.

11. (B) To purchase twelve tapes, Roy must buy six packages. At $2.98 per package, he spends $17.88. His change from a twenty dollar bill will be $20.00 − $17.88 = $2.12.

12. (D) Solving the equation $2x + 4 = 3x + 3$, first subtract $2x$ from each side.

$$2x + 4 - 2x = 3x + 3 - 2x$$
$$4 = x + 3$$

Now, subtract 3 from both sides.

$$4 - 3 = x + 3 - 3$$
$$1 = x$$

By plugging in the above value of x (that is, 1) for each of the answer choices, we find that 1 satisfies all the equations *except* choice (D).

$$\text{Does } x = -1? \text{ No.}$$
$$1 \neq -1$$

Therefore, (D) is the correct answer.

13. (B) Note that all choices except (B) are larger than $\frac{1}{2}$. Choice (B), $\frac{4}{9}$, is smaller than $\frac{1}{2}$.

14. (B) 210,000 is equivalent to $(2 \times 10^5) + (1 \times 10^4)$. A fast way of figuring this is to count the number of places to the right of each digit that is not zero. For instance,

   210,000   Note that there are 5 places to the right of the 2, thus 2×10^5.

   210,000   There are 4 places to the right of the 1, thus 1×10^4.

So 210,000 may also be written $(2 \times 10^5) + (1 \times 10^4)$.

15. (E) Since the chart does not distinguish how many houses are 3 years old or 4 years old, the answer cannot be determined.

16. (C) If the product of two numbers equals one of the numbers, then $(x)(y) = x$. If this product is more than 0, neither of the numbers may be zero. Therefore, y must be 1: $(x)(1) = x$.

17. (E) The best way to compute the area of the figure is to divide it into as few parts as possible, making each part a simple shape whose area is easily calculated (for instance, a triangle, rectangle, or square). Choice (E) divides the shape into a rectangle and a triangle.

18. (B) This problem requires an algebraic solution. First move the −50 to the other side of the equation, changing its sign in the process:

$$10m - 50 + 20p = 0$$
$$10m + 20p = 50$$

You want to find $m + 2p$, so divide the left side of the equation by 10. However, to keep the equation balanced, you must do the same to the right side as well:

$$\frac{10m + 20p}{10} = \frac{50}{10}$$
$$m + 2p = 5$$

19. (C) Rounding 0.14739 to the nearest thousandth means first looking at the digit one place to the right of the thousandths place: 0.147$\underline{3}$9. Since that digit is 4 or less, simply drop it. (There is no need to replace with zeros because they are not needed to the right of a decimal point.)

20. (E) Following the formula, plug in 3 for a, −2 for b, and 4 for c. This gives:

$$a\#b\#c = 2a - 3b + 5c$$
$$3\#(-2)\#4 = 2(3) - 3(-2) + 5(4)$$
$$= 6 + 6 + 20$$
$$= 32$$

21. (D) Since the large square has side 4 cm, then its area must be 16. By careful grouping of areas, you will see that there are four unshaded smaller squares and four shaded smaller squares (match the shaded parts to four squares). Therefore, half of the area is shaded, or 8 square cm.

22. (C) Note that only choice (C) raises one of the numbers by 5 while it lowers the other number by 5. Choice (C) will give the best approximation of the five choices.

23. (A) 16 out of 400 may be expressed as a percent as 16/400. Dividing 16 by 400 gives 0.04, or 4%.

24. (D) Using the probability formula,
$$\text{probability} = \frac{\text{number of "lucky" chances}}{\text{total number of chances}}$$
the chance of choosing a weekday = 5 weekdays/7 total days = $\frac{5}{7}$.

25. (E) Note that since there is a mark between +7 and +9, that mark must equal +8. Thus, each mark equals 1. Counting back, point Q is at +5. Therefore, 15 units to the left of +5 would be $+5 - 15 = -10$.

26. (C) The *product of two numbers* indicates the numbers must be multiplied together. Their *sum* means "add." Therefore,

$$\underbrace{\text{the product of two numbers}}_{(A)(B)} \underbrace{\text{equals}}_{=} \underbrace{\text{five more than their sum}}_{A+B+5}$$

27. (C) Only III is determined by division ($39 \div 3$). The others are determined by multiplication ($6 \times B$) and subtraction, respectively.

28. (D) Note that, for example, as the temperature decreased from $-10°$ to $-15°$, the average amount of snowfall per hour increased from 2 to 2.5 inches. (Watch out for the minus sign, which means the temperature drops when it goes from $-20°$ to $-25°$.) This relationship exists throughout the chart.

29. (B) Thirty percent off the original price equals a discount of $(0.30)(\$8000) = \$2400$. Therefore, the new selling price is $\$8000 - \$2400 = \$5600$.

30. (D) Since Harmon's sportscar averages 35 miles for each gallon of gas, on 12 gallons, he'll be able to drive 12×35, or 420 miles.

31. (D) Remember that a parallelogram has equal opposite sides. Therefore, its sides are 9, 7, 9, and 7. Its perimeter then is 32. If a square has the same perimeter, one of its sides must be one fourth of its perimeter (since the four sides of a square are equal). One fourth of 32 is 8.

32. (D) If each adult drinks $\frac{1}{5}$ of a gallon of lemonade, 1 gallon is consumed by each 5 adults. Since 28 adults attend the picnic, $\frac{28}{5} =$ slightly over 5 gallons.

33. (E) There are several quick methods of solving this problem. As in question 1, a ratio can be set up.

$$\frac{20 \text{ pgs}}{4 \text{ hrs}} = \frac{50 \text{ pgs}}{x}$$

Cross multiplying will give 10 hours for the answer. Or determining John's hourly rate (5 pages per hour) tells us he will need 10 hours to type 50 pages.

34. (B) Note that a total of 28 items were purchased, each costing 85¢. Therefore, the simplest way to compute the total amount spent would be 28×85¢.

35. (B) If team B's victories are called x, then team A must have $2x$ victories, team C must have $(2x - 5)$ victories, and team D must have $(x + 4)$ victories. All together these total $6x - 1$. We are told that the total equals 29 victories. Thus,

$$6x - 1 = 29$$
$$6x = 30$$
$$x = 5$$

Therefore, team D has $(x + 4)$ victories, or $(5 + 4) = 9$.

36. (D) If all dogs are green, and Bowser is a dog, then it must logically follow that Bowser is green. Bowser might also have blue in his fur, but this does not have to be true. Nothing in the statements allows us to reach any conclusions about cats. Choice (E) contradicts the statements.

37. (B) Note that on the graph a 30-degree drop in temperature on the line correlates with a 20% attendance drop (the fourth slash up the graph).

38. (E) Note that 30% of 50 may be expressed as 0.30×50 or $\frac{3}{10} \times 50$. Whichever way it is expressed, it will still total 15. The only answer choice that does not total 15 is choice (E), which totals $166\frac{2}{3}$.

39. (C) Plug in 3 for x:

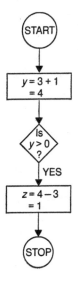

40. (A) Since the sum of the angles is 180°, we have

$$m + n + 72 + 25 = 180$$
$$m + n + 97 = 180$$
$$m + n = 180 - 97$$
$$m + n = 83$$

Hence, the sum of $m + n$ is 83°.

WRITING TEST: MULTIPLE-CHOICE SECTION

Part A

1. (C) The verb *made* should be *make,* a present tense consistent with the present tense used in the parallel verb *embarrass.*

2. (B) The pronoun *I* should be *me,* the objective case. It is the object of the preposition *between.*

3. (A) The verb *has consolidated* should be *consolidated,* the past rather than the present perfect tense.

4. (C) The preposition *to* should be replaced by *from.* The idiom is to *differ from* not to *differ to.*

5. (C) The verbal *satisfying* is incorrect. The first half of the sentence sets the action in the past (*scored*); to keep the tenses consistent, the verb should be *seems to have satisfied.*

6. (E) The sentence is correct as written.

7. (C) The correct verb form here is the past perfect *had fallen.* The past tense is *fell;* the past participle used to form the perfect tenses is *fallen.*

8. (C) Since the sentence begins by using the second person subject (*you*), the subject of the main clause should also be the second person (*you*), not the third person (*one*).

9. (E) The sentence is correct as written.

10. (C) There is a diction error here, a confusion of the past tense of the verb *to leave* (*left*) with the past tense of the verb *to let* (*let*).

11. (A) The past tense of the verb *to work* (*worked*) should be used here. The action described took place in the past, in the eighteenth century.

12. (B) The sentence contains a double negative. It should omit either the *not* or the *hardly; provides hardly any* or *does not provide any.*

13. (E) The sentence is correct as written.

14. (A) Since the subject of the sentence is the plural *races,* the verb should be the plural *are.*

15. (C) The adjective *skeptical* should be the adverb *skeptically,* modifying the verb *responds.*

16. (E) Though the *he* might be *she* or *he or she,* the sentence is grammatically correct.

17. (C) Since the two parts of the sentence contrast *most* with *a few,* the use of *and* as the coordinating conjunction makes no sense. The better choice is *but.*

18. (B) Since the subject of the sentence is the singular *population,* the verb should be the singular *is.*

19. (C) As it stands, the sentence has no main verb. A correct version would be *are rarely seen.*

20. (A) The problem is the phrase *in regards to.* The idioms the writer probably had in mind are *as regards* or *in regard to.* The sense of the sentence suggests that neither would fit as well as *in response to.*

21. (A) The correct verb here is the past tense, *sang; sung* is the past participle: *I sing; I sang; I have sung.*

22. (B) The subject of the sentence is the singular *rate;* the verb should be the singular *is.*

23. (C) Since the sentence begins by using the third person (*a person*) (*his*), the shift to the second person (*you*) should be corrected to *he.*

24. (A) The comma after *Ideas* should be deleted. The phrase *that now seem . . .* is restrictive.

25. (A) The conjunction *As* should be replaced by the preposition *Like.* The opening words are a prepositional phrase, not a clause.

Part B

26. (E) Choice (E) is grammatically correct, idiomatic, and more concise than choices (A), (C), and (D). In most cases, an adjective followed by an infinitive is idiomatic and preferable to an adjective followed by *for* and a gerund.

27. (C) Choices (A) and (B) join two complete sentences with a comma where a semicolon is needed. Given the meaning of the sentence, the conjunction *but* in choice (D) makes no sense. In (E), there is no main verb in the second clause, so the sentence is a fragment.

28. (B) Only choice (B) supplies the necessary main verb. In each of the other four versions, the sentence is a fragment lacking a main verb.

29. (A) Choice (A) correctly uses the past tense (*agreed*) and the infinitive (*to run*). It is grammatically correct and more concise than the other four choices.

30. (C) Choices (A) and (B) use a comma where a semicolon is needed to join two independent clauses without a conjunction. Since *results* is plural, the singular *it* in (D) is an agreement error. In (E), there is no main verb after the semicolon.

31. (E) The clause *that covertly hinted of devil worship* modifies *songs* and should be placed as close to *songs* as possible. Additionally, choices (A) and (B) use the wordier passive voice. Choice (C) changes the meaning of the sentence.

32. (A) Choice (A) is the most concise version of the sentence.

33. (B) There are parallelism errors in choice (A) and an extra *and* in (C). In (D), *fluent writing* is the object of *use;* in (E), the second clause is a fragment after the semicolon.

34. (D) The clearest and most concise version of this sentence is (D). The verbose *because . . . why* idiom should be avoided.

35. (A) Choices (B) and (D) use a comma where a semicolon is needed. Choices (C) and (E), by leaving out *one,* distort the meaning of the sentence.

36. (A) Choice (A) is correct and concise. The pronoun *who,* used in (D) and (E), should be used for people, not reptiles.

37. (C) Choice (A) misuses a comma for a semicolon. The phrase *being they* is not idiomatic or grammatical. In (E), the second clause is a fragment.

38. (C) The sense of the sentence suggests that *and* is not the correct conjunction. The verb tenses are incorrect in both (B) and (E), and the word order in (D) is awkward.

39. (D) The subject of the sentence is the singular *president.* The phrase *as well as senators from four states* is parenthetical.

40. (B) The participle (*watching*) at the beginning of the sentence modifies *I*, not *car.* To avoid a dangling participle, you must place the *I* after the comma. The adverb *nearly* should be next to the verb *ran.*

41. (B) *Is when* is not acceptable because *gerrymandering* is not a time. Choice (E) repeats this error. (D) is not best because it leaves vague whether *gerrymandering* is synonymous with *unfair division.* (C) is very general and vague.

42. (B) The original is flawed by faulty parallelism. *Fearless* is not parallel to *having great skill.* Choice (B) corrects this problem. *Fearless* is parallel to *skillful.* Choices (C) and (E) are both unnecessarily wordy.

43. (B) *Having finished* expresses the past tense by itself, so *after* is repetitious (its meaning is already implied in *having finished*). None of the other choices expresses the past tense both economically and clearly.

44. (C) The verb in this sentence should be *is* (not *are*) to agree with the singular subject, *actor.* A parenthetical phrase enclosed by commas and beginning with words such as *along with, including,* and *as well as* changes the number of neither the subject nor the verb. Choice (B) correctly uses *are* because the subject in this sentence has been made plural; however, the construction is awkward and wordy. Choice (D) retains the incorrect *are* and changes the meaning of the sentence. (E) leaves out the fact that the actor is on the train.

45. (B) When subjects are connected with *nor* or *or*, the verb is governed by the subject closest to it. In choices (A) and (D), the closer subject does not agree with the verb. (E) is awkward. In (B), the subject, *director*, agrees with the verb, *predicts.*

ANSWER SHEET FOR PRACTICE TEST 2

(Remove This Sheet and Use It to Mark Your Answers)

READING TEST

1 Ⓐ Ⓑ Ⓒ Ⓓ Ⓔ	21 Ⓐ Ⓑ Ⓒ Ⓓ Ⓔ
2 Ⓐ Ⓑ Ⓒ Ⓓ Ⓔ	22 Ⓐ Ⓑ Ⓒ Ⓓ Ⓔ
3 Ⓐ Ⓑ Ⓒ Ⓓ Ⓔ	23 Ⓐ Ⓑ Ⓒ Ⓓ Ⓔ
4 Ⓐ Ⓑ Ⓒ Ⓓ Ⓔ	24 Ⓐ Ⓑ Ⓒ Ⓓ Ⓔ
5 Ⓐ Ⓑ Ⓒ Ⓓ Ⓔ	25 Ⓐ Ⓑ Ⓒ Ⓓ Ⓔ
6 Ⓐ Ⓑ Ⓒ Ⓓ Ⓔ	26 Ⓐ Ⓑ Ⓒ Ⓓ Ⓔ
7 Ⓐ Ⓑ Ⓒ Ⓓ Ⓔ	27 Ⓐ Ⓑ Ⓒ Ⓓ Ⓔ
8 Ⓐ Ⓑ Ⓒ Ⓓ Ⓔ	28 Ⓐ Ⓑ Ⓒ Ⓓ Ⓔ
9 Ⓐ Ⓑ Ⓒ Ⓓ Ⓔ	29 Ⓐ Ⓑ Ⓒ Ⓓ Ⓔ
10 Ⓐ Ⓑ Ⓒ Ⓓ Ⓔ	30 Ⓐ Ⓑ Ⓒ Ⓓ Ⓔ
11 Ⓐ Ⓑ Ⓒ Ⓓ Ⓔ	31 Ⓐ Ⓑ Ⓒ Ⓓ Ⓔ
12 Ⓐ Ⓑ Ⓒ Ⓓ Ⓔ	32 Ⓐ Ⓑ Ⓒ Ⓓ Ⓔ
13 Ⓐ Ⓑ Ⓒ Ⓓ Ⓔ	33 Ⓐ Ⓑ Ⓒ Ⓓ Ⓔ
14 Ⓐ Ⓑ Ⓒ Ⓓ Ⓔ	34 Ⓐ Ⓑ Ⓒ Ⓓ Ⓔ
15 Ⓐ Ⓑ Ⓒ Ⓓ Ⓔ	35 Ⓐ Ⓑ Ⓒ Ⓓ Ⓔ
16 Ⓐ Ⓑ Ⓒ Ⓓ Ⓔ	36 Ⓐ Ⓑ Ⓒ Ⓓ Ⓔ
17 Ⓐ Ⓑ Ⓒ Ⓓ Ⓔ	37 Ⓐ Ⓑ Ⓒ Ⓓ Ⓔ
18 Ⓐ Ⓑ Ⓒ Ⓓ Ⓔ	38 Ⓐ Ⓑ Ⓒ Ⓓ Ⓔ
19 Ⓐ Ⓑ Ⓒ Ⓓ Ⓔ	39 Ⓐ Ⓑ Ⓒ Ⓓ Ⓔ
20 Ⓐ Ⓑ Ⓒ Ⓓ Ⓔ	40 Ⓐ Ⓑ Ⓒ Ⓓ Ⓔ

MATHEMATICS TEST

1 Ⓐ Ⓑ Ⓒ Ⓓ Ⓔ	21 Ⓐ Ⓑ Ⓒ Ⓓ Ⓔ
2 Ⓐ Ⓑ Ⓒ Ⓓ Ⓔ	22 Ⓐ Ⓑ Ⓒ Ⓓ Ⓔ
3 Ⓐ Ⓑ Ⓒ Ⓓ Ⓔ	23 Ⓐ Ⓑ Ⓒ Ⓓ Ⓔ
4 Ⓐ Ⓑ Ⓒ Ⓓ Ⓔ	24 Ⓐ Ⓑ Ⓒ Ⓓ Ⓔ
5 Ⓐ Ⓑ Ⓒ Ⓓ Ⓔ	25 Ⓐ Ⓑ Ⓒ Ⓓ Ⓔ
6 Ⓐ Ⓑ Ⓒ Ⓓ Ⓔ	26 Ⓐ Ⓑ Ⓒ Ⓓ Ⓔ
7 Ⓐ Ⓑ Ⓒ Ⓓ Ⓔ	27 Ⓐ Ⓑ Ⓒ Ⓓ Ⓔ
8 Ⓐ Ⓑ Ⓒ Ⓓ Ⓔ	28 Ⓐ Ⓑ Ⓒ Ⓓ Ⓔ
9 Ⓐ Ⓑ Ⓒ Ⓓ Ⓔ	29 Ⓐ Ⓑ Ⓒ Ⓓ Ⓔ
10 Ⓐ Ⓑ Ⓒ Ⓓ Ⓔ	30 Ⓐ Ⓑ Ⓒ Ⓓ Ⓔ
11 Ⓐ Ⓑ Ⓒ Ⓓ Ⓔ	31 Ⓐ Ⓑ Ⓒ Ⓓ Ⓔ
12 Ⓐ Ⓑ Ⓒ Ⓓ Ⓔ	32 Ⓐ Ⓑ Ⓒ Ⓓ Ⓔ
13 Ⓐ Ⓑ Ⓒ Ⓓ Ⓔ	33 Ⓐ Ⓑ Ⓒ Ⓓ Ⓔ
14 Ⓐ Ⓑ Ⓒ Ⓓ Ⓔ	34 Ⓐ Ⓑ Ⓒ Ⓓ Ⓔ
15 Ⓐ Ⓑ Ⓒ Ⓓ Ⓔ	35 Ⓐ Ⓑ Ⓒ Ⓓ Ⓔ
16 Ⓐ Ⓑ Ⓒ Ⓓ Ⓔ	36 Ⓐ Ⓑ Ⓒ Ⓓ Ⓔ
17 Ⓐ Ⓑ Ⓒ Ⓓ Ⓔ	37 Ⓐ Ⓑ Ⓒ Ⓓ Ⓔ
18 Ⓐ Ⓑ Ⓒ Ⓓ Ⓔ	38 Ⓐ Ⓑ Ⓒ Ⓓ Ⓔ
19 Ⓐ Ⓑ Ⓒ Ⓓ Ⓔ	39 Ⓐ Ⓑ Ⓒ Ⓓ Ⓔ
20 Ⓐ Ⓑ Ⓒ Ⓓ Ⓔ	40 Ⓐ Ⓑ Ⓒ Ⓓ Ⓔ

CUT HERE

ANSWER SHEET FOR PRACTICE TEST 2

(Remove This Sheet and Use It to Mark Your Answers)

WRITING TEST: MULTIPLE CHOICE

Part A

1 Ⓐ Ⓑ Ⓒ Ⓓ Ⓔ
2 Ⓐ Ⓑ Ⓒ Ⓓ Ⓔ
3 Ⓐ Ⓑ Ⓒ Ⓓ Ⓔ
4 Ⓐ Ⓑ Ⓒ Ⓓ Ⓔ
5 Ⓐ Ⓑ Ⓒ Ⓓ Ⓔ

6 Ⓐ Ⓑ Ⓒ Ⓓ Ⓔ
7 Ⓐ Ⓑ Ⓒ Ⓓ Ⓔ
8 Ⓐ Ⓑ Ⓒ Ⓓ Ⓔ
9 Ⓐ Ⓑ Ⓒ Ⓓ Ⓔ
10 Ⓐ Ⓑ Ⓒ Ⓓ Ⓔ

11 Ⓐ Ⓑ Ⓒ Ⓓ Ⓔ
12 Ⓐ Ⓑ Ⓒ Ⓓ Ⓔ
13 Ⓐ Ⓑ Ⓒ Ⓓ Ⓔ
14 Ⓐ Ⓑ Ⓒ Ⓓ Ⓔ
15 Ⓐ Ⓑ Ⓒ Ⓓ Ⓔ

16 Ⓐ Ⓑ Ⓒ Ⓓ Ⓔ
17 Ⓐ Ⓑ Ⓒ Ⓓ Ⓔ
18 Ⓐ Ⓑ Ⓒ Ⓓ Ⓔ
19 Ⓐ Ⓑ Ⓒ Ⓓ Ⓔ
20 Ⓐ Ⓑ Ⓒ Ⓓ Ⓔ

21 Ⓐ Ⓑ Ⓒ Ⓓ Ⓔ
22 Ⓐ Ⓑ Ⓒ Ⓓ Ⓔ
23 Ⓐ Ⓑ Ⓒ Ⓓ Ⓔ
24 Ⓐ Ⓑ Ⓒ Ⓓ Ⓔ
25 Ⓐ Ⓑ Ⓒ Ⓓ Ⓔ

Part B

26 Ⓐ Ⓑ Ⓒ Ⓓ Ⓔ
27 Ⓐ Ⓑ Ⓒ Ⓓ Ⓔ
28 Ⓐ Ⓑ Ⓒ Ⓓ Ⓔ
29 Ⓐ Ⓑ Ⓒ Ⓓ Ⓔ
30 Ⓐ Ⓑ Ⓒ Ⓓ Ⓔ

31 Ⓐ Ⓑ Ⓒ Ⓓ Ⓔ
32 Ⓐ Ⓑ Ⓒ Ⓓ Ⓔ
33 Ⓐ Ⓑ Ⓒ Ⓓ Ⓔ
34 Ⓐ Ⓑ Ⓒ Ⓓ Ⓔ
35 Ⓐ Ⓑ Ⓒ Ⓓ Ⓔ

36 Ⓐ Ⓑ Ⓒ Ⓓ Ⓔ
37 Ⓐ Ⓑ Ⓒ Ⓓ Ⓔ
38 Ⓐ Ⓑ Ⓒ Ⓓ Ⓔ
39 Ⓐ Ⓑ Ⓒ Ⓓ Ⓔ
40 Ⓐ Ⓑ Ⓒ Ⓓ Ⓔ

41 Ⓐ Ⓑ Ⓒ Ⓓ Ⓔ
42 Ⓐ Ⓑ Ⓒ Ⓓ Ⓔ
43 Ⓐ Ⓑ Ⓒ Ⓓ Ⓔ
44 Ⓐ Ⓑ Ⓒ Ⓓ Ⓔ
45 Ⓐ Ⓑ Ⓒ Ⓓ Ⓔ

Practice Test 2

READING TEST

TIME: 60 Minutes
     40 Questions

Directions: A question or number of questions follow each of the statements or passages in this section. Using only the *stated* or *implied* information given in the statement or passage, answer the question or questions by choosing the *best* answer from among the five choices given.

1. Recent studies show that aptitude test scores are declining because of lack of family stability and students' preoccupation with out-of-school activities. Therefore, not only the student's attitude but his or her home environment must be changed to stop this downward trend.

   Which of the following is one assumption of the above argument?

   (A) Recent studies have refuted previous studies.
   (B) Heredity is more important than environment.
   (C) Aptitude test scores should stop declining soon.
   (D) The accuracy of the recent studies cited is not an issue.
   (E) More out-of-school activities are available than ever before.

2. Once again, our city council has shown all the firmness of a bowl of oatmeal in deciding to seek a "compromise" on sheep grazing in the city. As it is wont to do more often than not, the council overturned a planning commission recommendation, this time to ban sheep grazing in the city.

The passage above uses the term "bowl of oatmeal" in order to

(A) condemn the actions taken by the city council
(B) add levity to the otherwise tragic situation
(C) imply that grazing sheep would prefer oats
(D) praise the city council for its recent vote
(E) urge the city council to overturn the planning commission

Questions 3, 4, and 5 refer to the following passage.

Recent studies indicate that at the present rate of increase, within two years a single-family dwelling will be unaffordable by the average family. Therefore, apartment living will increase noticeably in the near future.

3. Which of the following statements is deducible from the argument?

(A) The recent studies were for a five-year period.
(B) Condominiums are expensive but plentiful.
(C) The average family income will decrease in the next two years.
(D) Home costs are increasing more rapidly than average family incomes.
(E) The average family will increase within the next two years.

4. The argument would be weakened by the fact(s) that

    I. many inexpensive single-family dwellings are presently be-
ing built
    II. bank loan interest rates have increased
    III. apartment living is also becoming very expensive

    (A) I only
    (B) II only
    (C) III only
    (D) I and III only
    (E) II and III only

5. The argument presented assumes that

    I. the present rate of price increase will continue
    II. families will turn to renting apartments instead of buying
homes
    III. construction of apartments will double within the next two
years

    (A) I only
    (B) II only
    (C) III only
    (D) I and II only
    (E) II and III only

Questions 6 through 9 refer to the following passage.

From the U.S. Supreme court now comes an extraordinary decision permitting inquiries into the "state of mind" of journalists and
the editorial process of news organizations. This is perhaps the
most alarming evidence so far of a determination by the nation's
highest court to weaken the protection of the First Amendment for
those who gather and report the news.

The court last year upheld the right of police to invade newspa-
per offices in search of evidence, and reporters in other cases have
gone to jail to protect the confidentiality of their notebooks. Under
the recent 6–3 ruling in a libel case, they now face a challenge to
the privacy of their minds.

Few would argue that the First Amendment guarantees absolute
freedom of speech or freedom of the press. Slander and libel laws

(15) stand to the contrary as a protection of an individual's reputation against the irresponsible dissemination of falsehoods. The effect of this latest decision, however, is to make the libel suit, or the threat of one, a clear invasion by the courts into the private decision-making that constitutes news and editorial judgment.

(20) In landmark decisions of 1964 and 1967, the Supreme Court established that public officials or public figures bringing libel actions must prove that a damaging falsehood was published with "actual malice"—that is, with knowledge that the statements were false, or with reckless disregard of whether they were true or not.

(25) Justice Byron R. White, writing for the new majority in the new ruling, says it is not enough to examine all the circumstances of publication that would indicate whether there was malicious intent or not. It is proper and constitutional, he says, for "state-of-mind evidence" to be introduced. The court is thus ordering a CBS television producer to answer questions about the thought processes (30) that went into the preparation and airing of a segment of *60 Minutes*.

That six justices of the Supreme Court fail to see this as a breach of the First Amendment is frightening. The novelist George Orwell may have been mistaken only in the timing of his vision of a Big (35) Brother government practicing mind-control.

6. This article deals principally with

   (A) the U.S. Supreme Court's decisions
   (B) explaining the First Amendment to the Constitution
   (C) an attack on the freedom of the press
   (D) slander and libel laws
   (E) Big Brother in government

7. How many justices would have to change their minds to reverse this decision?

   (A) one
   (B) two
   (C) three
   (D) four
   (E) five

8. This writer feels the Supreme Court is wrong in this case because

    (A) newspapers were unsophisticated when the First Amendment was written

    (B) reporters are entitled to special rights

    (C) it challenges the privacy of a journalist's mind

    (D) Judge White has himself been accused of slander and libel

    (E) the Supreme Court is capable of malicious intent

9. What does "actual malice" (line 22) mean?

    (A) Knowledge that the statements were false

    (B) Reckless disregard of whether the statements were true or not

    (C) Either (A) or (B)

    (D) Libel

    (E) None of these

Questions 10 and 11 refer to the following passage.

Sometimes the U.S. government goes out of its way to prove it can be an absolute nuisance. Take the case of Southern Clay, Inc., which has a factory at Paris, Tennessee, putting out a clay product for cat-boxes best known as "Kitty Litter."

(5)   It's a simple enough process, but the federal Mine Safety and Health Administration insists that since clay comes from the ground—an excavation half a mile from the Kitty Litter plant—the company actually is engaged in mining and milling. Therefore, says MSHA, Southern Clay is subject to all the rules that

(10) govern, say, coal mines working in shafts several hundred feet down.

    The company has been told to devise an escape system and fire-fighting procedure in case there is a fire in its "mine." Southern Clay estimates it will lose 6000 man-hours in production time giv-

(15) ing its 250 factory workers special training in how to escape from a mine disaster.

    One thing that has always impressed us about cats, in addition to their tidiness, is that they seem to watch the human world with a sense of wise and detached superiority, as though they wondered

(20) what the hustle and bustle is all about. If they grin from time to time, as some people insist, it's no wonder.

10. The author's purpose in writing this article is to

    (A) explain how Kitty Litter is produced
    (B) describe the Mine Safety and Health Administration
    (C) show how tidy cats are
    (D) show that the government can sometimes be a nuisance
    (E) describe how to prevent fires in mines

11. What does the author mean by the article's last sentence?

    (A) Cats sometimes laugh at their own tidiness.
    (B) Cats sometimes seem to be amused by human antics.
    (C) People sometimes appear to be laughing at the antics of cats.
    (D) Some people think cats are laughing at the Kitty Litter plant.
    (E) Some people think cats are laughing at the futility of fire-fighting procedures.

12. The Jesuit Antonio Vieira, missionary, diplomat, voluminous writer, repeated the triumphs he had gained in Bahia and Lisbon in Rome, which proclaimed him the prince of Catholic orators. His two hundred sermons are a mine of learning and experience, and they stand out from all others by their imaginative power, originality of view, variety of treatment, and audacity of expression.

    The author's attitude toward Vieira may be described as

    (A) spiritual
    (B) idolatrous
    (C) indifferent
    (D) admiring
    (E) critical

13. While the 55-mile-per-hour speed limit was in effect, it not only lowered the number of accidents, it also saved many lives. Yet, auto insurance rates did not reflect this decrease. Therefore, insurance companies made profits rather than lower premiums.

This argument implies that

(A) the 55-mile-per-hour limit was unfair
(B) auto manufacturers agreed with insurance companies' policies
(C) insurance companies were taking advantage of drivers
(D) saving lives was of more importance than lowering premiums
(E) driving skills improved greatly while the 55-mile-per-hour limit was in effect

14. We all know life originated in the ocean. Science tells us so. Perhaps a bolt of lightning struck through the ammonia and methane gases of a volcanic planet, igniting some form of life in the primordial soup of the storm-tormented sea. But no scientific theory is sacrosanct. And now a group of scientists says we have it all wrong: Life originated in clay.

The passage above

(A) suggests that the earth began as clay, not water
(B) argues that science has been wrong about a certain theory
(C) implies that scientists are usually proven wrong
(D) presents an alternative theory about the creation of life
(E) denies the existence of life in the primordial ocean

15. What history teaches is this: that people and governments have never learned anything from history.

The statement above may be best described as a(n)

(A) ironic contradiction
(B) historical truism
(C) effective anagram
(D) derisive condemnation
(E) pragmatic condolence

Questions 16 and 17 refer to the following passage.

California once prided itself on being the state with the finest roads
in the nation. That is no longer true. Our gas taxes took care of
California's highway needs for years, but they no longer are adequate. One reason the present tax no longer covers the bill is that
modern cars are using less fuel. The main factor, though, is that
the cost of building and maintaining highways has gone way up
while the tax has remained fixed.

Certainly, California streets, roads, and highways need help.
Two thirds of city streets and 77 percent of country roads are sub-
standard. Ruts and potholes can be found almost everywhere, and
the longer they go without repair, the more they will cost.

16. Which of the following best summarizes the passage?

    (A) Deterioration of California's roads has resulted from in-
        creased costs and decreased funds.
    (B) The quality of California roads is now second in the nation.
    (C) Fuel-efficient cars cause more wear and tear on the roads
        than did cars of the past.
    (D) Every road in the state is marred with potholes.
    (E) Over three quarters of California's roads are substandard.

17. Which of the following is NOT a problem stated by the passage?

    (A) Inadequate tax revenue
    (B) Ruts and potholes
    (C) Increased cost of building highways
    (D) A fixed gas-tax rate
    (E) Demand for new highways

Questions 18 and 19 refer to the following passage.

At the outset of the Civil War, the North possessed a large population, a superior rail system, a greater industrial capacity, greater
capital assets, and a larger food-production capability than did the
South. Despite the North's apparent economic superiority, the South
did possess a few military advantages. Among them were fighting
a defensive war on their home ground and an established military
tradition. Most of the leaders of the pre-War army were from the
South, while the North had to train a new military leadership.

18. The final sentence of this passage functions in which of the following ways?

  (A) To support the general contention that most of the talent in the United States is concentrated in the South
  (B) To hint that the North found many of its military leaders in the South
  (C) To argue that the North entered the war without leaders
  (D) To further explain the South's "established military tradition"
  (E) To show that the South probably should have won the war

19. The author implies which of the following points in the passage?

  (A) The North did not have an economic advantage at the end of the war.
  (B) Previous to the beginning of the war, the South was already fighting another war and seasoning its leaders.
  (C) Almost all the banks in the United States were located in the North.
  (D) Military advantages are much more important than economic advantages.
  (E) The North had a greater capacity for enduring a prolonged conflict.

20. Few opticians have recognized the value of target practice for stimulating the eyes and improving vision. The value of a day on the rifle range surpasses that of a whole crop of fresh carrots.

The writer assumes that his or her readers are already convinced that

  (A) poor eyesight is a widespread problem
  (B) target practice is enjoyable and useful
  (C) carrots are good for the eyes
  (D) most people should own guns
  (E) the "day" mentioned is an eight-hour day

Questions 21 through 26 refer to the following passage.

(1) The Morrill Act (1862) extended the principle of federal support for public education, the earliest attempt being the Northwest Ordinance of 1787. (2) The Morrill Act established land-grant colleges in each state and specified a curriculum based on agriculture and mechanical arts. (3) Land-grant colleges often were a state's first institution of public higher education. (4) Public support and public control strengthened the concept of the state-university system. (5) The Civil Rights Act of 1875 was the first federal attempt to provide equal educational opportunity. (6) The progressive theories of John Dewey also had a profound effect on public education. (7) Dewey believed that education included the home, shop, neighborhood, church, and school. (8) However, industrialization was destroying the educational functions of these institutions. (9) Dewey believed that the public schools must be society's instrument for "shaping its own destiny." (10) To do this the schools had to be transformed in order to serve the interests of democracy.

21. If this passage were divided into two paragraphs, the second paragraph would begin with

    (A) sentence 3
    (B) sentence 5
    (C) sentence 6
    (D) sentence 7
    (E) sentence 8

22. The passage implies that one significant contrast between the Morrill Act and Dewey's theories was

    (A) Dewey's lack of faith in land-grant colleges
    (B) the fact that the Morrill Act was not a democratic law
    (C) the neglect in the Morrill Act of education's relationship to society
    (D) Dewey's lack of knowledge about the Morrill Act
    (E) the Morrill Act's stress on a heavily agricultural and mechanical curriculum

23. The word "also" in sentence 6 does which of the following?

   (A) Opens the question concerning whether Dewey himself would have supported certain government acts concerning education
   (B) Makes clear that Dewey's theories were innovative and inconsistent with government policy
   (C) Makes the point that Dewey's theories were somewhat identical to material in the Morrill Act
   (D) Suggests that the Morrill Act, Northwest Ordinance, and Civil Rights Act had a profound influence on public education
   (E) Suggests that Dewey's theories did more than affect public education

24. Which of the following statements, if true, would best support sentences 7 and 8?

   (A) Home, shop, neighborhood, church, and school each played an ever-increasing role in the world of learning.
   (B) Learning was equated exclusively with industrial progress, while moral, social, and artistic growth were undervalued.
   (C) Industry was shaping the destiny of the citizens, and Dewey was a strong industrial supporter.
   (D) Industry was transforming the schools so that they could serve the interests of democracy.
   (E) Sentence 3

25. This passage would be LEAST likely to appear in which of the following?

   (A) An encyclopedia article summarizing the major legislation of the nineteenth century
   (B) A brief survey of legislation and theories that significantly affected education
   (C) An introduction to the theories of John Dewey
   (D) An argument about the benefits of both progressive legislation and progressive educational theory
   (E) A discussion of the relationship between social needs and school curriculum

26. The passage allows us to conclude which of the following?

    (A) Beyond the legislation discussed in the passage, no other government acts addressed the issue of public education.
    (B) Theorists always have a more significant effect on education than legislators do.
    (C) The framers of the Morrill Act did not appreciate the value of moral education.
    (D) Dewey succeeded to some extent in transforming public education.
    (E) The state-university system was a concept long before it became a reality.

27. It is an important guideline to avoid discussing other students during a parent-teacher conference. Such comments often result in an emotional reaction by the parent and can interfere with the purpose of the conference.

    Which of the following facts, if true, would most strengthen the argument of the passage above?

    (A) The discussion of other students gives many parents a comfortable sense that the teacher understands the whole classroom "scene."
    (B) Most parents avoid taking the trouble to attend a conference.
    (C) The child's relationship with other students is most often the cause of problems that necessitate a conference.
    (D) Researchers witnessing parent-teacher conferences have verified that parents become angry in 90% of the conferences in which other students are discussed.
    (E) Emotional reactions by parents must be understood as the parents' legitimate expression of deeply felt concerns.

28. A test is valid if it measures what it is intended to measure. A test is reliable if it is consistent. Therefore, a test may be consistent even though it does not measure what it is intended to measure.

The author's primary purpose in this passage is to

(A) contribute to recent research in testing validity and reliability

(B) question whether we should use the terms "valid" and "reliable" to describe tests

(C) insist that all tests must be both valid and reliable

(D) call for the abolition of invalid tests

(E) explain the difference between validity and reliability

29. "Open houses" should be offered, as they enable a school district to present the school programs to the community. Effective open-house activities can further community participation in the educational process.

Which of the following is an unstated assumption of the author of this passage?

(A) Most participants in open-house activities do not take a whole-hearted interest in the enterprise.

(B) Without an open house, no members of the community would be aware of the available school programs.

(C) Open-house activities are very rarely effective.

(D) Community participation has a positive effect on the educational process.

(E) Many school districts never hold an open house.

30. The failure of the progressive movement to adjust to the trans-
formation of the American society spelled its ultimate collapse.
The progressive educational theories of the early 1900s did not
take into consideration the technological expertise of the nuclear
age.

Which of the following best expresses the point of this passage?

(A) At one time, the progressive movement served well the needs
of American education.
(B) The progressive theories were not adaptable to late-twentieth-century progress.
(C) The progressive movement collapsed soon after its heyday
in the early 1900s.
(D) The progressive movement was motivated by theories too
conservative to be useful.
(E) No American student these days could possibly benefit from
progressive educational theory.

Questions 31, 32, and 33 refer to the following passage.

The doctrine of association had been the basis for explaining memories and how one idea leads to another. Aristotle provided the basic law, association by contiguity. We remember something because
in the past we had experienced that something together with something else. Seeing a shotgun may remind you of a murder, or it
may remind you of a hunting experience in Wyoming, depending
on your history. When you hear the word "table," you are likely to
think of "chair." "Carrots" makes you think of "peas"; "bread"
makes you think "butter"; and so on. In each case the two items
had for you been *experienced* contiguously—in the same place or
at the same time or both. Today the terms stimulus and response
are used to describe the two units which have been associated by
contiguity.

31. The author of the passage would agree with which of the following statements?

(A) Many of the associations which Aristotle posited have become part of modern experience.

(B) There are a number of adults who have had no experiences and who therefore have no memories.

(C) When one smells coffee, one is not likely to think of eating a donut.

(D) No one thing is necessarily associated with any other thing in particular.

(E) Guns always remind people of an experience in which someone or something was killed.

32. Which of the following statements, if true, would most weaken the argument of the passage?

(A) Many people tend to become depressed when the weather is rainy.

(B) Only a very few researchers question the doctrine of association.

(C) More recent studies show that word-association responses are random and not determined by experience.

(D) Of 100 people tested, 96 of those given the word "bread" responded with the word "butter."

(E) Psychologists have found that we have many common associations.

33. The argument of the passage is best strengthened by which of the following statements?

(A) It is certainly possible to experience more than two items contiguously.

(B) The terms stimulus and response were never used by Aristotle.

(C) Those Londoners who endured the German "bombings" of World War II still become fearful when they hear a loud noise.

(D) Some people think of "butter" when they hear "carrots."

(E) Aristotle's own writing is full of very uncommon and unexplained associations.

Questions 34 through 38 refer to the following passage.

The question might be asked: how can we know what is "really" real? Defined phenomenologically, "reality" becomes purely a hypothetical concept which accounts for the totality of all condi-
LINE   tions imposed by the external world upon an individual. But since
(5)   other individuals are included in each of our fields of experience, it does become possible as we make identification of similarly perceived phenomena to form consensus groups. In fact, we often tend to ignore and even push out of awareness those persons and their assumptions regarding what is real which do not correspond
(10)   to our own. However, such a lack of consensus also affords us the opportunity of checking our hypothesis about reality. We may change our concepts about reality and thus in doing so facilitate changes in our phenomenal world of experience. Scientists, for instance, deliberately set out to get a consensus of both their pro-
(15)   cedures and their conclusions. If they are successful in this quest, their conclusions are considered by the consensus group as consti-
tuting an addition to a factual body of sharable knowledge. This process is somewhat in contrast, for example, to those religious experiences considered to be mystical. By their nature they are not
(20)   always available for communication to others. However, even the scientific researcher must finally evaluate the consequences of his research in his own, personal phenomenological field. To use a cliché: truth as beauty exists in the eyes of the beholder.

34. Which of the following is a specific example supporting the point of the passage?

(A) Certain established scientific facts have not changed for hundreds of years.

(B) Part of the phrase in the last sentence is from a poem by Keats.

(C) Reality is a given, unique experience in an individual's phenomenal world.

(D) We think of our enemies in war as cruel and regard our own soldiers as virtuous.

(E) The fans at baseball games often see things exactly as the umpire sees them.

35. Applying the argument of the passage, we might define a political party as

   (A) a political group to which few scientists belong
   (B) a consensus group whose individuals share a similar view of political reality
   (C) a consensus group whose members are deluded about what is really "real" politically
   (D) in touch with reality if it is a majority party and out of touch with reality if it is a minority party
   (E) a collection of individuals who are each fundamentally unsure about what political reality is

36. When the author says that "reality" is a "hypothetical concept" (lines 2–3), he or she means that

   (A) as for reality, there is none
   (B) we can think about reality but never really experience it
   (C) "reality" is not objective
   (D) "reality" is a figment of your imagination
   (E) "reality" is known only by scientists

37. According to the passage, one difference between a scientist and a mystic is that

   (A) the scientist sees truth as facts; the mystic sees truth as beauty
   (B) scientists are unwilling and unable to lend importance to religious experiences
   (C) the work of the mystic does not have consequences that affect individuals
   (D) the scientist is concerned with sharable knowledge, and the mystic may not be
   (E) the scientist cannot believe in anything mystical

38. To the question "how can we know what is 'really' real?" (line 1), this author would probably answer in which of the following ways?

    (A) If no one sees things our way, we are detached from reality.
    (B) Whatever we are aware of can legitimately be called real.
    (C) What is really real is whatever a group of individuals believes.
    (D) We can, if we use the scientific method.
    (E) We cannot know what is "really" real because reality varies with individual perspective.

Questions 39 and 40 refer to the following passage.

A lesson plan is basically a tool for effective teaching. Its primary importance is to present objectives and content in a logical and systematic manner; as such, it is an integral part of the instructional process.

39. Which of the following is an unstated assumption made by the author of this passage?

    (A) All features of the instructional process should have the same logical, systematic qualities as the lesson plan.
    (B) Students learn best when material is not presented in a disorganized or unplanned manner.
    (C) A teacher who is not a logical, systematic thinker has no place in the instructional process.
    (D) The lesson plan is by far the most important tool for effective teaching.
    (E) Teachers should not deviate from the lesson plan in any case.

40. The author uses the word "integral" (line 3) to mean

    (A) original
    (B) whole
    (C) essential
    (D) not segregated
    (E) modern

STOP: IF YOU FINISH BEFORE TIME IS CALLED, CHECK YOUR WORK ON THIS SECTION ONLY. DO NOT WORK ON ANY OTHER SECTION IN THE TEST.

MATHEMATICS TEST

TIME: 60 Minutes
         40 Questions

Directions: Each of the questions or incomplete statements below is followed by five suggested answers or completions. Select the best answer or completion of the five choices given and fill in the corresponding lettered space on the answer sheet.

1. Which of the following fractions is the largest?

   (A) $\frac{25}{52}$ (B) $\frac{31}{60}$ (C) $\frac{19}{40}$ (D) $\frac{51}{103}$ (E) $\frac{43}{90}$

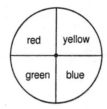

2. From the diagram of the spinner above, in spinning the spinner only once, what is the probability of spinning red, yellow, or blue?

   (A) 1/4   (B) 1/3   (C) 1/2   (D) 3/4   (E) 3/2

3. If $16\frac{1}{2}$ feet equal 1 rod, how many inches are there in 4 rods?

   (A) $5\frac{1}{2}$ (B) 22   (C) 66   (D) 792   (E) 2376

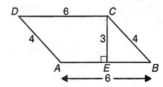

4. To compute the area of this figure, one would use

   (A) 6×4 (D) $6 + 3$
   (B) 12×3 (E) $4 \times (6 + 3)$
   (C) 6×3

5. All of the following ratios are equal EXCEPT

(A) 1 to 4   (D) 3 to 12
(B) 3 to 8   (E) 4 to 16
(C) 2 to 8

Undergraduate Expenses

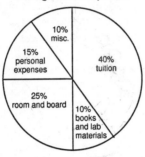

6. The chart above displays the costs in percentages associated with the average college undergraduate. If tuition for a given year is $4800, how much is spent on books and lab materials?

(A) $480—   (D) $1400
(B) $1000   (E) $1600
(C) $1200 —

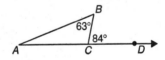

7. Given △ABC with ∠BCD = 84° and ∠B = 63°, find the measure of ∠A in degrees.

(A) 21   (B) 27   (C) 84   (D) 96   (E) 116

8. If Juan works 8 hours and receives \$4.75 per hour and Mary works 24 hours and receives a total of \$130, which of the following CANNOT be derived from the above statement?

(A) Juan's total
(B) Mary's wage per hour
(C) The difference between what Juan received and Mary received
(D) The average total received by Juan and Mary
(E) The hours Mary worked each day

9. If $3c = d$, then $c =$

(A) $3 + d$ (D) $1/3d$
(B) $3d$ (E) $(1+d)/3$
(C) $d/3$

10. On a map, 1 centimeter represents 35 kilometers. Two cities 245 kilometers apart would be separated on the map by how many centimeters?

(A) 5   (B) 7   (C) 9   (D) 210   (E) 280

11. Round off to the nearest tenth: 4316.136

(A) 4320   (D) 4316.106
(B) 4316.14   (E) 4316.1
(C) 4316.13

12. Which of the following is a prime number?

(A) 9   (B) 13   (C) 15   (D) 21   (E) 24

13. The fraction $\frac{1}{8}$ is between the numbers listed in which of the following pairs?

(A) $\frac{1}{10}$ and $\frac{2}{17}$ (D) 1 and 2
(B) 0.1 and 0.12   (E) $\frac{1}{9}$ and $\frac{2}{15}$
(C) 0.08 and 0.1

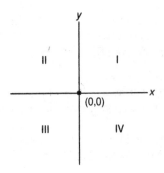

14. In the coordinate graph above, the point represented by (−3, 4) would be found in which quadrant?

(A) I
(B) II
(C) III
(D) IV
(E) The quadrant cannot be determined from the information given.

15. A class of 30 students all together have 60 pencils. Which of the following must be true?

(A) Each student has 2 pencils.
(B) Every student has a pencil.
(C) Some students have only 1 pencil.
(D) Some students have more pencils than do other students.
(E) The class averages 2 pencils per student.

16. A man purchased 4 pounds of steak priced at $3.89 per pound. How much change did he receive from a twenty-dollar bill?

(A) $4.34   (D) $15.56
(B) $4.44   (E) $44.66
(C) $4.46

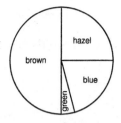

17. Sam tries to construct a pie graph representing eye color of his classmates. In his class of 24 students, 6 students have blue eyes, 12 students have brown eyes, 5 students have hazel eyes, and 1 student has green eyes. His teacher tells him that his graph (shown above) is not correct. In order to fix the graph, Sam should

   (A) increase the amount of green and decrease the amount of blue
   (B) increase the amount of blue and decrease the amount of hazel
   (C) decrease the amount of blue and increase the amount of brown
   (D) decrease the amount of hazel and increase the amount of brown
   (E) increase the amount of hazel and increase the amount of blue

18. If D is between A and B on $\overleftrightarrow{AB}$, which of the following must be true?

   (A) $AD = DB$
   (B) $DB = AB - AD$
   (C) $AD = AB + DB$
   (D) $DB = AD + AB$
   (E) $AB = AD = BD$

Questions 19 and 20 are based on the following graph.

A FAMILY'S EXPENSES

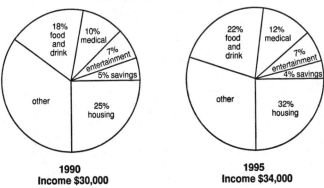

1990
Income $30,000

1995
Income $34,000

19. How much more money did this family spend on medical expenses in 1995 than in 1990?

(A) $800–$900   (D) $1100–$1200
(B) $900–$1000   (E) $1200–$1300
(C) $1000–$1100

20. What was the approximate increase from 1990 to 1995 in the percentage spent on food and drink?

(A) 4%   (B) 18%   (C) 22%   (D) 40%   (E) 50%

21. In a senior class of 800, only 240 decide to attend the senior prom. What percentage of the senior class attended the senior prom?

(A) 8%   (B) 24%   (C) 30%   (D) 33%   (E) 80%

22. What is the probability of tossing a penny twice so that both times it lands heads up?

(A) 1/8   (B) 1/4   (C) 1/3   (D) 1/2   (E) 2/3

23. 0.0074 is how many times smaller than 740,000?

   (A)   1,000,000
   (B)   10,000,000
   (C)   100,000,000
   (D) 1,000,000,000
   (E) 10,000,000,000

24. A suit that originally sold for $120 is on sale for $90. What is the rate of discount?

   (A) 20%   (B) 25%   (C) 30%   (D) $33\frac{1}{3}$%   (E) 75%

25. In the flow chart above, regardless of the number you select, the number at the end is always

   (A) 5
   (B) less than 14
   (C) the same as the original number
   (D) twice the original number
   (E) an odd number

26. To change 3 miles to inches, you should

   (A) multiply 3 times 5280
   (B) multiply 3 times 5280 and then divide by 12
   (C) multiply 3 times 5280 and then multiply by 12
   (D) divide 3 into 5280 and then multiply by 12
   (E) divide 3 into 12 and then multiply by 5280

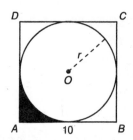

27. Circle O is inscribed in square $ABCD$ as shown above. The area of the shaded region is approximately

    (A) 10   (B) 25   (C) 30   (D) 50   (E) 75

28. Today is Lucy's fourteenth birthday. Last year, she was three years older than twice Charlie's age at that time. Using C for Charlie's age now, which of the following can be used to determine Charlie's age now?

    (A) $13 - 3 = 2(C - 1)$
    (B) $14 - 3 = 2C$
    (C) $13 - 3 = 2C$
    (D) $13 + 3 = 2C$
    (E) $13 + 3 = 2(C - 1)$

29. Angela has nickels and dimes in her pocket. She has twice as many dimes as nickels. What is the best expression of the amount of money she has in cents if x equals the number of nickels she has?

    (A) $25x$ (D) $5(3x)$
    (B) $10x + 5(2x)$ (E) $20(x + 5)$
    (C) $x + 2x$

30. Four construction workers build a house containing 16 rooms. If the house has 4 floors and they take exactly 4 months (without stopping) to build it, then which of the following must be true?

   I. They build 4 rooms each month.
   II. Each floor has 4 rooms.
   III. They build an average of 1 floor per month.
   IV. The house averages 4 rooms per floor.

   (A) I and II only
   (B) II and III only
   (C) III and IV only
   (D) I, II, and III only
   (E) I, II, III, and IV

**Annual Number of Calls
to Emergency Services**

Fire   Medical   Police

31. The annual number of calls to police emergency services exceeds the number of calls to medical emergency services by 200. Using the chart above, how many calls are made annually to emergency fire services?

   (A) 4   (B) 200   (C) 400   (D) 600   (E) 800

32. A square 4 inches on a side is cut up into smaller squares 1 inch on a side. What is the maximum number of such squares that can be formed?

   (A) 4   (B) 8   (C) 16   (D) 36   (E) 64

33. A color television set is marked down 20% to $320. Which of the following equations could be used to determine its original price, *P*?

(A) $320 − 0.20 = P
(B) 0.20P = $320
(C) P = $320 + 0.20
(D) 0.80P + 0.20P = $320
(E) 0.80P = $320

34. The areas of which of the following are equal?

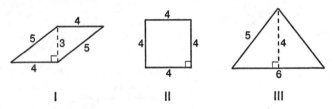

I   II   III

(A) I and II only
(B) I and III only
(C) II and III only
(D) I, II, and III
(E) None of them are equal.

35. Which of the following coordinate graphs displays a curved line passing through point (3, −2)?

(A)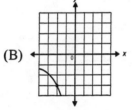

(D)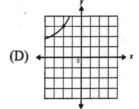

(B)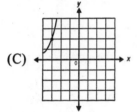

(E)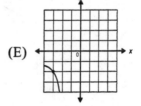

(C)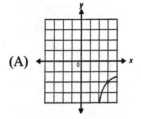

Questions 36 and 37 refer to the following graph.

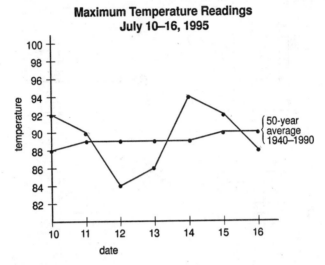

**Maximum Temperature Readings
July 10–16, 1995**

36. Of the seven days shown, about what percent of the days did the maximum temperature exceed the average temperature?

    (A) 3%   (B) 4%   (C) 43%   (D) 57%   (E) 93%

37. Between which two dates shown was the greatest increase in maximum temperature?

    (A) July 11–12   (D) July 14–15
    (B) July 12–13   (E) July 15–16
    (C) July 13–14

38. A furniture salesperson earns a 15% commission on each sale. If the salesperson sold a total of $1850 worth of furniture during one day, which of the following indicates that saleperson's commission in dollars for that day?

    (A) 15×1850
    (B) 1.5×1850
    (C) 0.15×1850
    (D) 0.015×1850
    (E) 0.0015×1850

39. How many paintings were displayed at the County Museum of Art if 30% of them were by Monet and Monet was represented by 24 paintings?

(A) 48   (B) 50   (C) 60   (D) 76   (E) 80

> The sum of two numbers equals
> one of the numbers.

40. If the above statement is true, which of the following best represents the relationship?

(A) $x + y = y + x$ (D) $x + y = y$
(B) $(x)(y) = 1$ (E) $x + y = x + 1$
(C) $x + y = 1$

STOP: IF YOU FINISH BEFORE TIME IS CALLED, CHECK YOUR WORK ON THIS SECTION ONLY. DO NOT WORK ON ANY OTHER SECTION IN THE TEST.

WRITING TEST: MULTIPLE-CHOICE SECTION

TIME: 30 Minutes
45 Questions

PART A

SUGGESTED TIME: 10 Minutes
25 Questions

<u>Directions</u>: Some of the following sentences are correct. Others contain problems in grammar, usage, idiom, diction, punctuation, and capitalization.

If there is an error, it will be underlined and lettered. Find the one underlined part that must be changed to make the sentence correct and choose the corresponding letter on your answer sheet. Mark (E) if the sentence contains no error.

1. The box of <u>nuts and bolts</u> <u>were</u> too heavy for the little boy to
           A   B
carry <u>by himself</u>, so he asked <u>his</u> mother for some help. <u>No error</u>
      C   D   E

2. <u>Not</u> able to keep a secret, <u>he announced</u> the stupidity <u>of his friend</u>
  A   B   C
to the <u>whole</u> class. <u>No error</u>
      D   E

3. <u>When</u> one wishes to be polite, <u>they</u> must <u>refrain</u> from eating food
   A   B   C
with his hands <u>when a knife</u> and fork have been provided.
             D
<u>No error</u>
  E

4. To have lain aside existential issues is to have adopted a certain
   A$$B
   rosy-cheeked naiveté that refuses to recognize sheer being as the
   C
   essence of ourselves and all that surrounds us. No error
   DE

5. Today's teenagers usually don't like any music that's played by
   ABC
   the Guy Lombardo Orchestra because the

   orchestra's arrangements make even new songs sound "old."
   D
   No error
   E

6. During the examination, two of the three hours will be allotted
   AB
   for writing; the third hour would be for editing your work.
   C$$D
   No error
   E

7. The only people in the movie theater on that stormy Monday
   A$$B
   night were the usher and me. No error
   C$$DE

8. Students who are not somewhat nervous about taking an exam
   A
   tend to subvert their ability by their very nonchalance. No error
   B$$CDE

9. The Japanese haiku form, brief and simple, lays somewhere be-
   AB
   tween the plainness of a wish and the elegance of a prayer.
   C$$D
   No error
   E

10. The words <u>"critic"</u> and "crime" have developed from a common
    A
    <u>linguistic root</u>; the reason for this <u>may be</u> <u>because</u> early speakers
    B C D
    had not distinguished the critical from the criminal. <u>No error</u>
    E

11. The <u>anger of</u> the opposing candidates <u>was obvious but</u> <u>neither</u>
    A B C
    <u>of them</u> insulted the other. <u>No error</u>
    D E

12. <u>Describing the auto accident</u> to a police officer, Tim <u>hopped</u> onto
    A B
    a bus and <u>rode away</u> from the wreck that <u>had once</u> been his sleek,
    C D
    flawless Ferrari. <u>No error</u>
    E

13. Everything that you, the voter, <u>needs</u> to know about the candi-
    A
    dates and <u>their</u> opinions is contained in the <u>newly published</u> voter
    B C
    information pamphlet written by the <u>Secretary of State</u>. <u>No error</u>
    D E

14. In opposition <u>to</u> President Carter's foreign policy <u>were</u> the <u>house</u>
    A B C
    Majority Leader and the Chairman of the

    <u>Ways and Means Committee</u>. <u>No error</u>
    D E

15. <u>Neither</u> my uncle <u>nor</u> my brother ever refused to share <u>their</u> lei-
       A   B   C
    sure time with <u>me</u>, and so I was never short of companions.
                   D
    <u>No error</u>
      E

16. <u>By</u> speaking to millions about the high incidence of heart attacks
     A
    suffered by unconditioned joggers, <u>Stanley Runabout</u> persuades
                                    B
    <u>one</u> to build speed and endurance gradually and monitor their
     C
    <u>progress continually.</u> <u>No error</u>
          D   E

17. Few scientists today expect <u>their</u> discoveries to be compared with
                               A
    <u>Einstein</u>, yet many work <u>hard</u> to advance knowledge by
       B   C
    <u>questioning and clarifying</u> the major discoveries of the past.
              D
    <u>No error</u>
      E

18. A strict and <u>highly disciplined</u> upbringing had its <u>effect</u> on my
               A   B
    cousin's later life; he treated his own children roughly and un-
    fairly, redoubling <u>the strictness</u> which he <u>had</u> experienced.
                       C   D
    <u>No error</u>
      E

19. Henry Kissinger, the former Secretary of State, once called for
                                       A
    bipartisan agreement among the members of Congress whom, he
        B   C   D
    declared, were slowing his efforts toward peace. No error
                                                      E

20. Standing alongside my friend and me in the hallway were Robert
                   A   B   C
    Redford and Dustin Hoffman, but we were too shy to step up and
                                       D
    say hello. No error
               E

21. By understanding what modern technology would have lost if
          A   B
    the steam engine would not have been invented, we become cer-
                        C
    tain that the Industrial Revolution was not an isolated and incon-
                                        D
    sequential event. No error
                      E

22. Both opinions are respectable, but the one which is supported by
                       A   B
    a specific plan should impress everyone as the most admirable.
                    C   D
    No error
    E

23. Only one of the dozen apartment units I inspected show any ne-
                 A   B   C
    glect on the part of the manager. No error
            D   E

24. At six A.M. <u>in the morning</u>, we trudged up the hill, <u>groggily</u>
                            A   B
<u>looking</u> forward to a <u>fifteen-mile</u> hike. <u>No error</u>
      C   D   E

25. A flock of <u>pigeons</u> <u>is</u> unexpected this time of year, and <u>its</u> espe-
                        A   B   C
cially surprising to see the birds winging through the city <u>amidst</u>
                                                                                              D

a snowstorm. <u>No error</u>
                              E

PART B

SUGGESTED TIME: 20 Minutes
20 Questions

Directions: Some part of each sentence below is underlined; sometimes the whole sentence is underlined. Five choices for rephrasing the underlined part follow each sentence. The first choice (A) repeats the original, and the other four are different. If choice (A) seems better than the alternatives, choose answer (A); if not, choose one of the others.

For each sentence, consider the requirements of standard written English. Your choice should be a correct, concise, and effective expression, not awkward or ambiguous. Focus on grammar, word choice, sentence construction, and punctuation. If a choice changes the meaning of the original sentence, do not select it.

26. That she neglected the children, that the house remained dirty and cluttered, and poor personal hygiene were reasons for firing the housekeeper.

    (A) That she neglected the children, that the house remained dirty and cluttered, and poor personal hygiene were reasons for firing the housekeeper.
    (B) That she neglected the children, house dirt and clutter, and poor personal hygiene were reasons for firing the, housekeeper.
    (C) That she neglected the children, dirty and cluttered house, and not good personal hygiene were reasons for firing the housekeeper.
    (D) Neglect of the children, poor housecleaning, and that she had poor personal hygiene were reasons for firing the housekeeper.
    (E) The housekeeper's neglect of the children, poor housecleaning, and lack of good personal hygiene were reasons for her firing.

27. Neither Barbara nor her friends <u>is invited to pledge the local so-rority</u>.

    (A) is invited to pledge the local sorority
    (B) are invited to pledge the local sorority
    (C) is pledging the local sorority
    (D) are pledging the local sorority
    (E) will pledge

28. As the shrill, piercing sound of the sirens <u>approached, several of my neighbors' dogs start</u> to howl.

    (A) approached, several of my neighbors' dogs start
    (B) approached, several of my neighbors' dogs started
    (C) approach, several of my neighbors' dogs starts
    (D) approach, several of my neighbors' dogs start
    (E) approach, several dogs of my neighbor started

29. After reconsidering my original judgments, I feel obliged to re-read <u>the book I maligned and which initially seemed so inconse-quential</u>.

    (A) the book I maligned and which initially seemed so inconse-quential
    (B) the book in which I maligned what first seemed so inconse-quential
    (C) the maligned book which I initially deemed inconsequential
    (D) the book I malign initially and inconsequentially
    (E) the book I will malign because of its initial inconsequential-ity

30. <u>On arriving at Los Angeles International Airport, his friends met him and took him immediately to his speaking engagement.</u>

    (A) On arriving at Los Angeles International Airport, his friends met him and took him immediately to his speaking engagement.

    (B) Arriving at Los Angeles International Airport, his friends who met him immediately took him to his speaking engagement.

    (C) When he arrived at Los Angeles International Airport, his friends met him and took him immediately to his speaking engagement.

    (D) When he arrived at Los Angeles International Airport, he was taken immediately to his speaking engagement.

    (E) After arriving at Los Angeles International Airport, he was immediately taken to his speaking engagement.

31. Among the members of the legal profession, there are <u>many who try to keep their clients out of court</u> and save their clients' money.

    (A) many who try to keep their clients out of court

    (B) ones who try to keep their clients out of court

    (C) they who try to keep their clients out of court

    (D) many of whom try to keep their clients out of court

    (E) a few who try to keep their clients out of court

32. <u>Whatever he aspired to achieve, they</u> were thwarted by his jealous older brothers.

    (A) Whatever he aspired to achieve, they

    (B) Whatever he had any aspirations to, they

    (C) Whatever aspirations he had

    (D) Whatever be his aspirations, they

    (E) Many of his aspirations and goals

33. Neither the scientists nor the ecologists knows how to deal with the lethal effects of nuclear power plant explosions.

   (A) Neither the scientists nor the ecologists knows
   (B) Neither the scientists nor the ecologists know
   (C) Neither the scientists or the ecologists know
   (D) Neither the scientists together with the ecologists knows
   (E) Not the scientists or the ecologists know

34. The job application did not state to whom to be sent the personal references.

   (A) to whom to be sent the personal references
   (B) to who the personal references should be sent
   (C) to whom to send the personal references –
   (D) to whom the personal references will be sent
   (E) to whom to send the personal references to

35. After battling hypertension for years, Marvin Murphy was relieved by the results of his doctor's annual physical examination, which indicated his blood pressure was normal.

   (A) his doctor's annual physical examination, which
   (B) his annual physical examination, that
   (C) his annual physical examination, which
   (D) an annual physical examination by his doctor, which
   (E) his doctor's annual physical examination that

36. When the Republican Party was the minority party, its ability to win a presidential election was determined by the number of Democratic and independent voters it attracts.

   (A) its ability to win a presidential election was determined by the number of Democratic and independent voters it attracts
   (B) its ability to win a presidential election is determined by the number of Democratic and independent voters it attracts
   (C) its ability to win a presidential election has been determined by the number of Democratic and independent voters it attracts
   (D) the number of Democratic and independent voters it attracts determines its ability to win a presidential election
   (E) the number of Democratic and independent voters it attracted determined its ability to win a presidential election

37. The boundaries of the Pleasant Valley School District <u>have and will continue to include</u> the small cities of Millerton, Cedarville, Granite, and Homersfield.

    (A) have and will continue to include
    (B) have included and will continue to include
    (C) has included and will continue to include
    (D) has and will continue to include
    (E) include and will include

38. Because she worked the night shift, <u>arriving at 10 P.M. and leaving at 6 A.M.</u>

    (A) arriving at 10 P.M. and leaving at 6 A.M.
    (B) having arrived at 10 P.M. and leaving at 6 A.M.
    (C) she arrived at 10 P.M. and left at 6 A.M.
    (D) with an arrival at 6 and a departure at 10
    (E) from 10 P.M. to 6 A.M.

39. <u>Laying low in the tall jungle grass was</u> a lion and his mate, both waiting for the opportunity to catch some food.

    (A) Laying low in the tall jungle grass was
    (B) The tall jungle grass concealing their low-lying bodies,
    (C) In the tall jungle grass, laying low, were
    (D) Lying low in the tall jungle grass,
    (E) Lying low in the tall jungle grass were

40. <u>Planning a career in business is often easier than to pursue it.</u>

    (A) Planning a career in business is often easier than to pursue it.
    (B) To plan a career in business is often easier than pursuing it.
    (C) Planning a business career is often easier than pursuing it.
    (D) The planning of a business career is often easier than its pursuit.
    (E) A business career plan is often easier than a business career.

41. A fight broke out when the foreign ambassador took a joke serious and punched the jokester hardly.

    (A) took a joke serious and punched the jokester hardly
    (B) took a joke seriously and hardly punched the jokester
    (C) hardly took a joke and seriously punched the jokester
    (D) took a joke seriously and punched the jokester hard
    (E) gave a hard punch to a serious jokester

42. The public soon became outraged at the Cabinet member whom
betrayed the public trust, and they demanded his ouster.

    (A) the Cabinet member whom betrayed the public trust
    (B) the untrustworthy Cabinet member
    (C) the Cabinet member with whom they betrayed the public
    trust
    (D) the Cabinet member who, after betraying the public trust
    (E) the Cabinet member who betrayed the public trust

43. Opinions about the ballot issue, of course, varies according with
the ethnic and economic status of each voter.

    (A) varies according with the ethnic and economic status
    (B) varies according to ethnic and economic status
    (C) changes with ethnicity and the economy
    (D) vary according to the ethnic and economic status
    (E) vary according to ethnic and economical status

44. While declaring his support for a nuclear weapons freeze, a small
bomb exploded some distance from the Cabinet minister, who
was startled but unharmed.

    (A) a small bomb exploded some distance from the Cabinet min-
    ister, who was startled but unharmed
    (B) a small bomb startled the Cabinet minister, but did not harm
    him
    (C) a small bomb startled the Cabinet minister from a distance,
    but did not harm him
    (D) the Cabinet minister was startled by a bomb that exploded
    some distance from him, but unharmed
    (E) the Cabinet minister was startled but unharmed by a small
    bomb that exploded some distance from him

45. Several disgruntled visitors had left the board meeting <u>before it</u> <u>had considered the new municipal tax cut</u>.

    (A) before it had considered the new municipal tax cut

    (B) before it considered the new municipal tax cut

    (C) before the members considered the new municipal tax cut

    (D) with the consideration of the new municipal tax cut yet to come

    (E) previous to the new municipal tax cut

STOP: IF YOU FINISH BEFORE TIME IS CALLED, CHECK YOUR WORK ON THIS SECTION ONLY. DO NOT WORK ON ANY OTHER SECTION IN THE TEST.

WRITING TEST: ESSAY SECTION

TIME: **30 Minutes**
        1 Essay

Directions: In this section, you will have 30 minutes to plan and write one essay on the topic given. You may use the paper provided to plan your essay before you begin writing. You should plan your time wisely. Read the topic carefully to make sure that you are properly addressing the issue or situation. **You must write on the given topic. An essay on another topic will not be acceptable.**

The essay question is designed to give you an opportunity to write clearly and effectively. Use specific examples whenever appropriate to aid in supporting your ideas. Keep in mind that the quality of your writing is much more important than the quantity.

Your essay is to be written in the space provided. No other paper may be used. Your writing should be neat and legible. Because you have only a limited amount of space in which to write, please do **not** skip lines, do **not** write excessively large, and do **not** leave wide margins.

Remember, use the bottom of this page for any organizational notes you may wish to make.

TOPIC

Think of a friendship that you've made anytime during your lifetime which you now realize was or is important to you. In the space provided, write an essay explaining why that friendship is or was so important to you.

ANSWER KEY FOR PRACTICE TEST 2

Reading Test		Mathematics Test		Writing Test Multiple-Choice	
1. D	21. C	1. B	21. C	1. B	24. A
2. A	22. E	2. D	22. B	2. E	25. C
3. D	23. D	3. D	23. C	3. B	26. E
4. D	24. B	4. C	24. B	4. A	27. B
5. D	25. A	5. B	25. C	5. E	28. B
6. C	26. D	6. C	26. C	6. D	29. A
7. B	27. D	7. A	27. A	7. D	30. C
8. C	28. E	8. E	28. A	8. E	31. A
9. C	29. D	9. C	29. A	9. B	32. C
10. D	30. B	10. B	30. C	10. D	33. B
11. B	31. D	11. E	31. E	11. B	34. C
12. D	32. C	12. B	32. C	12. A	35. D
13. C	33. C	13. E	33. E	13. A	36. E
14. D	34. D	14. B	34. B	14. C	37. B
15. A	35. B	15. E	35. A	15. C	38. C
16. A	36. C	16. B	36. D	16. C	39. E
17. E	37. D	17. B	37. C	17. B	40. C
18. D	38. E	18. B	38. C	18. E	41. D
19. E	39. B	19. C	39. E	19. D	42. E
20. C	40. C	20. A	40. D	20. E	43. D
				21. C	44. E
				22. D	45. C
				23. C	

SCORING YOUR PPST PRACTICE TEST 2

To score your PPST Practice Test 2, total the number of correct responses for each test. Do not subtract any points for questions attempted but missed, as there is no penalty for guessing. The scores for each section range from 150 to 190. Because the Writing Test contains multiple-choice questions and an essay, that score is a composite score adjusted to give approximately equal weight to the number right on the multiple-choice section and to the essay score. The essay is scored holistically (a single score for overall quality) from 1 (low) to 6 (high). Each of two readers gives a 1 to 6 score. The score that the essay receives is the sum of these two readers' scores.

ANALYZING YOUR TEST RESULTS

The following charts should be used to carefully analyze your results and spot your strengths and weaknesses. The complete process of analyzing each subject area and each individual question should be completed for this Practice Test. These results should be reexamined for trends in types of error (repeated errors) or poor results in specific subject areas. **This reexamination and analysis is of tremendous importance for effective test preparation.**

PRACTICE TEST 2: SUBJECT AREA ANALYSIS SHEET

	Possible	Completed	Right	Wrong
Reading Test	40			
Mathematics Test	40			
Writing Test	45			
TOTAL	125			

ANALYSIS—TALLY SHEET FOR QUESTIONS MISSED

One of the most important parts of test preparation is analyzing **why** you missed a question so that you can reduce the number of mistakes. Now that you have taken Practice Test 2 and corrected your answers, carefully tally your mistakes by marking each of them in the proper column.

	Total Missed	Simple Mistake	Misread Problem	Lack of Knowlege
Reading Test				
Mathematics Test				
Writing Test				
TOTAL				

Reviewing the above data should help you determine **why** you are missing certain questions. Now that you have pinpointed types of errors, focus on avoiding your most common type.

SCORE APPROXIMATORS

Reading Test

To approximate your reading score:
1. Count the number of questions you answered correctly.
2. Use the following table to match the number of correct answers and the corresponding approximate score range.

Number Right	Approximate Score Range
10–19	160–169
20–29	170–179
30–40	180–189

Remember, this is only an approximate score range. When you take the PPST, you will have questions that are similar to those in this book, however some questions may be slightly easier or more difficult.

Mathematics Test

To approximate your mathematics score:

1. Count the number of questions you answered correctly.
2. Use the following table to match the number of correct answers and the corresponding approximate score range.

Number Right	Approximate Score Range
0–10	150–160
11–20	161–170
21–30	171–180
31–40	181–190

Remember, this is an approximate score range.

Writing Test

These scores are difficult to approximate because the multiple-choice section score and the essay score are combined to give a total score.

Essay Checklist

Use this checklist to evaluate your essay.

Diagnosis/Prescription for Timed Writing Exercise

A good essay will:

_____ Address the assignment
     Be well focused
_____ Be well organized
     Have smooth transitions between paragraphs
     Be coherent, unified
_____ Be well developed
     Contain specific examples to support points
_____ Be grammatically sound (only minor flaws)
     Use correct sentence structure
     Use correct punctuation
     Use standard written English
_____ Use language skillfully
     Use a variety of sentence types
     Use a variety of words
_____ Be legible
     Have clear handwriting
     Be neat

ANSWERS AND EXPLANATIONS FOR PRACTICE TEST 2

READING TEST

1. (D) The author's entire argument is based on the recent studies indicating a downward trend in aptitude test scores. By extension, the author must assume that such studies are accurate.

2. (A) The term *bowl of oatmeal* is used sarcastically to condemn the actions of the city council. Choice (B) is not correct as the situation is certainly not *tragic*.

3. (D) Trends showing that within two years a single-family dwelling will be unaffordable by the average family indicate that not only must housing costs be going up, but the average family income will not meet the increased cost of housing.

4. (D) Both statements I and III weaken the author's argument. Statement I, if true, suggests that, in fact, there will be affordable single-family homes for the average family. Statement III suggests that average families may find it difficult to afford renting an apartment, thus weakening the author's final sentence.

5. (D) Both statements I and II are assumed by the author. First, the present trend (rise in housing cost) will continue, and second, families will turn to renting apartments (instead of, say, buying mobile homes or condominiums).

6. (C) In both the introductory and final paragraphs, the writer is concerned with attacks on the First Amendment and throughout the article emphasizes this concern with a detailed look at what he or she thinks is an attack on a particular group, the press, that is guaranteed a certain amount of freedom by that amendment. Therefore, choices (A) and (B) are much too broad, and choices (D) and (E) are supporting ideas rather than principal ideas; *slander and libel laws* and *Big Brother in government* are mentioned only briefly.

7. (B) Line 10 says a *6–3 ruling*. So if two justices change their minds, we would have a 4–5 ruling for the other side.

8. (C) Lines 10–11 say that reporters *now face a challenge to the privacy of their minds,* and the last sentence in the passage is a statement against *mind-control.* All other choices are not explicitly supported by material in the passage.

9. (C) As is stated in lines 22–23, actual malice is *with knowledge that the statements were false, or with reckless disregard of whether they were true or not.*

10. (D) As is often the case, the first sentence states the main idea of the passage. Choice (A) is incorrect, both because it is too narrow and because the passage tells the reader only that Kitty Litter is made from clay and does not tell how it is produced. Choice (B) is also too narrow. Choice (C) is incorrect because only one sentence mentions this fact. Choice (E) is incorrect because the article does not describe a method for preventing fires.

11. (B) The *they* in this sentence refers to *cats* in the first sentence of the paragraph. That first sentence describes cats watching the *hustle and bustle* with a sense of *superiority.* Given this information, we may infer that the grin described in the last sentence comes from watching the *hustle and bustle* of human antics, in this case, the antics of the U.S. government making itself a nuisance. Notice that all choices except (B) may be eliminated, if only because each describes cats *laughing* instead of grinning.

12. (D) The tone of the author concerning Vieira is certainly positive but not so much as to be idolatrous or spiritual. *Admiring* is the best choice.

13. (C) Since the fewer number of accidents did not result in lower premiums, one suggestion of the passage is that insurance companies pocketed the savings rather than pass them on to the consumer. Thus, the author implies that insurance companies took advantage of drivers.

14. (D) The brief passage introduces the possibility that life may have begun in clay instead of in water as scientists have believed. Choices (B), (C), and (E) are much too strong to be supported by the passage, and choice (A) refers to the earth instead of to life.

15. (A) The first part of the quotation begins, *What history teaches is this . . .*, implying that we have something to learn from history. The second part goes on to state that we *never learned anything from history.* This is a contradiction using irony.

16. (A) Choice (A) best summarizes the passage, citing two support points for the main idea—that California's roads have deteriorated. Choice (E) is incomplete, and the *over three quarters* is correct only in reference to the state's country roads.

17. (E) All the other choices are mentioned in the passage except the demand for new highways.

18. (D) The sentence explains that the established military tradition supplied the South with military leaders.

19. (E) The Northern advantages are all long-term, especially food production. Each of the other choices draws a conclusion beyond any implications in the passage.

20. (C) By mentioning carrots in connection with improved eyesight and not explaining that implied connection, the author is assuming that readers readily see the connection.

21. (C) Sentence 6 introduces a new topic; it shifts from a discussion of education legislation in general to a discussion of John Dewey in particular.

22. (E) Sentence 7 stresses Dewey's belief that education is concerned with many areas and experiences. This belief contrasts with the Morrill Act's stress on agricultural and mechanical arts as primary educational areas.

23. (D) *Also* indicates that Dewey's theories are being discussed in addition to previous information and that reference to the previous information is included in the statement about Dewey.

24. (B) Dewey's belief in a comprehensive education is inconsistent with a focus on industrialization, and choice (B) explains that inconsistency, thus supporting the statement that industrialization is destructive.

25. (A) The passage is about education and some related legislation but not about legislation in general.

26. (D) We are told that Dewey's theories *had a profound effect on public education.* Each of the other choices draws a conclusion beyond the scope of the passage.

27. (D) The passage states that discussion of other students has a negative effect on parents and on the conference; the fact expressed in choice (D) directly validates this assertion.

28. (E) Each of the other choices introduces information well beyond the scope of the passage.

29. (D) The author favors community participation in education; therefore, he or she must assume that such participation has a positive effect.

30. (B) If we replace *late-twentieth-century progress* in choice (B) with the synonymous term used in the passage, *technological expertise of the nuclear age,* we see that (B) clearly reiterates the point of the passage.

31. (D) Choice (C) flatly contradicts the argument of the passage, and (A) and (B) present information not touched on in the passage. Choice (E) is weak because associations are not universal; they depend on each individual's personal experience. This point—that associations are personal rather than universal—is expressed by (D).

32. (C) Choice (C) directly contradicts the point of the passage, which is that associations are determined by experience.

33. (C) Choices (D) and (E) neither weaken nor strengthen the passage, simply suggesting other examples of associations without explaining the stimulus which produced them; (A) and (B) are irrelevant issues. Choice (C) strengthens the argument of the passage by citing an example of experience reinforcing an association—or in other words, stimulating a response.

34. (D) The point of the passage is that "reality" varies according to who experiences it and what "consensus group" he or she is a member of. Along this line, a war is a conflict between two different consensus groups, and so the example given by (D) is appropriate.

35. (B) Both choices (B) and (C) mention consensus group, but (C) says that the members of the group are deluded about reality, which contradicts the author's argument that no view of reality is, strictly speaking, a delusion.

36. (C) Once again, the point of the passage is that different people or groups acquire different versions of reality based on their differing experiences. Reality is therefore subjective but not a mere figment of imagination.

37. (D) This choice is validated by sentences 8 and 9 (lines 15–19) of the passage.

38. (E) This choice has been explained above in the discussions of questions 34 and 36.

39. (B) By citing the value of planning the presentation of material in an orderly way, the author must assume that such organized instruction is beneficial. Each of the other choices draws conclusions beyond the scope of the passage.

40. (C) None of the other choices makes good sense when substituted for *integral,* and *essential* is one of the meanings of *integral.*

MATHEMATICS TEST

1. (B) Only choice (B), $\frac{31}{60}$, is greater than $\frac{1}{2}$. All the other choices are less than $\frac{1}{2}$.

2. (D) There are 3 chances out of 4 of spinning either red, yellow, or blue. Thus, the correct answer is 3/4.

3. (D) 4 rods = $(4)(16\frac{1}{2})$ = 66 feet
    66 feet × 12 = 792 inches

4. (C) Figure *ABCD* is a parallelogram. The formula for the area of a parallelogram is area equals base times height. Since the base is 6 and the height (a perpendicular drawn to the base) is 3, the area would be computed by 6 × 3, or answer (C).

5. (B) Ratios may be expressed as fractions. Thus choice (A), 1 to 4, may be expressed as 1/4. Notice that (C), (D), and (E) are all fractions that reduce to 1/4.

$$2/8 = 1/4$$
$$3/12 = 1/4$$
$$4/16 = 1/4$$

Only (B) does not equal 1/4.

6. (C) On the chart, tuition is 40% of total expenses. Books and lab materials represent 10%, so they are exactly one quarter of tuition. Since tuition is $4800 for the year, books and lab materials are one quarter of that, or 4800 divided by 4 = $1200.

7. (A) $\angle BCD = \angle A + \angle B$ (exterior angle of a triangle equals the sum of the opposite two angles). Then $84° = \angle A + 63°$, and $\angle A = 21°$.

8. (E) Mary worked a total of 24 hours, but we do not know in how many days. Therefore, we cannot derive the number of hours she worked each day. Each of the other choices can be derived from the statement.

9. (C) $3c = d$

$$\frac{3c}{3} = \frac{d}{3}$$
$$c = \frac{d}{3}$$

10. (B) $\dfrac{245}{35} = 7$ cm

11. (E) The tenth place is the number immediately to the right of the decimal point. To round off to the nearest tenth, check the hundredth place (two places to the right of the decimal point). If the hundredth number is a 5 or higher, round the tenth up to the next number. For instance, 0.36 would round to 0.4. If the hundredth is a 4 or lower, simply drop any places after the tenth place. For instance, 0.74356 would round to 0.7. Thus, 4316.136 rounded to the nearest tenth is 4316.1, which is answer choice (E).

12. (B) A prime number is a number which can be divided evenly only by itself and the number 1. Choices (A), (C), (D), and (E) can all be divided evenly by 3. Answer choice (B), 13, can be divided evenly only by itself and 1.

13. (E) The fraction $\frac{1}{8}$ equals 0.125.

$$\begin{array}{r} .125 \\ 8\overline{)1.000} \end{array}$$

Thus it would lie between $\frac{1}{9}$ (0.111) and $\frac{2}{15}$ (0.133).

14. (B) Points plotted on a coordinate graph are expressed (x, y), where x indicates the distance right or left and y indicates the distance up or down. Thus $(-3, 4)$ means 3 "steps" left and then 4 "steps" up. This will place the point in quadrant II.

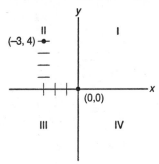

15. (E) The only statement which *must* be true is (E), "The class averages 2 pencils per student." Notice that 30 students could each have 2 pencils; so (C) and (D) may be false. Likewise, just one of the students could have all 60 pencils; therefore, (A) and (B) may be false. Only (E) *must* be true.

16. (B) Four pounds of steak at $3.89 per pound cost $15.56. Change from a twenty-dollar bill would therefore be $20.00 − $15.56, or $4.44.

17. (B) In order to have the pie graph represent blue-eyed students as 6 out of 24, the piece of the "pie" representing blue-eyed students should be 6/24, or 1/4. So the blue piece needs to be increased. Likewise, for hazel to represent 5/24, its piece of the pie should be slightly less than 6/24, so its size should be decreased.

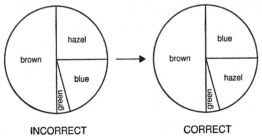

INCORRECT   CORRECT

18. (B) Since D is between A and B on $\overleftrightarrow{AB}$, we know that the sum of the lengths of the smaller segments $\overline{AD}$ and $\overline{DB}$ is equal to the length of the larger segment $\overline{AB}$.

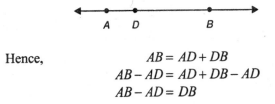

Hence,
$$AB = AD + DB$$
$$AB - AD = AD + DB - AD$$
$$AB - AD = DB$$

19. (C) In 1990, 10% of $30,000, or $3000, was spent on medical. In 1995, 12% of $34,000, or $4080, was spent on medical. Thus, there was an increase of $1080.

20. (A) There was an increase from 18% to 22%, or 4%.

21. (C) 240 out of 800 can be expressed 240/800, which reduces to 3/10, or 30%.

22. (B) The probability of throwing a head in one throw is

$$\frac{\text{chance of a head}}{\text{total chances (1 head + 1 tail)}} = \frac{1}{2}$$

Since you are trying to throw a head *twice,* multiply the probability for the first toss (1/2) times the probability for the second toss (again, 1/2). Thus, (1/2)(1/2) = (1/4), and 1/4 is the probability of throwing heads twice in two tosses. Another way of approaching this problem is looking at the total number of possible outcomes.

	First Toss	Second Toss
1.	H	H
2.	H	T
3.	T	H
4.	T	T

Thus there are four different possible outcomes. There is only one way to throw two heads in two tosses. Thus the probability of tossing two heads in two tosses is 1 out of 4 total outcomes, or 1/4.

23. (C) Changing 740,000 to 0.0074 requires moving the decimal point 8 places to the left. This is the same as multiplying by 1/100,000,000.

24. (B) The amount of discount was $120 − $90 = $30. The rate of discount equals

$$\frac{\text{change}}{\text{starting point}} = \frac{30}{120} = \frac{1}{4} = 25\%$$

25. (C) The final number is always the same as the number selected. For instance, try 10:

$$10 \times 2 = 20$$
$$20 + 14 = 34$$
$$34 \div 2 = 17$$
$$17 - 7 = 10$$

26. (C) To change 3 miles to feet, simply multiply 3 times 5280 (since 5280 is the number of feet in a mile). This computation will give the number of feet in 3 miles. Then multiply this product by 12, since there are 12 inches in each foot. The resulting product will be the number of inches in 3 miles.

27. (A) There are several approaches to this problem. One solution is to first find the area of the square: $10 \times 10 = 100$. Then subtract the approximate area of the circle: $A = \pi(r)^2 \approx 3(5^2) = 3(25) = 75$. Therefore, the total area inside the square but outside the circle is approximately 25. One quarter of that area is shaded. Therefore $\frac{25}{4}$ is approximately the shaded area. The closest answer is (A), 10.

    A more efficient method is to first find the area of the square: $10 \times 10 = 100$. Then divide the square into four equal sections as follows.

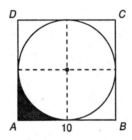

    Since a quarter of the square is 25, the only possible answer choice for the shaded area is (A), 10.

28. (A) If today Lucy is 14, then last year she was 13. Likewise, if Charlie's age now is C, then last year he was $C - 1$. Now, put these into an equation.

    $$\underbrace{\text{Lucy's age last year}}_{13} \overset{\text{is}}{\underset{\downarrow}{=}} \underbrace{\text{three years older than twice Charlie's age last year.}}_{2(C-1)+3}$$

    Transposing, $13 - 3 = 2(C - 1)$.

29. (A) The number of nickels that Angela has is x. Thus, the total value of those nickels (in cents) is $5x$. Angela also has twice as many dimes as nickels, or $2x$. The total value in cents of those dimes is $2x(10)$, or $20x$. Adding together the value of the nickels and dimes gives $5x + 20x$, or $25x$.

30. (C) Only statements III and IV *must* be true. If the house has 4 floors and it takes exactly 4 months to build the house, the workers average 1 floor per month. And since the house has 16 rooms on 4 floors, the house averages 4 rooms per floor ($\frac{16}{4} = 4$). However, I and II may not necessarily be true. To build 16 rooms in 4 months' time, the workers may not necessarily work at a steady pace, building 4 each month. They may, for example, build 5 rooms one month and 3 the next. Although they *average* 4 rooms per month, they don't have to build exactly 4 rooms each month. Likewise in II, just because a house *averages* 4 rooms on each floor does not mean the house necessarily has exactly 4 rooms on each floor. For example, the house could be built to have 6 rooms on the first floor, 3 rooms on the second and third floors, and 4 rooms on the top floor, which gives a total of 16 rooms.

31. (E) The question states that 200 more emergency police calls are made annually than emergency medical calls. Police calls are represented on the chart by 3 telephones, and medical calls are represented by 2 telephones. Since the difference between them is 1 telephone, each telephone represents 200 emergency calls. Thus, because calls for fires are represented by 4 telephones, 4 × 200 = 800 calls for emergency fire services.

32. (C) The maximum number of squares 1 inch by 1 inch will be 16.

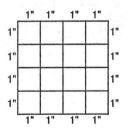

33. (E) If the color television is marked down 20%, then its current price is 80% of its original price. Thus, $0.80P = \$320$.

34. (B) The area of I, the parallelogram, equals *bh,* or $4 \times 3 = 12$. The area of II, the square, equals s^2, or $4^2 = 16$. The area of III, the triangle, equals $\frac{1}{2}bh$, or $\frac{1}{2}(6)(4) = 12$. Thus, I and III are equal.

35. (A) To locate the position of a point on a coordinate graph, you must know that the point's location is given in terms of (x, y). The first number is the x-coordinate, and it indicates the distance along the x-axis to the right or left of the origin (0). The second number is the y-coordinate, which indicates the distance up or down along the y-axis. Thus, the point $(3, -2)$ is 3 units to the right of the origin and 2 units down. The only curve that passes through that point is the curve in choice (A).

36. (D) There were 4 days (July 10, 11, 14, and 15) on which the maximum temperature exceeded the average; thus, $\frac{4}{7}$ is approximately 57%.

37. (C) The maximum temperature rose from 86° to 94° from July 13 to July 14. This increase was the greatest.

38. (C) To determine the saleperson's commission for that day, multiply 15% times $1850. Fifteen percent is expressed in decimal form by 0.15, so the answer is 0.15×1850.

39. (E) To find the total number of paintings, use the equation

$$\frac{\text{is}}{\text{of}} = \%$$

and simply plug in the given values. The question is essentially, 24 is 30% of how many? Therefore, 24 is the "is," 30 is the percent, and "how many" (the unknown) is the "of." Plugging into the equation, we get

$$\frac{24}{x} = \frac{30}{100}$$

Note that the fractional percent is used to simplify the math.

Cross multiplying	$30x = 2400$
Dividing both sides by 30	$\dfrac{30x}{30} = \dfrac{2400}{30}$
	$x = 80$

40. (D) The word *sum* indicates addition. The sum of two numbers is therefore $x + y$. If this sum equals one of the numbers, then the equation will be either $x + y = x$ or $x + y = y$.

WRITING TEST: MULTIPLE-CHOICE SECTION

Part A

1. (B) The subject is singular, *box*, so the verb must be singular, *was* instead of *were*.

2. (E) This sentence contains no error.

3. (B) *They* is meant to refer back to *one;* since *one* is singular, *they* (a plural) is incorrect. The correct pronoun is *one* or *he*.

4. (A) *Lain* should be changed to *laid*. *Lain* is used only when there is no object of the verb: "I have *lain* down."

5. (E) This sentence is correct as written.

6. (D) The second verb, *would be*, must be the same tense as the first verb, *will be*. So *would be* must be changed to *will be*.

7. (D) *Me* should be changed to *I*.

8. (E) This sentence contains no error.

9. (B) *Lays* should be changed to *Lies*, which is correct when there is no object of the verb.

10. (D) *Because* is unnecessarily repetitious, stating again the general meaning of *reason for this may be; because* should be changed to *that*.

11. (B) A comma is needed after *obvious* separating the two parts of the compound sentence joined by the conjunction.

12. (A) *Describing* should be changed to *having described* or *after describing*. Otherwise, the sentence seems to say that Tim was describing *while* he hopped on a bus.

13. (A) *Needs* does not agree with its subject, *you. Needs* should be changed to *need*.

14. (C) The first letter should be a capital *H* in *House*.

15. (C) *Neither my uncle nor my brother* is a singular subject; a plural compound subject uses *and* instead of *or* or *nor.* Since the subject is singular, the pronoun which refers to it must be singular, *his* instead of *their.*

16. (C) *One* (singular) does not agree with *millions* and *their* (plural). *One* should be changed to *them*.

17. (B) You cannot compare *discoveries* (things) with *Einstein* (a person), but you can logically compare *discoveries* with *Einstein's discoveries* or with *Einstein's*.

18. (E) This sentence contains no error.

19. (D) This is a pronoun error. *Whom* should be changed to *who*.

20. (E) This sentence contains no error.

21. (C) *Would not have been* should be changed to *had not been* in order to show that the invention of the steam engine is an *earlier action* than the probable loss by modern technology.

22. (D) Since only two opinions are being compared, *most admirable* (which correctly refers to more than two things) should be changed to *more admirable*.

23. (C) Since the subject of the sentence is singular, *one,* the verb must be singular, *shows* instead of *show.*

24. (A) *In the morning* is an unnecessary repetition of the meaning of *A.M.*

25. (C) The contraction *it's* (*it is*) is needed here.

Part B

26. (E) Choice (E) best expresses the parallel form called for in this sentence (*neglect, housecleaning, lack*—all nouns). The other choices contain the same "unparallel" structure of the original wording.

27. (B) Choice (B) contains the correct form *are* for the *neither . . . nor* construction. The verb in this case should be plural to match *friends,* which is the closer of the two subjects to the verb. Choice (D) correctly uses *are* but changes the meaning of the original.

28. (B) Choice (B) corrects the verb agreement problem in the original wording. The verbs must both be past tense or both be present tense. No other choice uses proper tense without introducing a subject-verb agreement error.

29. (A) The original is better than any of the alternatives. All other options are less direct, create ambiguities, or change the meaning of the original.

30. (C) Choice (C) clarifies the ambiguous wording of the original sentence. It is clear in (C) who is arriving and who is doing the meeting.

31. (A) The original wording is the best expression of this idea. Choice (E) changes the meaning. The other choices are either stylistically awkward or ungrammatical.

32. (C) Choice (C) best expresses the idea without changing the intent of the sentence as (E) does. The original and choices (B) and (D) are awkward.

33. (B) Choice (B) correctly supplies the plural *know,* which agrees with *ecologists.* The subject closer to the verb determines the number of the verb in this case. Choice (B) also retains the necessary *neither . . . nor.*

34. (C) Choice (C) best corrects the awkward wording in the original sentence. Choice (D), although grammatically correct, changes the meaning of the original.

35. (D) Choice (D) clarifies whose physical examination is in question, Marvin's or the doctor's. Choice (C) is straightforward and concise, also leaving no doubt as to whose examination it is; however, the *doctor* is not mentioned, and because one cannot assume that all physical examinations are administered by a doctor, this information must be included.

36. (E) Choice (E) is the most direct, concise wording of the original sentence. The verbs in these answer choices are the problem areas. Choice (B), for example, is incorrect because of the present tense *is* and *attracts.*

37. (B) Choice (B) corrects the verb problem in the original sentence. *Have and will continue to include* is better expressed as *have included and will continue to include.*

38. (C) The original sentence is a fragment; so are choices (B), (D), and (E).

39. (E) The verb *lying* (resting) is correct here; also, *were* is the correct verb because the subject, *a lion and his mate,* is plural. Choices (B) and (D) would make the sentence a fragment.

40. (C) The original is flawed by faulty parallelism. *Planning* is not parallel to *to pursue* (the former a gerund, the latter an infinitive). Choice (C) corrects this problem; *planning* is parallel to *pursuing.*

41. (D) Both errors in the original result from a confusion of adjectives and adverbs. *Seriously,* an adverb, correctly modifies the verb *took,* and *hard,* used as an adverb meaning *with strength,* correctly modifies *punched.* Choices (B), (C), and (E) significantly change the meaning of the original.

42. (E) The correct pronoun in this case is *who,* the subject of *betrayed.*

43. (D) The original contains two errors. *Varies* does not agree with the plural subject, *opinions,* and *according with* is not idiomatic. Choice (C) is a correct phrase but changes and obscures the meaning of the sentence.

44. (E) The introductory phrase is a dangling modifier, corrected by following *freeze* with *the Cabinet minister* to make clear to whom the introductory phrase refers. Choice (D) is not best because *but unharmed* is left in an awkward position.

45. (C) The original contains two errors. *It* suggests that the meeting, not the members, does the considering, and *had considered* is a verb tense simultaneous with *had left* and does not indicate that considering the tax cut occurred after the visitors had left. Choice (D) is unnecessarily wordy and leaves unsaid who did the considering.

FINAL PREPARATIONS: "THE FINAL TOUCHES"

1. Make sure that you are familiar with the testing center location and nearby parking facilities.

2. The last week of preparation should be spent on a general review of key concepts, test-taking strategies, and techniques.

3. Don't cram the night before the exam. It's a waste of time!

4. Arrive in plenty of time at the testing center.

5. Remember to bring the proper materials: identification, three or four sharpened Number 2 pencils, an eraser, and a watch.

6. Start off crisply, working the questions you know first and then coming back and trying to answer the others.

7. Try to eliminate one or more choices before you guess, but make sure you fill in all of the answers. There is no penalty for guessing.

8. Mark in reading passages, underline key words, write out important information, and make notations on diagrams. Take advantage of being permitted to write in the test booklet.

9. Make sure that you are answering "what is being asked" and that your answer is reasonable.

10. Cross out incorrect choices immediately. This strategy will keep you from reconsidering a choice that you've already eliminated.

11. Using the "Two Successful Overall Approaches" (page 6) is the key to getting the questions right that you should get right, resulting in a good score on the PPST.

PART VI

Testing by Computer

Computer-Based Academic Skills Assessments (CBT)

The Computer-Based Academic Skills Assessments (CBT) is another test in the ETS Praxis Series. It is classified in Praxis I along with the PPST and is very similar to it. The CBT is taken on computer, specifically on an IBM or IBM-compatible computer with a mouse. Like the PPST, the CBT contains questions that test skills in reading, writing, and mathematics that have been determined to be important for beginning teachers. Some states and educational institutions will accept a score from either the PPST or the CBT. The subject matter reviews, the content of the practice questions and answers, and the essay practice provided in this book will help you prepare for the CBT as well as the PPST.

The CBT is an adaptive test, that is, questions are computer-selected for the test taker based on the responses to previous questions. When a test taker answers a question correctly, the next question that appears on the screen will be at about the same level of difficulty or of greater difficulty. If a question is missed, the next question presented will be at about the same level of difficulty or of slightly less difficulty. In this way, the computer adapts the questions to finally reach the test taker's skill level.

CBT TUTORIALS

Immediately before taking the CBT, the test taker is required to be led through a tutorial program in order to be introduced to the computer system delivering the test and to practice. The types of questions given on the test are used in the tutorials, so the tutorials are good preparation for what you will encounter. The tutorials take approximately 30 minutes, and they explain

- how to use a mouse
- how to answer
- how to use the testing tools
- how to scroll
- how to use the word processor

A CLOSER LOOK AT THE TUTORIALS

How to use a mouse. You will be using a mouse to answer questions. Typing and other keyboard skills will not be needed. Be sure you are familiar with the use of a mouse.

- Point at items on the screen by moving the mouse in the appropriate direction.
- Point at an answer and click a button on the mouse to record your answer to test questions.
- To click, press and release any button on the mouse once.
- When you wish to go to the next screen, press and release any button on the mouse.

How to answer. This tutorial will let you practice using a mouse to answer different types of questions. For example, if the question is multiple choice, you simply use the mouse to move the pointer to the answer you wish to select. By clicking on the answer, the oval will become filled, showing your selection.

How to use the testing tools. The testing tool symbols you are given include

- Next—advance to the next question
- Confirm—confirm your answer before moving on
- Erase—remove or erase all selected answers to a question
- Time—view the time remaining (or hide the time remaining)
- Calc—view and use an on-screen calculator (or hide the calculator) to answer mathematics questions
- Exit—leave a section and move on
- Quit—leave the entire test

- Help—view directions and receive help on how to take one of the tests

How to scroll. This tutorial will teach you how to click on the scroll bar to view the passages in the Reading Test. Since some material may be too long to fit on one screen, you will need to scroll by using the scroll bar to view all of the material. The scroll bar will consist of an up arrow, down arrow, a scroll box, and the space between the scroll box and the arrows. Most word processing programs have similar setups for scrolling, so become familiar with this capability before your test. Practice scrolling during the tutorial also.

How to use the word processor. To respond to the essay topic on the Writing Test, you can either use the word processor on the computer or handwrite your essay. The word processor uses very common key functions. Keys available while typing include

- Backspace—moves the cursor to the left and deletes text
- Delete—deletes text to the right of the cursor
- Home—moves the cursor to the beginning of a line (without deleting anything)
- End—moves the cursor to the end of a line (without deleting anything)
- Arrows—move the cursor in the direction of the arrow (up, down, left, and right, without deleting anything)
- Enter—moves the cursor to the beginning of the next line
- Page up—moves the cursor up (back) one page
- Page down—moves the cursor down (forward) one page
- Tab—this key does not work

Practice using these keys on the tutorial. Also, before going to take the test, you can practice using these keys on most word processing programs.

A CLOSER LOOK AT EACH TEST

READING TEST

Time allotted: 90 minutes (Most test takers finish in less than 60 minutes.)

Number of Questions: 36

Format: Many types of questions may be used: choosing one or more answers, moving information, highlighting information, and marking or checking boxes in a table.

Contents: Passages and Questions

Reading passages may consist of 200 to 400 words, and some may be accompanied by a graph, chart, or diagram. The subjects of the passages are from social science, science and nature, the humanities, and education.

The questions are of two basic types: comprehension (60 percent) and analysis and application (40 percent). Comprehension questions delve into main ideas, supporting ideas, the organization of the passage, and summaries. Analysis and application questions may be about inferences, assumptions, arguments, consistency of logic, application of ideas to other situations, use of words, and understanding of context.

MATHEMATICS TEST

Time allotted: 55 minutes (Most test takers finish in less than 40 minutes.)

Questions: 29

Format: Many types of questions may be used: highlighting an answer choice, choosing one or more answers, moving numbers or symbols, completing a graph, marking a scale, checking boxes in a table, or entering a numerical response to a question. Scratch paper is available.

Contents:

• Number sense and operation sense	25%
• Mathematical relationships	20%
• Data interpretation	25%
• Geometry and measurement	20%
• Reasoning	10%

Number sense and operation sense. You will be required to

- order numbers, fractions, and decimals, recognizing equivalent numbers including square roots and powers
- understand characteristics of prime numbers, composite numbers, even numbers, odd numbers, multiples and factors, and fundamental operations
- perform computations in problem solving and estimating
- use a simple on-screen calculator to solve problems

Mathematical relationships. These questions will cover ratios, proportions, percent, simple probability, variable expressions, equations, inequalities, and word problems.

Data interpretation. These questions will cover

- interpreting, summarizing, constructing, and completing tables, charts, and graphs
- observing trends
- making computations
- evaluating and summarizing data using simple statistics

Geometry and measurement. These questions will require you to

- know basic patterns and formulas of simple geometric figures
- determine length, perimeter, area, and volume
- understand various systems of measurement, including the U.S. and metric
- make conversions within the same measurement system or from one system to another using a conversion table

Reasoning. These questions will require you to

- interpret logical "and," "or," and "if–then" statements
- interpret logical quantifiers such as "all," "some," and "none"
- use deductive and inductive reasoning
- draw conclusions
- evaluate the validity of conclusions

WRITING TEST

Time allotted: 66 minutes (26 minutes to complete the computer-adaptive questions and 40 minutes to write an essay)
Number of Questions: 35 and 1 essay
Format: Multiple-choice, error-recognition questions and an essay, either written on the word processor or by hand
Contents: Error-Recognition Questions and Essays

Error-recognition questions are multiple-choice questions that assess your ability to recognize errors in grammar (for example, with nouns, pronouns, verbs, modifiers, comparatives, and parallel structure), word choice, and mechanics (such as with punctuation and capitalization). You will also be required to recognize sentences that have no errors; that is, they are correct as written.

The 40-minute essay section assesses your ability to plan and write one well-organized essay. You will be given two computer-generated topics. You should select the topic that you feel most comfortable with and think would be the easiest for you to write about. The topics will ask you to take a position on an issue and use supporting details and/or examples from your own experience to write an effective essay. The topics do not require any special knowledge of a specific subject. The two essay topics that you will be choosing from are selected from a list of 72 topics given in the *Praxis I: Academic Skills Assessments, Tests At A Glance* bulletin available free from ETS or your local college testing office. Carefully review the list of topics given.

Again, you will have a choice of either handwriting your essay or using the computer's word processor. Select the method that you are the most comfortable with. If you decide to handwrite your essay, the proctor will give you the proper form (paper) and then two topics will appear on your computer screen. After selecting your topic, begin writing your essay on the form. If you decide to use the word processor to type your essay, a tutorial will appear on the screen explaining the features of the word processor. After viewing the tutorial, you may decide to use the word processor or change to handwriting your essay. This will be your last chance to choose between typing and writing. Once you have decided which method you wish to use, two topics will appear on the computer screen, and you will select one and start the essay-writing process. Regardless of the method you choose, you should always spend a few minutes prewriting—brainstorming, clustering or outlining, and carefully organizing your thoughts—before you start writing. Then be sure to leave time to proofread or review your essay.

Your essay will be scored holistically by readers trained to evaluate overall writing ability. The scoring is based on the criteria on pages 73–74. The method you use to write your essay, handwriting or typing, does not affect the scoring process, so be sure to select the one you are most comfortable with.

A NOTE ABOUT STRATEGIES

If you choose to prepare for the CBT, realize that the two successful approaches outlined at the beginning of this book for taking the PPST will not work for you. They are the "Plus-Minus" System and the Elimination Strategy (pages 6–7). Both of these helpful approaches require marking on the test booklet, which you will not have available on the computer. Additionally, in the reading, mathematics, and the multiple-choice part of the writing test, you may not skip questions to come back to them later, as is suggested in the "Plus-Minus" System. Recall that the computer is selecting more or less difficult questions for you based on whether you answer each question correctly or incorrectly.

Correctly answering difficult questions counts more than answering easy questions on the computer-adaptive portions of the CBT. If you aren't sure of an answer, ETS recommends that you try to eliminate as many of the answer choices as possible and then guess. You may find it helpful to quickly write the letters of the answer choices on your scratch paper and cross out the letters of the answers you have eliminated, so you don't keep reconsidering them.